D0871594

BLACKWAYS OF KENT

This volume is the second of the
Field Studies in the Modern Culture of the South
prepared under the direction of John Gillin,
sponsored by the Institute for Research in Social Science
of the University of North Carolina in
Chapel Hill

Previously published
Plantation County, by Morton Rubin

BLACKWAYS
of KENT

By

HYLAN LEWIS

1955
Chapel Hill

THE UNIVERSITY OF NORTH CAROLINA PRESS

Printed in the United States of America
VAN REES PRESS • NEW YORK
CMT

To Carole and Guy,
my daughter and son

FOREWORD

HYLAN LEWIS has written a unique book. It is an intimate account of Negro life in the South "from the inside." Although the anecdotal aspects of the narrative make fascinating reading, Lewis has nevertheless organized his materials according to a theoretical scheme that makes sense, not only to laymen but also to scientists who may wish to continue the type of investigation he has so brilliantly initiated.

Kent, a pseudonym, was chosen as one of six exhibits of the "Modern Culture of the South" * because it seems to embody most of the cultural aspects characteristic of a "typical" community of the Piedmont area. It has its elements of "old aristocrats," its "up-and-coming" middle class, its mill workers and textile factories, and a sizeable Negro population, herein described in cultural terms. Kent has "everything," and in this sense epitomizes the Piedmont subculture of the South.

The "white ways" of Kent—those of the aristocrats and the textile mill villagers—were studied respectively by Ralph Patrick, Jr. and J. Kenneth Morland. We hope later to publish their monographs. Dr. Lewis, a Ph.D. from the University of Chicago and now on the faculty of Atlanta University, worked closely with these two social scientists during the field work and afterwards. Dr. George L. Simpson, Jr., Research Associate

* The Field Studies in the Modern Culture of the South, directed by this writer, were financed by the Rosenwald Fund and the University of North Carolina through the Institute for Research in Social Science.

vii

in the Institute for Research in Social Science, a former newspaper man and an author in his own right, has coordinated the editing of the three reports on Kent, in addition to contributing the introductory statements in this volume.

One of the extraordinary things about this study is the fact that Dr. Lewis was able to penetrate and portray in everyday human terms the way of life of the lower-class Negroes of Kent—the "nonrespectables," as he calls them in keeping with the local label. Other Negro investigators have made notable contributions to our knowledge of the Negro in the South, but few, if any, have succeeded in "getting to" people, especially those of the lower class, in the man-to-man way here demonstrated. In short, Dr. Lewis has shown that he is a scientist with the common touch.

I would like to add my personal appreciation of the always efficient service of Dr. Katharine Jocher, who has seen this volume through the press in her role as editor of the publications of the Institute for Research in Social Science.

JOHN GILLIN

Chapel Hill
August 19, 1954

PREFACE

It will be clear to the reader of *Blackways of Kent* that the central findings are based upon participant observation, a technique custom-made for social science research. Not so obvious are the hazards—methodological and moral—and the rewards that are components of this kind of research behavior. It is highly probable that "the stories behind the stories"— that is, how particular students met and tried to resolve the dilemmas of participant observation—might be fully as useful contributions as many of the versions of people's behavior and motivations that get placed upon library shelves.

The degree to which I was permitted to share in the activities and thoughts of the people of Kent was in a large measure a function of the extent to which I came to know and to reciprocate the affection and confidence of many Kentians. This sharing paid dividends in personal satisfactions, continuing friendships, and kinds of knowledge not obtainable otherwise. It also posed the crucial ethical problems related to the fact that on one level persons and relationships came almost inevitably to be ends and on the other they came necessarily to be means or data. And the need to be constantly and acutely aware of the subtle or crude ways in which one's own background, the ordinary pleasures and pains of in-group living, the normal imperatives of friendship, and the very presence of one's self in the field of study might possibly blind, censor, or distort was a constant source of anxiety; but it was also the best guarantee of self-correction and scientific humility.

If participant observation has anything to recommend itself in both scientific and moral terms, it is probably just this paradoxical fact that it does permit (or enforce) the treating and experiencing of persons and social situations as both means and ends. (Incidentally, the participant observer himself is also variously experienced and viewed by his data in both means and ends terms.) If many of the people of Kent had not sensed and reciprocated their primary value for me as persons, they could have hardly become the means by which I was able to share an inside view as well as to observe and to place in context much of that which is external. The truth values of science were reinforced rather than violated by viewing subjects as ends. Given the life-context of the Negro in Kent and the logic of my role there, the implicit aims of friendship and con-genial association—the byproducts of empathy—came to be the same as those of science: accurate description, explanation, and prediction. Anything short of trying to approximate these would be breaking faith with Kentians, with myself, and with my fellow students who grapple with these same problems as they try to develop a science of human relations.

This is the place to lay bare a bias, a sense of inadequacy, and a haunting fear. The people of Kent are too important in personal as well as scientific terms to be described inaccurately or incompletely; but at best this version is incomplete, selective, and approximate. The Negro society of Kent is not a "closed system"; and it is just as impossible to "catch it all" as it is to convert all of my "private" knowledge into "public" knowl-edge. There is reasonable fear that the limitations of language, the strictures of "objective" reporting and of publication might possibly devitalize or even caricature the people to whom I owe so much both as a person and as a practicing social scientist. If this happens at any point, it is because I have failed in an attempt to solve the language and moral problems involved in trying to synthesize and to communicate two kinds of knowledge. For the inadequacy of a technique and for any human ineptness, I am supremely confident that the people of Kent will forgive me—and probably more quickly than my colleagues! The Negro people of Kent and people like them need make no apology nor do they need one made for them; it is rather the "tough" culture that shapes their behavior and the social science techniques that but approximate the truth and meaning of their lives that need examination and correction.

My greatest indebtedness—and one that transcends this study —is to the people of Kent, and especially to I.N.W., A.N., T.B., and B.W. I wish to express my deep appreciation to Professor John Gillin and his colleagues of the Institute for Research in Social Science of the University of North Carolina for giving me the opportunity to make this study and the necessary support. I voluntarily took many conceptual and practical cues from Dr. Gillin. A rewarding feature about our relationship was that he was always as graceful and unobtrusive in "giving me my head" in tackling methodological and personal problems as he was unstinting and warm in his support and confidence. I am also grateful to Dr. George L. Simpson, Jr. and to Dr. Katharine Jocher for performing the many editorial and mechanical chores incident to publication.

The manuscript upon which *Blackways of Kent* is based was submitted as a dissertation to the Department of Sociology of the University of Chicago. For expediting its acceptance, I cherish the aid and the incisive comments of the late Professor Louis Wirth, and the warm support of Professors W. F. Ogburn, E. W. Burgess, E. C. Hughes, and C. W. Hart. My wife, Audrey Carter Lewis, spent the last four months in the field with me. I am deeply indebted to her for moral support and for much practical assistance.

HYLAN LEWIS

Atlanta, Georgia
October 15, 1954

CONTENTS

⇢ PART THREE ⇠

FIGURES

TABLES

INTRODUCTION

HYLAN LEWIS has written of one part of the town of Kent, a town of about 4,000 people in the heart of the Piedmont South.

It is true, of course, that the Negro life which Dr. Lewis presents to us is in many fundamental and subtle ways separate from the remainder of Kent. Yet the integral elements of the Negro subculture have evidence in the context of the total community, white and black. They play against, so to speak, integral elements of white culture. And then, as Dr. Lewis shows us, the lines of inter-connection between white and black are numerous and amazingly complex.

It is well to know, then, that Kent is an old town, a county seat. There is no dearth of significant, even compelling, local history in Kent. People who know Kent almost always remark first that it is quite like many of the old towns of the Coastal Plain and Tidewater South. But these same people will not neglect to point out that there are in Kent four cotton mills, and that change and resistance to change in way of life in all parts of the community are virtually preoccupations.

Over wide areas of the Piedmont South the two names "Scotch-Irish" and "Presbyterian" have always been factors to reckon with, and still are. These words, properly understood, describe the people who first settled the countryside from which Kent grew and who to this day figure largely in the life of the town.

This rather remarkable cultural group began to develop early in the sixteen hundreds as an instrument of English domination of Ireland. After 1611, Scotch people of strong Presbyterianism were sent as settlers to Northern Ireland and given lands, so that they might begin to populate Ireland with succeeding generations who would be loyal both to the English kings and to Protestantism. There was no miscalculation here. These doughty, hard-working Scots were fertile in propagation and firm in faith. By the middle of the seventeenth century there were perhaps 300,000 of these Scotch-Irish in Northern Ireland and by 1700 about a million. By the turn of the century, however, complications arose. The settlers in Northern Ireland had turned their hands so successfully to manufacturing, as well as to farming, that they were competing with English manufacturers. As a result, in 1698, English legislation was passed restricting manufactures in Northern Ireland, and shortly thereafter religious disabilities were inflicted on Scotch-Irish Presbyterianism. Their schools were closed; marriages performed by their clergymen were declared invalid; and they were forbidden to hold anything but petty governmental posts. As a result, these Scotch-Irish began, especially after 1720, to come in great numbers to the American colonies.

They migrated at first mainly to Pennsylvania. But in the 1750's and 1760's great numbers began to move up the long funnel of the Shenandoah Valley, some stopping there, but others fanning out into the southern Piedmont.

They were rural people. Their communities grew up around the Presbyterian churches they established early, with names like Bethel, Mt. Zion, Shiloh, and Ebenezer. Traditionally, the ministry was well educated, and soon college trained ministers came in to fill the pulpits on Sundays and to conduct schools during the weekdays. This trinity of family farm life, school, and church was powerful and integrated. Though life of necessity was sanguine and utterly real in the frontier conditions, it was not worldly. Thrift and hard work as economic necessity and religious duty were the compelling patterns of life which this trinity propagated. Out of it all there emerged a strong, vigorous farm life. With all their attachment to kinsmen and church, these people individually kept their own conscience and counsel and did their own thinking.

They thought long and hard on the subject of revolt and joined the Revolution grudgingly and late. They were not averse to fighting for liberty. They wanted, though, to be sure that liberty was what they would get, and their experience in the Piedmont had raised some doubts. This Piedmont to which they had come was "back country" to the older and more influential people of the low country rice and indigo plantations. Ever since their coming, the Scotch-Irish had found themselves without voice in a government dominated by royal appointees and low-country planters and merchants. It was the low country people who urged revolution, and the back country people could see little benefit in changing matters. In the early years of the war emissaries from the low country rode the back country seeking cooperation and troops with little success. Not until the British moved their forces inland and began to pillage the back country did the Scotch-Irish of the Kent area enter the war wholeheartedly. And, as it turned out, two important victories were won in Kent County with the substantial collaboration of the Kent County people themselves.

The war over, the people of the Kent area resumed their rural life. The town of Kent, which is the concern of this book, gradually emerged, as did many other towns in the Piedmont, from this rural settlement. As early as 1771, there was a crossing of two wagon roads at the present site of Kent, known as Ferguson's Cross-roads. When Kent County was marked off in 1785, this Cross-roads was about in the middle of the new county. The courthouse was erected there, and the little settlement began to be known as Kentville.

Kentville grew slowly in the service of the surrounding rural communities. By the early 1820's there were 8 lawyers, 2 physicians, 1 clergyman, and 52 "mechanics." There were eight stores and five taverns, a male and a female academy, a post office, and a printing shop which issued two weekly newspapers. Two things stand out. On the one hand, the existence of two academies, two newspapers, and as many lawyers as are in Kent today, shows a vital and somewhat unusual development along these lines. On the other hand, the presence of but one clergyman and of no regularly established church reveals the continuing vitality of the rural church communities.

Actually, over the years after 1800, a major transformation was taking place around Kent, for during these years cotton was coming into what had been an area of general agriculture. In time, large areas of the rolling Piedmont country went over to cotton as thoroughly as did the middle and low country areas, where the classic plantation complex reached full development. There was in general the difference, however, that the Piedmont raised its cotton with very few slaves on small farms worked mainly by white owners. Both the cultural background of the people and the hilly topography of the Piedmont contributed to this type of development. Kent County, however, was something of an exception to this Piedmont rule. Situated on a relatively level and rich plateau between two large rivers, some large plantation development was possible, and did, in fact, take place.

So it was that during the ante-bellum period a large number of plantations developed around Kentville, with slaves and a style of life and prestige for the owners typical of the southern plantation system as a whole. The flowering of plantation life was of great importance in establishing standards of life and achievement in the area. Kentville began to reflect these developments. It prospered from the agricultural bounty. Sons of the plantation and large farm families frequently turned to professional life and settled in Kentville. Daughters married merchants and other townspeople. Townspeople themselves, as they prospered, adopted as far as possible this way of life, and it was reflected in their thinking, the style of their homes, in their aspirations, and even in the purchase of plantations.

There was something of a climax to these developments in the eighteen-fifties. Prior to that time the population of the town had not exceeded 900, but during the next ten years it doubled. Kentville was incorporated in 1849, and on January 1, 1850, the town council met for the first time. By 1852, Kentville energy and capital had brought in a railroad. Subsequently, the streets were macadamized, hotels, business buildings, and imposing homes were built. It was during this period that the First Presbyterian Church, which today is considered one of the most beautiful church buildings in the Piedmont South, was erected. In 1855 two young men established the Liberty Military Academy, and Kentville became something of an educational center.

By 1860, Kentville was a town of importance in its section of the Piedmont, and for itself a place of promise and good living. It went to war in 1861 with all its young men, its resources and its hopes. The war over, many of its young men were gone, along with almost all of its resources and hopes. Defeat was bearable though bitter, but military occupation, Reconstruction, and the forcible reordering of many social and economic relations were resented and contested bitterly. These defensive exertions assumed major proportions in the life of the town. White Kent's reaction was to shift from its ante-bellum interest in the future to a considerable preoccupation with the past.

Following Reconstruction, Kent moved along as a mercantile and court center for a rather wide area, with little change in population and activities. It was during this period, however, that industry—primarily cotton mills—was coming to

the small towns of the Piedmont to take advantage of cheap
and abundant labor, power, and the proximity of the cotton
fields. While towns on all sides were energetic in this development, Kent held aloof and did not participate. The passage of
a main trunk railroad line through Kent was vetoed by influential townspeople. Foregoing this golden opportunity re-
tarded industrial development both in time and quantity.
Beyond this, there was little initiative in the town for the
establishment of mills, and outsiders were not encouraged.
During the same period Kent turned down the state's offer to
locate the state normal school for girls there.

It was not, in fact, until 1896 that a group of Kent people
got together to establish a cotton mill. Between then and 1907,
three other mills were built. These were all relatively small,
and none has been established since 1907.

To work the mills rural people came to Kent from the surrounding countryside. These were not strangers; not foreign-
ers. These people also were the descendants of the original
settlers of the Piedmont South, largely Scotch-Irish though not
exclusively so. They were small farmers and tenants, in many
ways the backbone of the area, who had remained on the farms
and had suffered the vicissitudes of cotton culture. They came
for the weekly wage of cash money, bringing their rural her-
itage of strong individualism with them. To house the new
labor, cheap housing was required. The mills at Kent, as was
the custom, built rows of houses all alike close by the mills and
rented them to the workers. So they became "mill people,"
looked down upon by the town, isolated, and in turn conscious
of their separateness. This condition, originating in the ills of
cotton culture and in the original ecological grouping of the
mill workers in mill villages, exists to this day.

The mills were the last main structural addition to Kent.
Since the early years of the century, the town has remained
virtually the same in size, in interests, and in its considerable
preoccupation with the past. To say this is not to say that Kent

has been totally static. It has been influenced by other nearby communities where these last fifty years have been ones of industrial growth and of social change. Twenty-eight miles away, on the railroad which Kent rejected, there has grown up a large textile center of about 20,000 people. Here also is the state normal school for girls which Kent turned down. In any direction one might take from Kent, the roads soon pass through the new industrial villages and towns of the Piedmont South. Within Kent itself, there have been in varying degrees over the years individuals and groups who have wanted to come to closer grips with the new developments. It is not incorrect to say that here in Kent is found an example par excellence of the climactic old coming to grips with the new.

Thus far very little has been said about the Negroes of Kent, who constitute the third major element of the community. In historical perspective, the importance of the Negroes in Kent has derived from their presence rather than from their specific actions. There has existed that rather remarkable cultural phenomenon in which whites and blacks have met daily face to face, often in intimate and close ways, but without any accepted meeting of their respective cultures. Generalization from the individual Negro to either his basic nature or to his culture has always erected a wall between white and black. The Negro, individually, was passive in slavery, but his presence shaped ways of living and thinking and contributed to the contention that led to Civil War. Similarly, since the war it has been the Negro's presence, often as an issue, that has motivated thinking and behavior of whites both in and outside of Kent.

While the main stream of time and events has passed around them, the Negroes of Kent have had a culture as real and as genuine as that of the whites, and to them the white world has been a fact of life, a constant element to all of which they have adjusted, and part of which they have adapted. It is of these things that Hylan Lewis writes. But as he writes there appears time and again evidence of change in the older order, change in the Negro subculture itself, and change between white and black. This is not the change of newspaper headlines but change in basic cultural elements.

GEORGE L. SIMPSON, JR.

PART ONE

INTRODUCTION TO THE SUBCULTURE

INTRODUCTION TO THE SUBCULTURE

B LACKWAYS OF KENT is a study—after the manner of the cultural anthropologist and sociologist—of the customs of the Negro in this bi-racial community of the Piedmont South of today. The characteristic practices of the Negro are viewed as one of the many subcultures that go to make up contemporary America; they constitute one of the many versions of American culture. The Negro in Kent as a group has created, adopted, and adapted selected ways and instruments to meet the demands of on-going existence in this setting. The organized ways—patterns of action, thought, and belief—are seen in the abstract as parts of a system, in this case, a subsystem. Obviously this subculture can not and does not exist in a vacuum: it is responsive to, and incorporates, local, regional, national, and international influences. It is only in terms of the specific geographic location and a unique organization of customs that this culture—or any phase of modern American culture—can be thought of as "local."

The Study of a Subculture

CHAPTER 1 — THERE ARE three major versions or styles of living in Kent: that of the "town" whites,[1] that of the "poor white" mill villagers, and that of the Negroes. These three groups form the larger society of Kent.[2] Each exhibits a distinctive organization of customs, attitudes, and values. Each is a subculture—a variation of American culture, Southern Piedmont style.

In order to understand the Negro subculture, it is important to bear constantly in mind that within Kent Negro society itself there is a basic cleavage that results in two distinctive styles of life—the respectable and the nonrespectable.[3] These ranked categories which are recognized and designated by

1. Although about three-fourths of the mill villagers actually live within the town limits, they tend to cluster in distinct, segregated areas. The designation "town" white refers to those whites who are not mill workers (top management and owners excluded) regardless of where they live. The population of Kent is overwhelmingly a native-born American population; the 1940 U.S. Census reported only 11 foreign-born persons, all of whom were white.

2. These three groups were studied independently by three investigators between 1947 and 1949 under the auspices of the Institute for Research in Social Science, Chapel Hill, North Carolina. Although each investigator shared the common interest in the culture of the groups, each worked out and followed his own techniques and organizing questions. The field notes of the other two investigators were available during the last stages of writing this manuscript.

3. See pp. 233 ff. for a discussion of these categories and the types and statuses distinguishable within them.

Negro and white Kentians [4] have the characteristics of sub-cultures themselves.

These facts about this cleavage should be borne in mind: there appear to be no organized group activities which are participated in exclusively by persons of either of the categories; it is difficult in this small society for a person to confine his contacts or associations solely to respectables without suffering extreme isolation. The designations respectable and nonrespectable refer to aspects or emphases of total behavior, the great bulk of which for both categories is neutral or conventional and without value implications in this sense. Nonrespectable behavior tends to be more dramatic, unrestrained, and public, and therefore it looms larger in the public eye; and the persons who practice it contribute more heavily to the over-all tone of the society. Subsequent chapters will indicate some of the reasons why this subculture almost necessarily has a heavy non-respectable cast.

In broad terms, behavior and attitudes with respect to whisky, sex, family, the law, and the use of leisure time define respectability and nonrespectability. The nonrespectable person will have one or more of these characteristics: a reputation for excessive drinking or public drunkenness, nonconventional family life or sex promiscuity, an arrest record, the habit of frequenting taverns. These are major traits. Often accompanying them may be any or all of these: apparent resignation toward or bland acceptance of the risks of jail and bodily harm, carrying a knife or pistol, hair-trigger responses in self-defense or to insult or fancied insult, and unrestrained use of profanity.

In general, the characteristics of the respectables would be the converse of the nonrespectables. In the main, they are peo-

4. This does not mean that Negro and white evaluations always coincide; however the emphasis upon public conduct and morality is a constant. For the whites a respectable Negro is also necessarily a respectful Negro. Although all Negroes tend to be overtly respectful with reference to whites, it is not an idealized or intrinsically valued trait in the Negro community.

ple who are careful of their public conduct: they do not get in trouble and they are proud of their lack of contact with the law and the courts. They are likely to be people who strive to maintain "nice homes" and stable families, who evince thrift, and who have or have had a measure of economic security.

The study was conceived as a comprehensive treatment of culture in a subgroup. The minority status of the Negro and the course of race relations in Kent and elsewhere in the United States were seen as highly significant facts in the total cultural situation; but they were not in themselves the prime focus. These questions outlined the research task as it was first conceived:

1. What factors are involved in the life adjustment of the Negro group in Kent? Out of what materials has he organized a way of life?

2. What is the content of the Negro subculture of Kent?

3. How and to what extent are Negro customs organized and integrated?

4. What is the relationship between Kent culture and individual behavior?

If we resist the temptation to push the analogy too far, the Negroes of Kent may be thought of as acting out a life drama in accordance with an imaginary "script" that each person "carries in his head." The delineations of action and thought about which there is agreement are designated cultural patterns by the social scientist. Their existence is inferred from the observed behavior of individuals going through their routinized paces. The life drama of any group takes place in a particular setting with which it is more or less consistent, and the ongoing behavior is facilitated by appropriate objects and tools— "props"—and innumerable cues to action. The quality and tone of life in the group are functions of the "script": some scripts are more tightly knit and balanced than others, and the particular demands made by each upon the individual vary. Lack of clarity and the intrusion of competing ways tend to confuse and make for poor or indifferent performance.

The task of this investigator was to ascertain and record as much as possible of the prescriptions that outline and give some uniformity to the behavior of Negroes in this small town of the Piedmont South, and to describe the manner in which typical or actual persons interpret and act out their roles. There is also a basic interest in the satisfactions sought and achieved in this subculture.

Radcliffe-Brown has stated the rationale of studies such as this:

Social anthropology has for its aim to discover valid and significant generalizations about human society and its institutions. The only method by which this aim can ever be attained is by the comparison of a sufficient number of sufficiently diverse types of society. . . .

What is required . . . is a knowledge of how individual men, women, and children live within a given social structure. It is only in the everyday life of individuals and their behavior to one another that the functioning of social institutions can be directly observed. Hence the kind of research that is most important is the close study for many months of a community which is sufficiently limited in size to permit all the details of its life to be examined.[5]

In keeping with this aim "not only to consider 'culture as culture,' but also to relate culture to actual human behavior," [6] the materials to a large extent have been analyzed and organized in terms of an adaptation of the theories and concepts of John Gillin's *The Ways of Men*. Among the core conceptions used or adapted here are (1) "the position that culture consists of patterned and functionally interrelated customs common to specifiable individual human beings com-

5. Introduction to John Embree's *Suye Mura, A Japanese Village* (Chicago: University of Chicago Press, 1939), pp. x-xi.

6. John Gillin, *The Ways of Men* (New York: D. Appleton-Century Company, 1948), p. vii.

posing specifiable social groups or categories"; [7] (2) the concept "cultural situation" [8] which permits us to distinguish and label the different components involved in the adjustment of customs; (3) a scheme for classifying the content of a culture in terms of its complexity: unit-customs, cultural complexes, institutions, orientations and objectives, value systems; [9] and (4) some detailed aspects of the integration of cultural systems: [10] relatedness, functional linkage, consistency, and balance.

The relative smallness of the community and the maximum class mobility of the investigator meant that within the limits of time, purpose, and skill, coverage was reasonably complete and the data representative. Accuracy implies faithfulness in catching meaning as well as action. It is suggested that the intimate contact resulting from the role played aided in getting a close approximation of the meaning of this subculture to those who practice it. Necessarily, much of this "meaning" is inference; yet a certain degree of accuracy was assured by checks other than those that came from my own observations: key informants strategically placed in all levels and in all sections helped to verify or deny conclusions. In many cases, actual counting or the availability of pertinent records gave statistical support for generalizations. A content analysis of the field notes of this study was independently done [11] and has served as a valuable check and partial validation of findings, particularly those that have reference to the orientations and values of the subculture.

The manuscript for this case study of a subculture was

7. *Ibid.*, p. 181.
8. *Ibid.*, p. 198.
9. *Ibid.*, pp. 492-97.
10. *Ibid.*, pp. 516-31.
11. Gertrude D. Stevens, Application of Content Analysis to Anthropological Field Notes (unpublished master's thesis, Department of Sociology and Anthropology, University of North Carolina, 1949).

written in the field and is based primarily upon field notes. Findings are presented without elaborate cross references to cultural studies which are more or less comparable. This does not mean that these studies have been ignored; on the contrary, knowledge of such studies [12] affected research orientation and field operations in many ways. The knowledge of what others have done gave clues as to what to do and what not to do, as well as to what added kinds of information are needed about the behavior of people in this setting.

The goal of this investigation has been essentially modest and realistic; there is no feeling or claim that all aspects or elements of this subculture have been probed or presented; rather the interest, as indicated, is in noting the essential character and efficacy of the "script" that outlines the conduct of the Negro in this particular setting and the range of individual interpretations and performances.

12. Cf. John Dollard, *Caste and Class in a Southern Town* (New Haven: Yale University Press, 1937); L. Warner and P. Lunt, *The Social Life of a Modern Community* (New York: Harper and Brothers, 1941); E. C. Hughes, *French Canada in Transition* (Chicago: University of Chicago Press, 1943); Allison Davis, Burleigh Gardner, and Mary Gardner, *Deep South* (Chicago: University of Chicago Press, 1941); St. Clair Drake and Horace Cayton, *Black Metropolis* (New York: Harcourt, Brace and Company, 1945); John Gillin, *Moche, A Peruvian Coastal Community* (Washington: Smithsonian Institution Institute of Social Anthropology, 1947); John Embree, *Suye Mura* (Chicago: University of Chicago Press, 1939); James West, *Plainville, U.S.A.* (New York: Columbia University Press, 1945); and other studies.

The Cultural Situation

CHAPTER 2   BEFORE WE begin a description of the culture of the Kent Negro we have a concern for the setting that provides the materials for that culture and which, at the same time, conditions its practice. Gillin points out that "no culture exists and functions in a void: it is always faced with a situation." [1] The general components of cultural situations are: "(1) the human component; (2) the environmental component; (3) the social component; (4) the not invariably present foreign cultural component.... They lay down the conditions under which the culture must operate." [2]

THE HUMAN COMPONENT

THE human animal factor in relation to culture is considered first because "customs must necessarily be adapted to the performance capacities of the group members." [3] Do the biological equipment and the physical characteristics of the Negro in Kent place any conditions upon social life and custom? A thoroughly competent answer would require detailed and accurate data as to racial characteristics, body size and type, and the incidence of organic abnormalities and disease. Thorough research

1. John Gillin, *The Ways of Men,* p. 198.
2. *Ibid.*
3. *Ibid.*

9

into these problems on the local scene was not practicable. However, some data and scientific conclusions are available, and certain reasonable assumptions can be made about the significance of the biological characteristics of the local Negro for culture.

Observation and genealogies indicate that the Kent Negro represents a genetic mixture of Negro, white, and American Indian elements. Although the modal Negro is brown-skinned, the individual Negro may be very dark or he may be very fair-skinned: "race" is social rather than biological. But granting the differences in modal physical types and different combinations of genes—of what significance are they for culture? [4] Lacking precise data on the local situation, we are nevertheless justified in assuming that there is nothing peculiar or abnormal about the biological Negro of Kent; and that genetically the only significant limits to culture creation and practicing are those that are common to the human species. The weight of the evidence from anthropology is that biologically there are no fundamental physical differences in all stocks and races, that biogenetic potentials are shared equally by all stocks and by all races.[5]

We achieve the best results in interpreting and predicting culture by proceeding, for the present, on the assumption that all normal hereditary varieties and subgroups of the species (excluding, of course, obviously mentally deficient and diseased groups) are fundamentally equal in cultural ability.[6]

There are, however, secondary physical characteristics and acquired physical conditions in the Kent Negro group that affect social practice. Despite great variability, there is a modal Negro who has brown skin, a relatively flat nose, and

4. There is no concern at this stage for the social definition of physical characteristics. The question is, what direct bearing do these traits have on culture?

5. W. M. Krogman, "What We Do Not Know About Race," *Scientific Monthly*, LVII (August 1943), 97-104.

6. Gillin, *op. cit.*, p. 143.

short, curly hair. Excluding the one very fair Negro who is a resident in the community now (there have been more in the past and there are others in nearby communities), the range of color is from light brown to dark brown or black. In terms of direct influence on behavior, these physical traits are only significant in the area of personal adornment.

And, as a matter of fact, a major complex of habits, values, and experts has arisen around the "need" for special treatment of Negro hair—and, to a lesser extent, the skin.[7] The Negro's use of cosmetics and his treatment and styling of hair are in keeping both with his physical characteristics and the dominant beauty values of the larger community: customs are conditioned by the length and texture of the hair and darker skin color, on the one hand, and the general cultural drive to approach prevailing standards of beauty and sartorial acceptability on the other. Hair stylings are approximations or adaptations of current modes. A strong secondary drive, developing from these different physical characteristics, creates the demand for special adaptive techniques and inventions. The more effective these techniques, the closer the Negro "version" of hair approaches prevailing types and styles of the larger community.

Disease and bodily vigor have obvious implications for custom. Much of disease is "functional" and related to hygienic factors. Complete and reliable data with reference to the health and energy potential of the Negro in Kent proper are lacking but there are some facts and data that support inferences and assumptions. For the nation as a whole, the sickness and death rate of the Negro is significantly higher than the white rate for the following: pellagra, syphilis, homicide, pneumonia and influenza, and tuberculosis. In 1940, the registered infant mortality rate in the United States was 69 per-

7. See the later treatment of the "Dress and Grooming Complex," pp. 53-64.

cent higher among Negroes than among whites; the maternal mortality rate for the same year was two and one-half times as high.[8] In the Southeast region in which Kent lies the ratio of Negro rates of death to white rates for all causes was 1.5 in 1940.[9]

The health picture of the Negro in Kent tends to conform to the national and regional patterns, if available vital statistics for Kent County are taken as representative. Table 1 shows that the mortality rate for the Negro in the Kent area was 30 percent higher than the white rate, and that the Negro rate was significantly higher in infant and maternal mortality and deaths due to tuberculosis, pneumonia, syphilis, apoplexy, and diseases of the kidneys.[10] On the other hand, the Negro rate was less for cancer, diabetes, heart diseases, influenza, and accidents.

Although exact Selective Service data for the town of Kent are not available, further evidence of differential morbidity among Negroes of the area is provided by figures for Kent County. During the years 1940 to 1946 inclusive, Negroes constituted about one-third of the total registrants examined, but they represented 42 percent of county registrants rejected for physical reasons.[11] On the other hand, they constituted

8. Gunnar Myrdal, *An American Dilemma* (New York: Harper and Brothers, 1944), I, 174.

9. Rupert B. Vance, *All These People* (Chapel Hill: University of North Carolina Press, 1945), p. 349.

10. The fact that approximately three-fourths (76.4 percent in 1940) of the Negroes of Kent County are classified as rural in contrast to slightly less than 50 percent (46.5 in 1940) of the whites might be used with caution to explain part of the differences in rates between the races in Kent only in the cases of infant and maternal mortality; with few exceptions, urban mortality rates are higher for both racial groups as is shown in a comparison of city and county rates for South Carolina. In the South in general, there has been a tendency for the gap in rates between the racial groups to be wider in the cities than in the rural areas (for both age-corrected and crude rates). See *ibid.*, pp. 347-49.

11. All calculations are based upon summary tables in the published report of the State Director of Selective Service of South Carolina: Holmes B. Springs, *Selective Service in South Carolina, 1940-1947* (Columbia, S.C.: Vogue Press, 1948), p. 132 and *passim.*

TABLE 1. SELECTED VITAL STATISTICS BY RACE,
KENT COUNTY, 1946

	Race		Ratio Negro Rate to White Rate
	White	Negro	
Births [a]	22.6	26.0	1.18
Deaths [b]	7.0	9.1	1.30
Deaths by selected types and causes			
Tuberculosis	3.9	21.3	5.46
Pneumonia	11.6	58.5	5.04
Maternal [c]	1.7	8.2	4.82
Syphilis	10.1	47.3	4.68
Apoplexy, Embolism, Thrombosis	61.6	170.2	2.76
Infant [c]	32.6	57.4	1.76
Kidneys	57.8	101.1	1.70
Accidents	65.5	53.2	0.81
Heart	223.4	154.3	0.69
Diabetes	19.3	10.6	0.55
Influenza	23.1	10.6	0.46

a. Rate per 1,000 population.
b. Rate per 100,000 population.
c. Rate per 1,000 live births.

Source: *Sixty-Eighth Annual Report of the State Board of Health of South Carolina for the Period Beginning July 1, 1946 and Ending June 30, 1947.*

63 percent of those rejected for mental deficiency, and 33 percent of those rejected for mental disease.[12] Thirty-five

12. These three causes accounted for 52 percent of the Negro registrants rejected and 25 percent of the rejected white registrants. Since the rural areas probably contributed a disproportionate share of these rejections, it is reasonable to assume that the induction rate for Negroes in the town of Kent was higher than the summary figures for the county indicate. The State Director reports a lack of uniformity in interpretation and notes that "several boards in agricultural counties dependent upon an abundance of farm labor were inclined to classify Negroes as mentally or educationally deficient when some of them could have been accepted." (*Ibid.*, p. 85)

percent of all registrants in the county were rejected for all reasons. The rate of rejection for Negroes was 57 percent for all reasons, and for whites, it was 24 percent.[13]

Despite the lack of specific data on productivity and job performance, it is reasonable to believe that on the average the energy potential of the Kent Negro is lessened and work habits are influenced by higher sickness and death rates. There are so many factors affecting the local economic pattern of the Negro—types and amount of work available, and incentives, for example—that it would be difficult to measure the effects of illness accurately in a study of this kind. The important point is to recognize that these physical facts are significant for customs and attitudes. Shorter life expectancy, a heavy incidence of widows—by actual count, there are 56 Negro widows in Kent [14]—the characteristic social and economic role of the mother, smaller families, broken families and family disorganization, and the attitudes and values related to these tie in with higher sickness and death rates. Myrdal points out:

Ill health reduces the birth rate in ways other than killing off mothers in their child-bearing period. In the first place, it increases sterility among men and women. That there is more sterility among Negroes than among whites is shown by the fact that there are more childless women, both married and unmarried, among Negroes and that the higher Negro birth rate is due to a higher average number of children per mother. This sterility is

13. As of August 1, 1945, the rejection rate for all white registrants examined in the United States was 27.9 percent; the nation-wide rate for Negroes was 47.0 percent. In the same period, the white South Carolina rejection rate was 33.9 percent, and the Negro rejection rate of 56.6 percent was the highest of any State in the Nation. It is significant to note that the South Carolina rejection rate for whites was higher than the West Virginia and New Jersey rejection rates for Negroes (33.0 percent).

14. In 1930, 14.5 percent or one in seven Negro females in Kent was a widow; only 4.4 percent of the Negro males or about one in twenty-five were widowers. *Negroes in the United States, 1920-1932* (Washington: Government Printing Office, 1934), p. 64.

not innate ... but is caused by general diseases, venereal diseases, induced abortion and organic deficiencies.[15]

Sickness, pain, and death loom relatively large in the experiences and customs of the Negro of Kent; mutual aid, insurance, religion, burial practices—all have a functional significance in these terms. It is likely that attitudes toward life and death are colored by these conditions that tend to be an expected, taken-for-granted aspect of group life.

THE ENVIRONMENTAL COMPONENT

TOPOGRAPHY, resources, and climate make three natural divisions of the state: the Blue Ridge Province, the Piedmont Plateau, and the Coastal Plain region. Distinctive differences in life in each are related to the manner in which historical factors have combined with topographical in selecting persons and activities. Kent is in the Piedmont Plateau; people of the upcountry have historically thought of themselves as different from low-country people, reflecting the different styles of life carved out in different geographic settings. Land in the Piedmont Plateau is of a rolling character with occasional hills. Much of the underlying rock is granite, and soils tend toward a sandy loam. Much of the Piedmont today is marked by severe erosion. The plantation style of life and economic activity was historically a product of the flat coastal plain, although not unknown in this area. Slaves were fewer in this section, as Negroes are relatively today. Farms have been— and are—smaller; the growing season is significantly shorter. Industry got a head start in this area, spurred by access to water power and transportation.

The comparative manner in which the natural environment has been adapted to and utilized in this section is indicated

15. Myrdal, *op. cit.*, pp. 174-75.

in these figures: of the 46 counties of the state, Kent ranks

    8th in population
    11th in percentage of white population
    9th in number of farms
    23rd in average size of farms
    4th in percentage of population employed in
        manufactures
    5th in the value of manufactured products

The Kent Negro has adapted to and used the soil, climate, topography, and animal and vegetable life according to a regional pattern which he helped to shape as slave and free man. There is no evidence that he exhibits special or unique ways of adapting to or coping with the natural environment. Basically, his occupation and tools, housing, diet, clothing, attitude toward nature, and leisure-time activities conform to the regional pattern.

Natural factors are significant for the behavior of the local Negro in the same sense as they are significant for the local white. They color his behavior and interests sufficiently to give him a feeling that his way of life is different in some degree from peoples of other sections: low-country people or mountaineers, for example.

THE DEMOGRAPHIC VARIABLE

POPULATION size, age and sex composition, spatial distribution and mobility, and birth and death rates are consequences in part of the function and way of life of a community; but at the same time population structure influences greatly the quality of life in a community. There is a reciprocal relationship between demographic and cultural structures and processes: the population characteristics of societies differ in part because of social organization and custom; the potentialities of societies for social interaction differ because behavior and custom in each case must adjust to such basic facts as size of group, distribution of persons in space, and the age and sex composition. What relevance do these facts have for the culture of the Kent Negro? [16]

The size of the group affects the quality and amount of Negroes' interaction in Kent society. The Negroes of Kent represent less than one-third of the town's population; the ratio for Kent County is about the same. This ratio between the racial groups is characteristic of the Piedmont section and contrasts markedly with the state as a whole where the total Negro population is just slightly less than the total white population. This Piedmont area is not marked by the same fear of "black domination" that has traditionally characterized the lower parts of the state. This accounts in part for what locals describe as relatively good race relations and the feeling among some Negroes that "you can do a lot of things here that you can't do in other places."

In Kent "everybody knows everybody else." Each person tends to be placed in terms of who he is and what he does; consequently, strangers are objects of curiosity and comment. Relationships tend to be more nearly those of "status" rather than of "contract." They are tinged with informality and personal reference and claim. The more detached persons— those who are not natives, the exceptionally educated, those who have left the community permanently, those who have traveled extensively—are prone to make invidious comparisons: "These people around here don't know nothing; they ain't had contact with nobody but themselves." This, of course, is exaggerated, but it suggests the limitations of size on diversity and the fostering of a certain amount of cultural inbreeding.

The size of the group affects the elaboration of functions and institutions in a society; but in the case of the Kent Negro

16. Some of the implications of differential morbidity and mortality for the quality of life in the Negro community were discussed in a previous section. See pp. 12-15.

subgroup, it is not the only factor affecting the range of activities and services within the group. Although size sets limits, there is a question as to whether, with larger size, Negroes of Kent would develop a full complement of institutions and agents. The Negro lives in a relationship with the white community that involves the exchange and "borrowing" of services and agents. Religious, educational, recreational, and personal service resources are, in the main, manned, though not necessarily controlled, by Negro personnel. Professional, commercial, and governmental and protective services flow from a common service agent or are "borrowed." Some services are obtained from other communities. Size of subgroup does not necessarily limit access to needed services or means of satisfying wants: living in a bi-racial community, the Negro has created or has worked jointly to create, or has had imposed upon him, ways and procedures to get access to certain—if not all—desired services or values. The consistency, the effectiveness, and the psychological derivatives of these means of satisfying the wishes or needs of the Negro, and of distributing a joint stock of goods and services are problems that must be treated later.[17]

The fact that the range of callings is small and true specialties few in Negro Kent is related to size as one factor. Only a minority of the gainfully employed function with reference to the direct and specific needs of the local Negro group. Operating with prime reference to the local Negro community are:

11 teachers in the local school
5 small store operators
5 part-time barbers
5 part-time bootleggers
4 active midwives (out of a total of 8)
4 part-time hairdressers

17. See Chapters 4 to 9.

3 full-time preachers, each of whom services
  another church in addition to the local charge
3 morticians, connected with a firm that services
  an area much wider than Kent
2 numbers agents
1 full-time and 4 part-time tavern operators
1 filling station operator (with mixed patronage)
1 pool parlor attendant
1 part-time electrician

Working for the most part with reference to the demands of the white community are:

8 painters
5 skilled construction helpers
4 carpenters
2 automobile mechanics
1 part-time paperhanger
1 motion picture machine operator
1 drugstore porter-clerk

With the exception of farmers and agricultural workers, all other employed persons perform domestic service, semi skilled or unskilled labor. The amount of occupational differentiation and the number of specialty callings have significance for income and status, manners of dress and living, and interests and outlooks. These will be described in Part Two, the "Content of the Subculture."

Negro females in Kent outnumber males in practically every age bracket.[18] There are roughly 8 Negro males to every 10 Negro females. In 1940, the sex ratio for Kent Negroes was 79.7 as compared to 91.6 for the Kent white. The sex ratios for the state as a whole were: Negro, 93.7

18. All figures in this section are based upon the United States Census figures for 1940 for Kent, South Carolina, and the southeastern region.

and native white, 105. The high incidence of females reflects the following possible factors, in addition to the sex differential in death rates: a more stable employment pattern for women; a relatively smaller rate of out-migration for women and a greater tendency for women to return for retirement; and the fact that women as a whole exhibit fewer anxieties about economic matters. (For example, one in every seven females over 21 is a widow, and the great bulk of them are looked upon as being relatively secure and "well fixed.")

The Negro population is heavily weighted with adults. In 1940, three out of every five Kent Negroes were over 21 years of age; one in five was over 50 years of age. Slightly less than three out of every five white Kentians were over 21 and slightly less than one in six was over 50. The proportions of aged people in the respective populations are very close to each other and do not vary significantly from the national figures (20.4 percent over 50); but they do differ from the figures for the region and the state as a whole. One in every six Negroes in Kent was between 5 and 14 as compared to one in every five for whites. The ratio of children under five to women 15 to 44 (the fertility ratio) indicates an even sharper contrast: 255.9 children per thousand women of child-bearing age in the Negro community and 352.4 in the white, as compared with the state rate of over 425.

The relatively small number of children in the Kent Negro population is probably related to certain factors that are generally operative in the Negro population. There is a relatively high percentage of childlessness in the Negro community. Vance points out that "27 percent of Negro women have no births as compared with 19.1 percent of white women, while 28.8 percent Negroes have one birth as compared with 17.8 percent of white women." [19] Out of a sample of 123 Kent Negro families with children in school, 30, or nearly one in

19. Vance, *op. cit.*, p. 99.

four, had but one child; another 30 had two children; thus it appears that nearly one-half of the families have two children or less.[20] Also operative in Kent is the fact that a significant proportion of the population is either beyond the child-bearing age or is widowed.

The facts of sex and age affect certain obvious areas of cultural adaptation and development. A high percentage of the population is married; unmarried females tend to outnumber unmarried males—the male who is unmarried or has never been married is rare. For the girl who stays in the community, the chances are that she will marry on her own level or on a level below her, rather than upward. Although only partly related to numerical facts, there is a large amount of non-marital sex activity with attendant conflict and suspicion.[21]

The high proportion of older people in the population means that many of the community's activities revolve around their interests and needs and are controlled by them—the church and property, for example. Institutional control is largely in the hands of older people, thus fostering some indifference and lack of participation on the part of younger people; aside from some few activities centering around the church and the school, there are no organized activities for youth or young adults. The bulk of Kent property is controlled by older people; this tends to enhance their independence and to elicit, at the same time, some envy, respect and deference from younger persons. The conservatism and inertia that mark much of the culture can be seen concretely in the cases of those older people who are financially able to make improvements in living conditions—such as housing—and who hesitate to do so for the expressed reason that they are not sure that they will live long enough to enjoy the benefits. The old ways are good enough for them, and then,

20. See Tables 2 and 3, p. 22.
21. See Chapter 4, "Courtship, Marriage, and the Family."

TABLE 2. NUMBER OF CHILDREN IN 123 KENT NEGRO FAMILIES

Number of Children	Number of Families	Percent of Total
1	30	24.5
2	30	24.5
3	20	16.3
4	14	11.3
5	9	7.3
6	5	4.0
7	5	4.0
8	3	2.4
9	3	2.4
10	1	0.8
11	1	0.8
12	2	1.7
Total	123	100.0

TABLE 3. SIZE OF FAMILIES OF 123 KENT SCHOOL CHILDREN

Size of Family	Number of Families	Percent of Total
2	7	5.6
3	30	25.0
4	26	21.0
5	20	16.3
6	13	10.5
7	7	5.6
8	6	4.7
9	5	4.0
10	2	1.7
11	4	3.2
12	0	—
13	3	2.4
Total	123	100.0

too, many of them lack the significant family ties that would encourage changes in living conditions.

To the aged themselves, being old does not seem a harsh experience. It is essentially a time of waiting for death, and those who have ceased significant economic activity show by conversation and manner that they are waiting and thinking about death with poise and assurance. It is in this perspective that one must understand the force of religion for these older people and their power in the church. In the later stages of life, they have a stake in the church superior to that of young people, not only for the assurance it offers, but also because they are no longer active in other areas. Heightened church activity is the last phase of the natural history of most lives in this subculture.

In general, the attitude of younger people toward the aged is one of respect and kindness; there tends to be marked filial respect and obedience among all groups. This may seem inconsistent with a great deal of the delinquent and nonrespectable behavior of the community but actually it is not, because to a great extent this latter is extra-family and extra-home behavior; in crucial decisions relating to family and home, there is the disposition to do—or at least *say* one will do—what the mother or father desires. Mother and father are significant sentimental and sacred symbols that are frequently invoked. As noted, a significant amount of the respect for the older persons is related to the following facts: they control a significant part of the wealth or means of support as propertied heads of families or as widows; pension payments give many a measure of support and release them from dependence upon relatives or friends. Many old people are still active as workers, and many still provide support and care for children and grandchildren. The older women, in particular, have a lively interest in what is going on in the community; the literate ones—a number have recently learned to read in government-sponsored classes—read with great interest the papers from

Stone Valley and Metro City. All exchange news, gossip, and evaluations of community happenings. They decry much of the behavior of youth, but, instead of being bitter, they tend to accept much of it as "the way things is done nowadays." They tend to be intensely grateful for attention from younger people and, in general, good-humored.

The older people play another important role in Kent society; they are not only significant links with the ways of previous generations of Kent Negroes, but they are also significant links with present and past generations of Kent whites. The relationship of older people to whites in the community has a different flavor from the relationships of Negro youths to whites. Many older Negroes have cordial sentimental relations with whites with whom they grew up or for whose families they have worked. Many of the women point to their "sons" and "grandsons"—white persons they helped to raise and with whom they have kept in touch. Some of these relationships have practical significance in terms of gifts, favors, and intercessions; many of the younger generation benefit by virtue of being identified with older people who are sentimental favorites of influential whites. These relationships, that derive from another day but which are still retained to some extent by older people, are important residual elements in the culture, although younger people may not fully appreciate or accept them.

Older peoples' expectations of youth are generally not in terms of possible future support for themselves nor in terms of outstanding achievements by the young people. Their concern is that youth be able to earn a living and to stay out of trouble. Few youths themselves exhibit a real restlessness or strong competitive urge. A few speak with some bravado about leaving to join relatives in the North or to go to places like Norfolk, Virginia, to work in the shipyards, but they seem to lack conviction. Actually, the excessively ambitious Negro youth in Kent would suffer significant isolation and acute frustration. Many of the male youths are in this dilemma: they express distaste for heavy manual labor, preferring lighter work or white collar work; but even if they were qualified, few such jobs are available in Kent. Getting the kind of job he wants is probably the greatest anxiety that the Negro youth of Kent has; but he tends to be fatalistic about it, and, if he stays in Kent, he eventually "makes peace" on some level. Youth is not overtly evaluated or lauded by older people as a particularly happy status; when older people speak about the happy times of their youth, they are referring to the youth of another generation, not the times of contemporary youth—times that they see as marked by job problems and the constant threat of getting in trouble.

The Negro lives in every section of Kent, but the majority live in four well-defined areas that rim white communities. They live "down in" the Jackson Street area, "over in" Mason City and Scotland, and "out in" Foggy Bottom—Southside. The residential neighborhoods are without significant formal organization. These neighborhoods are shown on the accompanying map (Figure 1). The components of each are listed below the map.

There are less than a dozen Negro residences scattered in other sections of the town. In general, when a Negro leaves his neighborhood, he must pass through a white neighborhood or commercial zone to get to where he is going. There are no great barriers to travel or communication among the areas except the hazards and deterrents of unpaved or poorly kept streets. Nine-tenths of the Negroes live on streets that are unpaved and without sidewalks, streets and walks that follow the alternating pattern of dust and mud. In general, streets in white neighborhoods are paved, and the paving stops where the Negro neighborhood begins. Aside from possible effects upon clothing, housing, and attitudes, unpaved streets in the Negro district are the basis of an important hope: the Negro

FIGURE 1

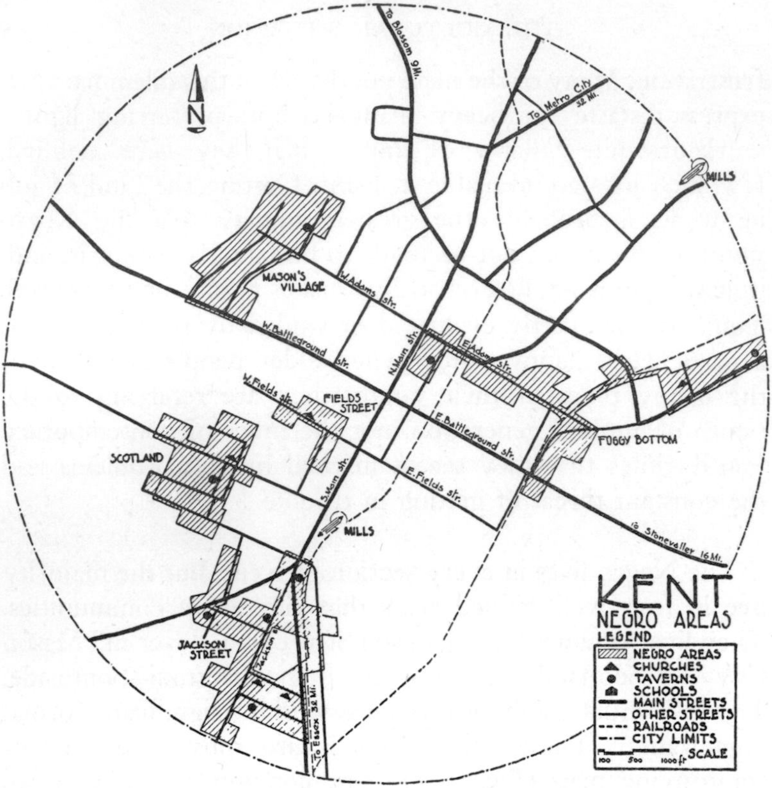

KENT
NEGRO AREAS
LEGEND

░░░	NEGRO AREAS
▲	CHURCHES
●	TAVERNS
▣	SCHOOLS
——	MAIN STREETS
—	OTHER STREETS
---	RAILROADS
-·-	CITY LIMITS
▬▬	SCALE
100 500 1000 ft	

The Jackson Street Area
76 residences
3 church buildings
3 taverns
1 store
1 store-cafe
1 pool parlor
1 filling station
1 beauty parlor
1 school

Foggy Bottom—Southside
67 residences
3 stores
2 taverns
1 barber shop
1 church

Scotland
50 residences
2 stores
1 tavern-store
1 church
1 lodge hall
1 ball park and
   fair ground

Mason City
46 residences
1 tavern

Fields Street
8 residences
1 church
1 lodge hall

looks forward to improved streets as one of the first signs of improved status—and incidentally, as a reward for political activity.

There is no single center of dominance or point of focus in the Negro community. The only Negro institution that serves or touches the community at large is the school in the Jackson Street area. The poolroom is a specialized center. Each area, with the exception of one, has at least one church; however church attendance tends to follow preference lines rather than locality lines. Each area (with the exception of Fields Street) has one or more taverns, and it is the tavern that vies with the church as the dominant symbol of interest and activity in the neighborhood.

Each neighborhood has a local history. Although identification of person with area is not strong enough to foster neighborhood organization, it is strong enough to mark individuals off from one another in terms of residence and to lessen the total solidarity and unity of Negroes in Kent. Discrete neighborhoods rank with denominations as divisive tendencies. There are many persons who have frequent contact with persons of other areas only in churches, the main business district, taverns, or the balcony of the one local theater. The existence of these four discrete areas certainly lessens the sense of strong community solidarity among Kent Negroes; identification tends to be in terms of the local area of residence. In any large gathering there is bound to be a large number of persons who are "away from home," and behavior and sensitivities indicate mutual awareness of the handicap of distance in terms of travel and frequent contact.

The Foreign Cultural Component

SURROUNDING and impinging ways of life are in varying degrees "foreign" to the Kent Negro's way of life; his local customs adjust to a constant stream of influences from the outside. The changes that occur in Kent Negro society are aspects of an acculturation process that goes on constantly, involving it and influences from relatively different societies and value systems. Among the more pertinent influences that affect the local Negro are: local white ways, Negro life and activities in other parts of the nation, rural and urban, and national and international forces and trends.

The very existence of this Negro subculture is a function, in the main, of local white customs and values. The Negro way of life, no matter what its content and emphases may be, is essentially a forced way of life. The color or race line is the most important single factor making for a Negro world distinct from the local white world. Consciousness of color or race is an all-pervading influence. All aspects of life tend to be race-ridden; this is among the most crucial of the thoughtways that result from contact with the "foreign" ways and values of the white community.

The world of white folks tends to be, from the point of view of the Negro, a world marked by the different incidence of material objects and with more sophistication and polish on the average. It is characterized by emphases and values related to public status and power, and it is marked by easier access to what are essentially common goals. From the point of view of the minority, these are the things that are foreign about the way of life of the dominant group; they are facts to which the Negro must adjust his ways. There seems to be no major disposition for the local Negro to hold on to Negro ways and values, as such—in fact, although they are accepted and adjusted to, they are often the objects of significant shame and criticism. A recurrent expression among Negroes is, "After all, you've got to live here!" Their behavior and values tend to be realistic adaptations to that theme. There is explicit common-sense recognition on the part of the Kent Negro that the ways of white folks are different (and that the ways of Negroes are different when dealing with whites): "White

folks is white folks," "I was going to do just like the white
folks," "He treats her just like a white woman," "You can't
talk to white folks like that," "A colored man is just different,
I don't care what you say. A Negro will mess up every
time." [22]

Local white culture has many functions or effects. This
white culture restricts Negro life, while at the same time com-
plementing it in such a way as to make possible its continued
existence; the white culture gives a kind of enforced unity to
Negro culture, while at the same time disrupting and making
for low morale; the white culture serves as a model for the
conventional and accepted, and yet certain facets are rejected
or held inferior by group-conscious Negroes; it restricts and
censors much behavior, and on the other hand encourages
certain behavior by tolerance and indifference.

The adjustment of the local Negro to rural influences is
not a difficult one and involves no problems that are recognized
as crucial. Kent culture itself has a significant rural streak, and
the majority of the Negro adults have a rural background.
Contact and social and economic interchange with the rural
areas are constant and basic to the local style of life. The
situation is congenial to the retention of many rural practices.
Apparently the adjustment to "modern" agriculture—mechanization, diversification, soil conservation—has been made
easily by the Negroes in the town of Kent who are primarily
farmers. One Negro farmer owns a tractor, and many small
operators—usually part-time farmers—hire mechanical equipment by the hour for breaking the land. The shortage of agricultural labor in the rural areas of the county makes easier

22. Although this statement was made by a male teacher, an outsider,
sardonic judgments of this type are not unusual at any level. Such expressions are not necessarily believed to be literally true. They are for ingroup
consumption.

the transition to the "new farming" for both Negro and white farmers. Despite the importance of farming in the surrounding area and Kent's indirect dependence upon it, the primary functions of the town as a marketing and processing area mean that the impact of new agricultural methods upon the average Negro tends to be indirect and has the character of interesting news for persons who are not now directly involved, since they are townspeople.

The Kent Negro—along with the rest of the population—has adjusted his ways to the features of urban penetration which have modified expenditure and consumption patterns, transportation and communication, recreation and leisure-time activity, and the use of modern conveniences. The chain stores and national advertising affect expenditure and consumption patterns although local enterprisers still get a significant share of Negro trade: habit, personal relationships, and added services of the private merchant, such as credit, make for the continuing patronage of small local merchants by both Negroes and whites. The Kent Negro reads the news of the outside world and county happenings from the three out-of-town papers. Three out of every five Negro households take at least one of the papers from nearby larger centers. The circulation of the nearby Stone Valley daily is slightly higher among Negroes than the circulation of the two Metro City papers.[23] The circulation of the national Negro weekly newspapers was uneven and unpredictable: one Negro family ("Chick" Thorpe's) received the *Pittsburgh Courier* by mail; during a span of three weeks, a Negro barber served as distributing agent for the *Baltimore Afro-American,* and he and his sons never quite sold their full allotment of fifty copies; about thirty subscribers received the *Capitola Beacon,* a militant paper with primarily an urban state circulation, for a three-

---

23. One Negro, a native of the town who had just returned to teach school, had a mail subscription to the *New York Times* for six months of the year.

month period,[24] and six of that thirty became regular subscribers on an annual basis.[25]

The relatively limited circulation of Negro newspapers is no real measure as to the circulation of news about Negroes in other communities: Negro newspapers (and magazines like *Ebony* and *Our World* which can be picked up on newsstands in nearby cities) are shared and passed around to a greater extent than the daily papers. Daily papers and magazines carry an increasing amount of news about Negro sports figures, political activities and issues, and distinguished achievements—and news of crime and violence involving Negroes has always had circulation in these papers. Thus news of significant happenings and persons in the Negro world is passed around and shared and becomes a rallying point for identification, pride, invidious comparisons, shame, and resentment. Fresh news about other Negroes, no matter what its source, is probably the most important element linking the local Negro to the larger Negro community; at the same time that it makes him more group-conscious it widens his horizons and brings him and his ways into a closer relationship to the national culture.

There is one movie house with a balcony for Negroes that holds 115 persons. Tickets for the balcony are sold on the stairway by the Negro man who has charge of changing the marquee and posting the notices of current and coming attractions; he is relieved by the Negro woman (the wife of

24. This was a tie-in deal with the financing of the efforts of the state Negro political organization with headquarters in Capitola to force by court action admission of Negroes into primary elections and to encourage Negro use of the ballot. The persons who paid their dues in the local branch of the organization, the Fair Deal Democratic Club, were given a three-months' subscription to the *Beacon* which served as the unofficial organ for the leaders of the Fair Deal Democratic Party who directed activities from the largest cities of the state, Capitola and Seaton.

25. These were the local leaders of the Fair Deal Democratic Club (the minister of the African Methodist Episcopal Zion Church, a non-native), a school teacher-minister, a lady insurance agent, a filling station operator, a farmer, and a barber.

a Negro tavern-store operator) who doubles as the maid for the white proprietor who is one of the "aggressive newcomers" to the town. Aside from the regular small-town fare of second-run features, westerns and serials, about once every three months a special midnight show featuring a film with Negro actors or a film especially slanted for Negro audiences is presented. White attendance at these features is usually small but Negroes are always restricted to the balcony regardless of the size of audience. The people who attend the movies regularly are predominantly school age children and young adults. The movie habit tends to be confined to these age groups; men and women over forty rarely attend.

The radio is well-nigh universal, with four out of five households having at least one set. Although Kent itself has no radio station, the town is the center of a good receiving area. It receives strong daytime signals from more than twenty stations which are scattered in the nearby towns of two states; the two stations in nearby Stone Valley and the four stations in Metro City are most frequently tuned in. In each of these cities and in several of the surrounding communities, special programs of jazz, blues, and gospel singing are beamed at the Negro audiences of the area. During the spring and summer months, the most popular daytime station among men listeners is a North Carolina station some eighty miles away which broadcasts daily a big league baseball game. The fortunes of the Brooklyn and Cleveland baseball teams and the records of the Negro stars on those teams are followed avidly through the press and radio and are matters of great interest to practically all males from adolescence on and to many younger women.

The incidence of "modern conveniences" gives further clues to urbanization among Negroes: more than 90 percent of the residences are wired for electricity; approximately two-thirds of the residences have running water, but in about three out of every four of these cases the water comes from a spigot in the front or back yard. (The people who have no running water of their own usually get it from neighbors; they are often thought of as "cheap" or lacking resourcefulness.) Less than 10 percent of the households have flush toilets and bath tubs; no Negro residence is on a city sewer line and hence the septic tank is the rule in all these cases. The number of families with telephones is even smaller; [26] there are but seven —assigned to "Chick" Thorpe, the undertaker; his mother, "Miss Phoebe" Thorpe; his aunt, "Miss Rose," the storekeeper; "A. B." Green, the taxicab driver; the Methodist Episcopal parsonage (which was vacant more than half the year with the exception of week-ends because the pastor then assigned was a student in a theological school in Atlanta and commuted the 250 miles every week); Bradley, the attendant at one of the town's larger service stations; and "Blood" Roberts' service station. About one in seven households has electrical refrigeration. There are about seventy-five cars and trucks in the possession of Negroes—or one for every fourteen persons; they are invariably second hand cars with the most frequent type being more than twelve years old.

The Kent Negro exhibits no special difficulties in adjusting to those features of urban and rural life that influence him here. Up to this time his ways have been flexible and diversified enough to incorporate elements from each without creating general problems. The crucial problems of his society have their sources in other areas.

The local Negro's knowledge of what goes on in other Negro communities, the experiences which many have had in those communities, and the local activities of agents from interest groups in those communities have an increasingly important influence on the behavior, attitudes and expecta-

26. The telephone company began to string new lines into Negro neighborhoods in late summer of 1949; and the number of phones doubled immediately.

tions of the local Negro. The most significant of these influences come from the centers of Negro population in the urban North and to a lesser degree from southern urban centers. Their effects are seen in economic behavior; fads and fashions in dress, grooming, music and dancing; fraternal and religious policy; Negro participation in local politics; and race pride and consciousness. In some degree, local images of "what Negroes are doing in other places" serve functions similar to the images that circulate of "what white folks are doing": some tend to be models of the conventional and the successful; others are rejected or held inferior to local Negro ways. For example, fashions, items of conspicuous consumption, expressions of political or economic achievement are likely to be looked upon favorably and stimulate imitation, but the Negroes who remain in Kent tend to reject any suggestion that the style of life of Negroes in northern urban centers and the manner in which they are treated—by law enforcement officers, as an instance—are necessarily better. From the point of view of the outsider, the Kent Negro may exhibit a perverse loyalty to regional and local ways, but it seems highly probable that to him it is only occasionally that such loyalty is consciously seen as inconsistent or ironic. The overall design which gives meaning to his life in Kent would probably collapse without the sentiment that Kent is a good— and in some ways, a superior—place to live.

The many relatives and friends of Negro Kentians who are scattered for the most part in eastern urban centers are one of the more important factors in communication and identification with other centers. It seems as if every family and practically every adult individual has some tie of sentiment or recognition with relatives or friends in urban centers. This identification with persons and places tends to be strong even though letters and direct communication may be infrequent. References to Negro Kentians who are living elsewhere indicate two major patterns of migration in the past twenty years:

first, the relatively short movement to nearby cities; and second, the longer movement to eastern centers, the most important of which are New York City, Philadelphia, and Washington. Many migrants follow the custom of the annual vacation visit to family and friends. Death and illness in the family are other important reasons for the temporary return of the migrant. A small number of persons return to Kent to live the remainder of their lives after having spent many years away. For the most part such persons are older men and women who have no conjugal families of their own who return to live with sisters or brothers or to set up their own households. These persons bring a certain sophistication and many memories; their conversations are sprinkled with such expressions as "When I was in service in New Jersey...." and "Before I decided to come back here...."

The Kent Negro population itself is made up overwhelmingly of South Carolinians who were born in Kent or adjacent counties. Up Country Kent Negroes tend to look down upon Low Country Negroes, North Carolinians, and Georgians. The Kent Negro has few meaningful contacts or identifications with southern centers outside of the state.

The typical adult Negro Kentian is a person who has traveled and had some personal contact with persons in other centers. These travels may be classified as follows: the trips to nearby cities for shopping, work, professional care, recreation, and education; the trips to more remote centers for work, vacations or holidays; and the trips to urban centers incidental to service in the armed forces. The greatest and most constant flow of Negro travel is between Kent and Stone Valley. This rapidly growing industrial and commercial center of the county has a population of over 25,000 of whom about 7,000 are Negroes. Stone Valley has in its Negro community two physicians, three dentists, one pharmacist, a night club, two church-supported junior colleges, the largest and best equipped Negro high school in the county, and a very active

NAACP. The physicians and the dentists attract few Kent Negro patients (most Kent Negroes patronize the local white professional men); the night club is familiar to young Negro Kentians but it attracts no regular patronage from Kent; Kent Negroes are called upon in their churches to help support the junior colleges and they tend to share Stone Valley's pride in the more successful of the two—the Baptist-supported Amity College—as "our school." During the course of this study no Negro from Kent was enrolled as a regular student at either of the colleges, but two veterans commuted daily to take building construction courses in the special "veterans' classes" subsidized by the federal government. During 1947 and early 1948, about forty Negro Kent men—mostly veterans—commuted daily to Stone Valley to help in the construction of the big Maximum Plant; at the time of this writing, three Negroes from Kent have jobs in the completed plant. The Maximum Plant in Stone Valley provided something that Kent has never been able to do: jobs at premium pay ($.87½ to $1.60 per hour) for a large group of semi-skilled and skilled Negroes.

Comments of Kent Negroes indicate that they look upon the Negro community of Stone Valley with mixed feelings: they seem to recognize it as a community where some Negroes make a great deal of money and exhibit a high level of living as measured in types of homes, automobiles, travel, and entertainment; and they also concede that the fraternal groups and the NAACP are stronger and better led. Younger people who refrain from going to Kent's taverns frequently refer to Stone Valley as a place where one can do things by way of recreation that cannot be done in Kent. On the other hand, the typical Negro Kentian tends to be highly critical of the "superior airs" of many Stone Valley Negroes and the manners and untrustworthiness of Stone Valley's nonrespectable Negro population. Some balm for any feelings of inferiority and envy that Kent Negroes may have with respect to Stone

Valley Negroes comes from the fact that Kent's Negro high school basketball team has consistently beaten Stone Valley's team for the past five years.

Travel to Metro City, the metropolis just over the state line, is less frequent and more selective. One Negro male who works there during the week returns to Kent every weekend; similarly, two Negro domestics return from their Metro City jobs once a month. Four or five families which are better situated economically make seasonal shopping trips to the larger department stores of Metro City. Younger men frequently organize groups to drive over for the periodic dances at the City Auditorium which feature nationally famous Negro bands and musical attractions. Metro City has a Negro college from which four current residents of Kent have graduated: "Chick" Thorpe, the undertaker; his nephew, Tom Thorpe, who returned to Kent to work with his father in construction work; the preacher-teacher, Reverend Williams; and his son, John, who teaches at the local high school. "Chick" Thorpe's sisters who are teachers in the county have also attended summer sessions at the Metro City college. For the average Negro Kentian, Metro City is known through its newspapers and radio stations far more than through frequent and regular visits; and the trips that are made tend to be related to the specialized services of a metropolis rather than to general participation in the Negro community.

The town of Blossom is closer to Kent than either Stone Valley or Metro City, but it is smaller than both and probably exerts less influence on Kent than either. The baseball teams of Blossom and Kent are traditional and spirited rivals, and when one team plays in the other's town, large numbers of rooters accompany it. There are several courting relationships between the men and women of the two towns, particularly among the nonrespectable group; gossip frequently links persons in the two communities. Blossom is nearer Textile City across the state line than it is to Kent, and since Textile City is larger than either, it probably exerts a stronger pull on the Blossom Negro than does Kent; hence very few Blossom Negroes come to Kent for services. Some local Negroes claim that although Blossom is smaller than Kent and has a smaller Negro population, the Negroes there are more "progressive," civic-minded, and independent than the Kent Negroes: Blossom Negroes have a uniformed high school band, and a Negro policeman; Kent has neither.

The Negro Kentians who make regular vacation trips to larger and more remote centers are few, but there are those like the porter-clerk at Field's Drug Store and the lady insurance agent who have successful children in northern cities whom they visit annually. Others of the young and middle-aged adult group have made brief visits to centers where they have usually visited a brother or a sister who had preceded them. References to such visits and experiences are frequent. And then there is a small group of men, about eight, who went together with a larger group in 1929 to a small town in New York to work in a brick kiln; they drifted back in the early 1930's. Similarly, there are one or two older men who speak of experiences when they were recruited to work on the construction of levees on the Mississippi during the 1930's.

One of the effects of contacts with other Negro communities is the awakening political interest and activity of local Negroes. Negro leaders from the state capital who were working closely with the national officers of the National Association for the Advancement of Colored People relayed political information and instructions to local Negroes prior to the election of 1948. This was done mainly through a mass meeting held in one of the local churches at which a person from the outside interpreted the federal court ruling [27] admitting Negroes to the Democratic primary and instructed local

27. In 1947, a federal judge ruled that Negroes could not be excluded from the Democratic primary. The ruling was sustained by the Fourth Circuit Court of Appeals and the Supreme Court. In the 1948 primaries, Negroes voted freely for the first time since 1876.

Negroes on registration and balloting procedure and strategy.[28] The local person who worked closely with state leaders and who led the way in registration of Negroes was the pastor of the African Methodist Episcopal Zion Church, a native of an adjoining state who had been in the community but one year.

Other Negro societies in the United States not only provide local Negro Kentians with a stream of stimuli and images of different ways of doing things but they also provide some of the leadership and pressure for reform which the local community does not possess or cannot exercise.

The depression of the 1930's, the New Deal of President Roosevelt, World War II, and the civil rights program of President Truman, are significant landmarks in the minds of adult Negroes; they reflect a consciousness of the importance of larger and outside influences upon their way of life here. They represent changes in expectations. "Back in Hoover times" is a frequent reference of the older generation. The interest of many in the candidacy of Truman for the presidency, aside from the civil rights question and the "Dixiecrat Revolt," was in the possibility that a Republican would be elected. One person, referring to "Hoover times," said "A Republican would be bad for the Negroes and poor people." Older persons still recount with humor how they fared during the period. In the same sense that Hoover was the villain, Roosevelt remains a hero—a person who championed their cause and made them acutely aware of the power and interest of the government. The "government" and the "government man" have come to be important personifications of personal aid, fear, and hope. Direct relief, work relief, the Civilian Conservation Corps, old age pensions, unemployment compensation, crop controls, and subsidies have shaped new patterns of action and expectations.

28. See pp. 172-176.

World War II, aside from the changes it made in normal routines, took the large majority of male youths and younger male adults out of the country. Of the approximately one hundred and sixty Negro males between 18 and 40 years old, about three out of four or roughly one hundred and twenty-five were inducted into the Armed Services.[29] Of those who left the community to serve in the Armed Services, about one in three did not choose to return to Kent—or if he did return, he did not stay.[30] The highest ranking person to return was Lieutenant "Blood" Roberts (who now operates the filling station); he was promoted while in the field in the South Pacific, and is the only Negro from Kent who achieved officer status.[31] A good majority of those who returned were persons who were married when they were inducted, or who got married shortly after their return. Very few veterans returned to claim jobs they held before induction. This is in part due to the fact that most of the better and steady jobs for males—such as janitors in the mills or store porters—have been held by older males.

The veterans who have returned to Kent to stay have for the most part adjusted to the local routine of life; but they are persons with important memories, different conceptions of themselves and their worth as human beings, and a more

29. This figure is based on the Roll of Honor of Kent Negroes who served in World War II, published in the 1947 high school year book, the *Jacksonian*.

30. This estimate is based on a listing of the known veterans living in Kent during the summer of 1949. The listing of 77 persons was based on the investigator's person and family file, the designations of informants, and a checking of the town's roll of those persons eligible to pay the annual street tax (all adult males under 65 are required to pay an annual street tax of five dollars, unless exempted for service given in the voluntary fire department).

31. This is an important factor in his conception of himself now. He constantly refers in conversation to his leadership role during the war and the fact that he billeted with white officers and commanded both Negro and white troops on some of his noncombatant details. He comments wryly on the irony of his being unable to join the local National Guard.

personal interest in national and world affairs.[32] The chief
themes of veterans' conversations about their wartime status
and experiences are: educational aspects of service in the
armed forces, pleasant and unpleasant experiences as Negroes
in foreign and domestic service, avowals of what they will do
or not do or "take" or "not take" on the domestic scene,
status in the "52-20 Club," [33] the things they did when they
first returned and the subsequent changes in attitudes and
financial status, and the chances of war with Russia.

In the general population there is evidence of sensitivity to
the national and international discussion of peace, freedom,
and human rights, but characteristically, the greatest sensitivity is to those issues which are seen as affecting them directly.
"Do you reckon Truman's going to be able to give us those
civil rights?" was a recurrent question that caught much of
the attitude toward the civil rights controversy. There is no
expectation of radical change in status immediately—the Kent
Negro is realistic above all—but there is a promise and an expectation of improvement that is generally shared, even by
the most skeptical. Civil rights are rarely defined or conceived in specific terms, rather they are thought of in such
general terms as justice, opportunity, and respect. The only
specific item that got frequent mention during the study
was the right to the ballot.

32. However, as a whole, the group has shown little or no interest in
organizing or channeling such interests. They are not affiliated with any
local or national veterans' interest group; they are poorly represented in
the ranks of the local NAACP, the Fair Deal Club, and the Parent-Teachers'
Association which are devoted to local improvement. Their interest in national affairs is expressed as the interest of discussants wondering how and
when changing events would affect them individually.
33. Federal unemployment compensation for veterans.

· PART TWO ·

THE CONTENT
OF THE SUBCULTURE

THE CONTENT OF THE SUBCULTURE

THIS SECTION IS primarily an inventory of the customs of the Kent Negro; it is a description of action and belief and the bases of consensus in this society. Some practices and uniformities are explicit, others are implicit and must be inferred. Linton points out that the contents of a culture can be divided into three categories—universals, specialties, alternatives, "these being derived from the extent to which the elements ... are shared by the society's members." [1] This description of content will include indications as to what persons practice, or may practice, the indicated customs, and when.

An exhaustive listing of every element or pattern is impractical and would be of little value in terms of the ends of this study. In keeping with the fact that the parts of a cultural system may be seen as representing an ascending order of organization of elements —culture traits, cultural complexes, institutions, orientations, value systems [2]—it is assumed that the substance of this subculture can be caught through examining the higher orders of custom patterning.

1. Ralph Linton, *The Study of Man* (New York: D. Appleton-Century Company, 1936), pp. 272-73.
2. John Gillin, *The Ways of Men*, p. 492.

Cultural Complexes

CHAPTER **3** In Kent Negro society, there are a number of cultural complexes that catch the action or interest of practically every normal adult; the person tends to be aware of them or affected by them even if he is not an active participant. Some of these complexes are parts of larger institutional patterns. Among the complexes are: church-going, insurance, cotton, whisky, burying, hunting and fishing, sex play and dalliance, baseball, idling, one-story frame dwelling, white patron or friend, nicknames, lodge and "society," and dress and ornamentation. Descriptions of some of the more important or characteristic complexes of the subculture are included in this chapter. Churchgoing, burying, sex play and dalliance, and white friend or patron will be described later as parts of related institutions.

The Frame Dwelling Complex

Since there are but two brick buildings used as residences for Negroes, the chances are about 125 to one that the Negro of Kent lives in a wooden frame building; the chances are fifty to one that it is a one-story building; and the chances are about eight to one that it is a house badly in need of major repairs. In a tabulation of 239 residences occupied by Negroes, 219, or 91 percent, were owned by Negroes; 147, or 61 percent, were owner-occupied; 72, or 30 percent, were rented by Negro landlords; and 20, or 9 percent, were rented by white landlords.

The modal house has three or four small rooms that are unpapered and probably in need of paint; if an old house—and the majority are more than 25 years old, according to the residents—it rests unevenly on rock pilings; it has a small front porch, an unfenced front yard with flowers in season, a back yard that normally contains an outhouse, the invariable black wash pot, and a small vegetable garden. For 90 percent of the houses, the unpaved street without sidewalks is a part of the complex.

An 11-year old student's description of "The House I Live In" approaches the modal type of house.

My house has three large rocks and a spigot in the front yard. It has a sycamore tree in the front yard. It has four rooms and two porches. It has a tin top.

As you go in the front door you enter the front room. To the left is a bedroom. The door at the right in the first bedroom leads to the kitchen. The door at the right in the kitchen leads to another bedroom. There are two bedrooms, a living room, and a kitchen.

The living room has two windows, wall paper on the walls. The bedrooms have two windows and wall paper on the wall. The kitchen has an oil stove and a kitchenette. The people living in the house are mother and father, two brothers, one sister and myself.*

Housing has some status and pride connotations, as is indicated by the general attitudes toward deviations from the typical. Although the vast majority of the houses are in poor condition, there are a few that are looked down upon as outside the mode, and the residents are thought of as being indifferent or particularly unfortunate: the residents of Barry

* In this and following excerpts throughout the book, the attempt has been made to reproduce case material exactly as it was written or spoken. The use of "*sic*" to indicate errors, therefore, has been avoided.

Lane, whose houses furnish meager protection against the elements and are in imminent danger of falling down; the two families that live in converted railroad box cars; and the five families that live in the congested quarters of "Brick Building."

A student's description of this type of housing went like this:

My house is an old three room shack on side of a road. It has a tin top on it and a front porch. Some of the window panes are broken out. We have one fire place and a heater. In the kitchen is one table, ice box, kitchen cabanet and a stove. It is seven living in the house, my two sister, mother, aunt, cousin, grandmother.

On the other hand, there are the differentiated few who live in painted houses and/or have "modern conveniences." These are "nice houses." The appointments of one of these "nice houses" were described at length by a student:

It is a six room structure with bath. On the right side of the house is the living room, dining room, and kitchen. The living room has pink and white wallpaper, a couch, three armchairs, two wine ones and one green one, at each end of the couch are end tables with big white lamps on them. On each side of the room there are end tables with flowers on them. In front of the couch is a coffee table. Beside the front window is a large radio that plays records. In the corner is a very large whatnot. On the whatnot is a selection of beautiful novelties.

There are green and white curtains at the windows. There are two straight chairs on the right side of the room. There is a heater in the middle of the room. The rug on the floor has large roses on it with a light tan background.

Next is the dining room it has pink and white wallpaper. There is a large china closet on one side of the room. On the other side is a sideboard with two candles and a mirrow on it, and on the other side of the room is an electric refrigerator. In the middle of the room is a small dinner table with six chairs.

And next is the kitchen it is painted yellow. It has a wood stove and beside it is the kitchen sink. Behind the stove is a small cabinit and beside this is another large cabinit where the can goods are kept, and beside this cabanit is another large cabanit where the dishes, pots, and pans are kept. There is also a table with four chairs in the middle of the room.

On the left side of the house is my mother and father's bedroom. Next is my grandmothers and aunts bedroom and the next bedroom belongs to R- - - and me and last of all the bathroom.

My mothers room has blue, pink and white wallpaper it has pink and white curtains, a bed, dresser, fire place, two chester drawers, a sewing machine a small table with radio on it. There is a big straight chair by the fireplace and over the fireplace is a mantle piece with a large gold mirrow over it. There is also a rocking chair in front of the fireplace.

My grandmothers room has wallpaper with flowers on it. She has blue and white curtains. First there is the bed, chester drawers, babies bed, the heater and over it is a very large brown mirrow. And then the close closet and the dresser.

And then next is R - - -'s and my room it has blue, pink and white wallpaper. It also has white curtains. First there is the dresser, bed, and table over the dresser is a little shelf where I keep my airplanes and train.

Last of all is the bathroom. It has blue and white walls. First is the stool then the tower rack and the sink. Over the sink is a mirrow. Next is the window it has blue and white curtains and then the bath tub at both ends of the tub there are tower racks. The bath tub has hot and cold running water.

Lacking objective measurement of a "nice house," varied individuals were asked what they meant by the expression. The most frequently mentioned characteristics, in order: plenty of room, good condition, painted, good furniture, modern conveniences, rugs on the floor and pictures on the wall. A jury of three was then asked to list the "nice houses" occupied by Negroes. There was agreement on 34, or about one in every eight of all the houses occupied by Negroes. There are 11 residences equipped with "modern conveniences"—flush toilets, possibly accompanied by bath tub, and hot and cold running water. Nine of the 11 residences with "modern conveniences" were also on the "nice house" list.

Of all the items of equipment in the housing complex, the piano seems one of the best crude indexes to higher economic and social status and its correlates—the design for respectability and mobility in selves and children, stable family, education, and community leadership. Of the 24 families who owned pianos, 21 were among the 34 families listed with "nice houses."

In one sense, the housing complex presents a paradox. Most of the houses are in need of paint externally, in poor repair, and tend to be overcrowded, but the level of housekeeping on the inside is generally high. Furnishings may be meager, of poor quality or makeshift in character, but generally speaking the rooms are kept clean and relatively ordered. In many small crowded homes, the bed is the central piece of furniture and it gives tone to the whole interior. The bed is omnipresent because so many of the rooms do double- or triple-duty as living, sleeping, and eating places. The style and quality of the bed are frequently not in keeping with the other furnishings. In many cases, this is because the bed or the bedroom set is one of the first things bought by the couple beginning housekeeping or the couple seeking to improve living conditions. In any case, beds, as central pieces, are usually neatly made up and frequently colorfully covered. Among older women, collections of spreads have great importance. In a house lacking other distinction, the spread is often a showpiece proudly exhibited to the visitor. Similarly, the kitchen stove is the central piece of that part of the house. Generally speaking, the level of housekeeping in the kitchen is below that of the bedroom and the living room.

Formal and ritualistic visiting, except in the case of the minister's visits or the entertainment of church clubs, is infrequent. Most visiting is informal and casual and takes place in the daytime. Exchanges of pleasantries and gossip generally take place on the porches and in the front yards. Most people spend a great deal of their leisure time on their front porches. Generally speaking, the house and its arrangements are geared primarily to the eating and sleeping of household members; inter-family activity in homes is limited and occasional. A few homes serve as headquarters for teen-age cliques; a few serve as places for social card playing (whist) among a small group of men.

Older people are most concerned about owning a home or the possibility of "building me a house." Custom and security seem to loom larger than display and comfort as values here, although home ownership does have high prestige value. For young people, "having a nice house" is a more important value; they show more anxiety over the quality of housing than do their parents. A student who lives in one of the houses rated as a "nice house" wrote voluntarily:

In my home I would change the conditions that we live under. I would remodel it and have a modern equipped home built. I would halt the confusion between the family and make it peaceful and comfortable.

How does the Kent Negro get to own or occupy a house? And what considerations are involved? The following general patterns are apparent:

(1) Inheritance from spouse or parents. This is an important factor in the relative security and independence of many of Kent's widows and the good "head start" of many younger couples. Such people are considered fortunate. The disposition of the property of widows upon their eventual death, especially when they are without close heirs, is a matter of considerable interest and speculation. In a few cases, persons who are interested have sought to make agreements such as this: transfer of the property with the understanding that the aged person will have a home as long as he or she lives. In any case, property ownership makes the widow the subject of some envy and deference and she often is under more or less subtle pressure as to its use and disposal.

(2) Purchase or rental of "heir property." Descendants of property owners who live in remote communities sell or rent property which they do not intend to occupy. The ownership of every piece of property is generally known and interest in what absentee heirs will do is always acute. The behavior of the heirs is generally impersonal and unpredictable. In two recent cases, heirs sold very desirable property in Negro neighborhoods to white millworkers; in another case, property was "sold out from under" a renter who had a verbal option to buy it and was prepared to meet any price. The white lawyer-executor-adviser is often an important figure in deciding who gets what.

(3) Purchase or rental of investment property. Investment property may be held by whites or Negroes. In some cases, such property has been in families for a long period; in other cases, houses may be built with a special interest in the Negro market or for some particular person. One white widow makes a practice of renting her properties only to Negroes who are willing to work for her. Building houses for sale or for rent, or buying up available properties for investment purposes, represents one of the few ways in which the ambitious or enterprising Negro can make money. One such person in speculating about the possibilities of better housing for Negroes commented: "Negroes going to have to learn to pay more rent; they are wanting modern conveniences and they have got to pay for them." The average rent for the older "Negro houses" is between $7.00 and $12.00 per month; the sale price between $800.00 and $1100.00. Some recently built houses that are very small but that have some modern conveniences are offered at $35.00 per month with a portion being credited on the purchase price. These were built by a local farm implement distributor and the first house was occupied by one of his employees.

(4) Gift from parents or family. A few of the more stable families have provided significant aid to younger members of the family in the acquisition or building of a house. In one or two instances a house for a son or a daughter has been built on an adjoining lot.

(5) Gift of property from white employers or benefactors. There are at least a half dozen houses occupied by Negroes which fall in this category. These persons are considered very fortunate and as a rule are themselves substantial persons in the community. The houses are better than average quality. One widow, now deceased, gave four homes to her cooks and maids and provided her chauffeur with a house for his lifetime.

(6) "Building me a house." This normally involves the purchase of a lot—usually some time before the actual building begins—and obtaining some means of financing it. Most of the financing is done through one of the two local banks. One of the banks has a building and loan arrangement and the president is familiarly spoken of in the Negro community as a sharp dealer "who owns many a Negro around here." In a few instances, the financing and much of the actual construction of the house are now done by the person who is to occupy it.

The Cotton Complex

Cotton growing and cotton processing set the pace of economic and social activity for the Negro of Kent. This is true whether he is involved directly or not. There are at least thirty Negroes in the community who are actively growing cotton. Between twenty and fifty Negroes are normally employed in the five local mills. At least six of the men who were laid off from the mills during the course of this study turned to part-time cotton farming as a means of supplementing income. Six Negroes work for the cotton warehouses and brokers. A number of Negroes work as domestic servants for mill workers, mill executives, and local businessmen whose income stems directly from cotton. During the periods when extra manpower is required for hoeing and picking cotton, the unemployed and the casual workers are busy. The weather in relation to crops, the progress of the crop, the price of cotton and the wages for working it are matters of general interest and conversation. Church and school attendance are affected, particularly among rural residents. Major church and community events are timed to coincide with the progress of the crop: spring revival meetings tend to coincide with the completion of planting and later summer meetings with the picking. The Kent County Colored Fair comes in the early fall, and its promoters anticipate the newly acquired spending power of cotton workers. The buying of heavy goods and luxury goods tends to coincide with the sale of crops.

The pattern of idling and leisure-time activity ties in with the rhythm of cotton production. As one Negro farmer just outside the city limits put it:

Whenever I hears a clap of thunder or a dark cloud comes up, I jumps on my mule and comes uptown to see what's going on.... Just as soon as I gets my cotton in, I gets out my gun and dogs and heads for the field to hunt.

The Dress and Grooming Complex

MANNER of dress and adornment is generally recognized by student and layman as one of the significant features distinguishing peoples and cultures—and status groups within a society. In a gross sense, the dress, adornment, and grooming of the Kent Negro follow the American regional pattern, with appropriate differentials in terms of sex, age, occupation, and income. Differences within the Negro community indicate that there is no basic "Negro dress pattern," as such, and that there is a basic strain toward conventionality. There are, however, certain traits that are common to Negroes or that apparently have a greater incidence in the group. What often occurs in the case of dress and grooming can be attributed to a "distortion" of the conventional: psychological or status factors may operate, or the distortion may be due to the not wholly successful absorption or practicing of available or model customs in the larger community.

The small range of occupational differentiation and the fact that a large percentage of the population—both male and female—work or are candidates for work mean that work clothes are dominant styles for everyday wear. The only males who regularly wear ties are the few preachers, the teachers, the undertakers, and one of the tavern owners—a total of less than a dozen. There are certain pressures that operate from the white community with respect to dress and manner. The Negro is aware of these pressures even if he doesn't always bow to them. The Negro male who dresses well consistently (i.e., without overalls or work clothes on week days), or who in his bearing or manner does not suggest a certain deference or humility, or the Negro who wears glasses, is in danger of being labeled a "smart nigger." The least he can expect, no matter what his occupation or interest, is to be called (with some degree of patronage) "preacher" or "teacher." As one young Negro put it, "They don't like nobody who don't wear overalls and don't work like digging ditches. If a man dress decent, he's a smart nigger."

Among the distinctive but not necessarily universal features of dress and grooming among local Negroes are these: gaucheries in dress and adornment, hair treatment and styling, stylings of men's headwear, and the incidence of gold teeth and fillings.

Gaucheries of dress and adornment are most common among the lower status persons, who are often the most recent rural migrants, and among older persons. Among women, the deviations may take any of these forms: several layers of clothing,[1] mixture of male and female articles, cheap or ill-fitting versions of current styles, obviously cast-off, second-hand clothing such

---

1. A fellow student in the local community after observing a Negro woman with newspapers inside her stockings on a cold day, suggested the following hypothesis: "That, in lower status groups, the function of clothing is closest to its original function of affording protection from the elements; and that, as the social scale is ascended, this original function becomes more and more secondary, with the prestige factor becoming more important, often letting fashion supersede protection from the elements."

as worn fur coats and incongruously fancy dresses and accessories. Among men, the deviations may take the form of mis-
placed or inappropriate accessories such as pins or chains and
odd ties, or tielessness when otherwise "dressed-up." A part
of this impression of awkwardness given the observer is due
to the self-consciousness of workingmen and women on the
special occasions when a manner of attire that is different from
the usual is indicated.

Several factors support and reinforce this pattern, among
them the sources of clothing and the basic lack of purchasing
power. Some merchants tend to stock and prominently display
a line of goods that is supposed to appeal to the low-income
Negro and rural trade. Choice of the consumer is limited; by
custom he usually deals with the same merchant or merchants
over a period of time and often on a credit basis. By custom,
too, a significant amount of the Negro's clothing is handed
down from whites or is bought secondhand. As a consequence,
fittings in many cases are likely to be approximate, and color
and style blendings off. On Saturdays throughout the year,
several temporary sidewalk stands featuring a wide range of
used clothing are set up; they cater primarily to low-income
Negroes and whites. A Negro woman is the distributing agent
for the regular shipments of used clothing that come in for
the residents of a local institution. The white officials, instead
of distributing the clothes that are sent in from all over the
country, sell them through this agent. Whites and Negroes
are among her regular customers. The chances are that the
average purchaser thus has access to better quality clothes
than he would or could ordinarily purchase, albeit at the ex-
pense of accurate fit and harmonizing.

It should be stressed that this awkwardness of dress is in
the nature of a lag that diminishes as education, income, and
contact with the conventional increase. Evidences of change
(acculturation) are most striking among younger women. An
ex-teacher was asked what changes she had noted among the

students during her 20-year stay in the community; she replied:

I think the really remarkable changes have been in the way the girls dress and take care of themselves now. When I first came, the girls were unbelievably crude; they didn't know anything and their parents hadn't been anywhere, so they couldn't tell them. But now they dress and groom themselves and generally look nice. Watching the younger teachers and the people uptown have had something to do with it. Some of the country girls are still a little crude but it doesn't take them long to catch on. The kids do much better than their parents.

Types of hair among Negroes run the gamut of length and texture, but the modal type is short in length and coarse in texture. The ideal type is long and straight or wavy. In this particular setting, the evidence is that hair texture is probably a more important criterion than skin color for beauty. Usually when the beauty, or lack of beauty, of a woman is remarked upon, the quality of the hair will be mentioned before her color. A test question was asked of a small sample of 20 persons: "If you were to be born again and could decide, which would you prefer, good hair or light skin?" The majority answered "good hair." [2] One brown-skin person said jocularly:

If I got to be a nigger, give me the hair. Don't care how light you is, if they say you a nigger, you a nigger.

However, a person with darker skin said:

If I was the right color and went somewhere away from here, I could do something about that hair.

2. In a community that is relatively homogeneous in color, it may be that hair is emphasized as a differentiating factor and thus becomes more important generally in sex selection. There is also the factor that there is some antipathy toward and suspicion of "half-white Negroes." And finally, there is the practical fact that it is easier to modify hair texture than skin color.

It also appears to be true that hair epithets, "hard" jokes and banter are most frequent—and more tolerated—than color epithets and jokes, although both have significant circulation. The emphasis in the following is significant:

One little boy called another a "nappy-headed son of a bitch." The other replied, "Gone! Your head would have been as nappy as mine if your old lady had paid her insurance." [3]

Samples of hair-derision or epithets go like this:

She got hair 'bout this long (indicating tip of forefinger). You short-haired son of a bitch! Pepper Head! or Clinker Top!

These are examples of in-group perversity—the use of traits that are important bases of shame and frustration in jest or taunt.

The concern about the hair is particularly pronounced among young school girls. A number indicated that they wanted to become hair dressers or beauty parlor operators. One 14-year old girl wrote in her autobiography:

When I was small I want to be a hair dresser. I want other people hair to look good.

When girl students answered the question, "If you had the power or the ability, what would you change about yourself?" they stressed appearance and personality. The mentions of hair and feet far outstripped color, although a number spoke generally of changing their "looks." These are typical comments:

If I had the ability I would change myself. I would have a beautiful shape, long silky hair, good health, and plenty of education.

3. It is a rather interesting point that this same joke is cited by John Dollard as being told some twelve years earlier by a white upper class woman in Southerntown, a deep south community. See Dollard, *Caste and Class in a Southern Town.*

Naturally, I would change my hair for a smoother texture.

When I was a baby, I had curly hair and one little lock laid on my forehead at all times. Well, as you can now see, as time passed so did my curly hair.

If I had the power or ability...I would make my hair grow longer, have a round plump fat face with dimpers in my jaws. And made up streamline.

To satisfy this drive for "better" hair and to meet the need for different treatment of the Negro's hair there has developed a cluster of habits, material equipment, special knowledge, and experts. The straightening iron and special grease or oils are standard equipment for the female; "doing my hair" or "getting my hair done" comes to be a personal ritual. A large number of the women "do" their own hair or get it done by experts or friends on special occasions. Even those who regularly have their hair done by trained operators use home treatment between visits. Special preparations for the Negro market are advertised and distributed in practically all stores with significant Negro trade. Two agents for national companies make the rounds of this community and the surrounding area, supplying regular customers with hair and beauty preparations. Barber shops and beauty shops feature charts with Negro models demonstrating approved or appropriate hair stylings, and national Negro magazines and newspapers feature advertisements and informational articles in the area of beauty and charm for the Negro.

One local agent's catalog uses Negro models and advertises more than three hundred beauty preparations. Among the products for women:

Presso helps release the twist and tight curl of stubborn hair and makes it easier to arrange in styles becoming to you. Presso is a hair straightener and makes curly, twisted hair straighten out and lay in position, more easily arranged, better and longer looking. Presso adds lustre and sheen to harsh, dry hair.

And for men:

MEN, USE ACE HIGH—BE ACE HIGH

1 Makes Hair Stay in Place
2 Makes Hair Slick and Glossy
3 Makes Hair Look Stylish
4 Makes Hair Straighter
5 Makes Hair Stay Combed
6 Makes Hair Easier to Train
7 Makes Hair Feel Softer
8 Makes Hair to be Proud of

In general, the social pressure is greater on the woman to achieve "better" hair; the competitive handicap for the man with "bad" hair is not as great. In truth, the man whose hair styling is too obviously artificial or extreme is subject to mild censure and derision. There are about four young men in town who affect a long, straight hair style that is termed a "conk." The "conk" is an import from urban Negro centers; one variation on it is the "mop," which is an imitation of long-haired male motion picture stars. One young Negro who had just had his "mop" cut off said,

Man, I had mine cut off; that man in the barber shop ruined me; he didn't know how to do that stuff. These people around here ain't know nothing about them; I picked it up in California—everybody out there wears them. J - - - - was the onliest other fellow around here who had one; he had one when he came back from the Army that was "mad," but he had it cut off because these people 'round here hadn't ever seen them. Did you see that "mop" that Caesar Romero had in that picture? Man, that cat was "mad" and "real gone."

Treatment of Negro women's hair follows through four steps and involves certain basic equipment. The basic procedure is the same whether done at home or in the beauty parlor: hair washing or shampoo, oiling or greasing of scalp and hair, "pressing" or straightening with heated straightening combs, and marcelling and croquinole-curling. Marcelling consists of waving the hair with hot curlers. In croquinole-curling, the hair is wrapped on the curling iron in such a manner as to produce a curl that may be combed upward or downward. There are five women in the community with some degree of special training in beauty culture. Three are licensed and one is serving an apprenticeship preparatory to licensing. All of them are in effect part-time operators. One uses a shop that is simply equipped, and the others use portions of their homes. The beautician's function and status come to be important ones. They approach professional status as trained and licensed specialists; their establishments are centers for the exchange of local gossip and news, and, therefore, to some extent they play a confidant-listener role.

A pattern that fits in with the character of Negro hair and the "needs" of the woman is the use of the headcloth by some women. Very old women, lower status women, and ruralites are given to wearing headcloths of varying colors and materials. Some of the older women wear them only in the house or within the confines of their own yards. It is difficult to tell whether the headcloth custom is a carry-over from former days or whether it is an adaptation of a current style or vogue. I have seen young whites using essentially the same styling, but it was apparently after their heads had been shampooed. Some Negroes use them for the same purpose. Questioning of those younger persons who wear them frequently in the open indicates that they are an economical type of headwear and that they serve effectively to hide short, ungroomed hair. There are individual differences in styling, but the most common is the turban-like wrap with a knot in front and the top of the head open. The constant and indiscriminate use of the head rag comes to be a symbol of servant status and coarseness to those women who frown upon its use.

Special treatment of hair is a universal for women, but

this is not true for men. In general, among men, good grooming dictates a short haircut every two or three weeks; small
amounts of grease or oil may be used, especially for "dress-up"
occasions. The occupational and sex demands for "good"
hair are not as great among men. Extremely unkempt hair or
excessively styled hair among men are both deviate forms in
Kent. Straightening grease has some slight vogue and the
"conk" [4] has been mentioned. There is no "cult of conk" here
as may be true of larger communities. Aside from the few
locals who affect the "conk," the chief patrons of the barbers
for such a treatment are a few youths from rural communities
or nearby smaller towns. Pegged pants and the black hat with
a wide colored ribbon band go with the "conk."

The wearing of some sort of headpiece on all occasions
with the exception of certain taboo situations is a constant
among Negro males. For some males the practice is to keep
the headpiece on in practically all situations among their own
group, except where respect and deference are obviously indicated.

The factors involved in the wearing of the hat are many.
There is first the possibility that it is related to the texture and
length of hair. Possibly there is more or less unconscious incli-
nation to keep under cover a low-prestige physical characteristic. The latter possibility is given some support by such jest-
ing remarks as: "Man, if I had as bad hair as you, I wouldn't
never be without a hat; I'd even wear one in bed." The fact

---

4. "Conking" involves the following procedure. The male's hair is allowed to grow longer than usual. After washing, the barber treats the damp
hair with a strong patented chemical that has the effect of straightening it.
With the application of heavy grease or oil the hair takes on a patent leather
finish. When given in a barber shop, the treatment costs $1.25 and is sup-
posed to last for about six weeks. To be effective, care should be taken. The
hair may turn reddish (the chemical acts like a lye-like bleach) or the scalp
may receive painful burns if not well greased before application. The nape
of the neck and the sides of the head must be watched lest the growing
hair in these areas present a contrast to the "conked" portion. These areas
are usually periodically shaved clean.

that the hat is very frequently kept on in theaters and while dancing or sitting with females in taverns may stem from practical considerations: the fact that there are no checking facilities, the possibility of theft, and the possibility of having to make a quick exit.

It is likely, however, that the hat's importance lies in its being a symbol of manhood and a very important means of expressing individuality. Type of hat, the characteristic angle at which it is worn, the manner in which the crown is creased or dented and brim bent, and the decorations sometimes used— all these seem to have a psychological significance: they mark the individual off; they express a certain bravado, aggressiveness, or recklessness; and they often serve as clique badges.

This meaning of the headpiece must be juxtaposed to its meaning in the interracial situation. In some situations that have caste implications, the pattern is for the Negro male to doff his hat or keep it in his hand. For some males, "hat in hand" is a tool that is more or less cynically used. In telling of their approach to whites in a situation where they wanted something, they will stress ". . . and I put my hat in my hand." For most Negroes, "hat in hand" is something that must be done. It is not approved behavior: unnecessary obsequiousness is a source of embarrassment and resentment. The situations in which the Negro male must doff his hat are apparently decreasing; he doesn't have to do it in stores, and the pattern is mixed in the banks and the courthouse and city hall. In the drugstores, Negroes stand at the soda fountain with hats on to purchase goods, but they do not consume them there.

The hat among women does not have the same functions or psychological meaning that it has among men. For the working woman, the hat tends to be functional in terms of ordinary street wear—that is, the main purpose is to protect the head from the elements and provide comfort. The style or display element is secondary. For such reasons, hat types among women on a weekday may cover a wide range that includes wide-brimmed straws and cast off men's felts. However, a hat of style is a must for church and special occasions—every woman has a "dress-up" hat or hats.

Ordinarily, among men the type of headpiece bespeaks the occupation. For both men and women there are "occasion" hats for church, etc. The somewhat awkward manner in which these are sometimes worn is due in part to the lack of frequent wearing.

The incidence of mouth gold among Negroes is high. Spot checks in public gatherings and a review of adult acquaintances indicates that about one in four male adults and one in three female adults have noticeable gold in the mouth. A check of rural visitors on the downtown streets on Saturdays indicates a higher incidence. Teeth fillings have had a significant prestige as well as functional value. The incidence is related to status, contact, and social distance from rural life. There are many factors involved: the incidence of dental troubles, the costs of dental care in relation to income, the customs or preferences of the group, and the customs or expectations of the professional practitioners with respect to Negro clientele.

An older informant points out that when she was young a gold tooth was highly valued, and that she was anxious to lose a tooth in order to get a gold one put in. She spoke of persons she knew who had sound teeth drawn in order to get gold replacements. She pointed out that "folks ain't as crazy about gold in their mouth as they used to be; at one time, it was just the thing." Another woman in the community is pointed out as one who had a plate made that was filled with many gold teeth to match those drawn. She later became ashamed of the excess gold and subsequently ordered a plate without ornamentation. For the less sophisticated and more rural, gold teeth are matters of both pride and utility; they are pleasing to look at and represent a type of conspicuous consumption. For increasing numbers, gold is a matter of utility and when used should be made as inconspicuous as possible; ostentatious display is a form of vulgarity. The use of gold teeth as a type of conspicuous consumption can be understood under some circumstances: it is permanent, portable, personal, and easily displayed. It may be that with sophistication the conspicuous consumption drive has shifted into other channels, such as autos and clothing, for example.

The Tavern Complex

THE seven "colored" taverns share rank with the churches as major symbols of the Negro community of Kent. The church and the tavern are the great focal points of interest and activity outside of home and the job. Although they are ostensibly polar symbols representing the extremes of nonrespectable and respectable behavior, activities and attitudes with respect to them have a similarity. For many, the church and tavern are places of regular ritual-like attendance; they are places where one can be somebody. Each provides a ready-made pattern of relief from care and relatively unrestricted behavior; each has its regular clientele; and each is run by and for Negroes.

Although it is true that four of the seven taverns are owned or sponsored by "church people," there is a recognized gap between those who attend taverns and those who do not. Taverns are frequented by persons who are held by their opposites to be "the low element," or "bad niggers." All groups—those who frequent and those who do not—concede the taverns to be "dangerous" places where the risk of getting hurt or in trouble is high:

I had to stop going to Zeke's; I used to go there lots when he first opened up, but every time I went there I had to run.

I never goes over to Jim Bass' because I'm going to have to carry me my pistol and as sure as I got my pistol in my pocket, I'm going to have to take it out and shoot some drunken fool.

A number of habits and tastes tie in with the tavern; it tends, too, to select certain types. For instance, whisky drinking is well-nigh universal among adult males and very frequent among lower status women. A line, however, is drawn between those who drink in public and those who drink in private or with select company. Among those who drink in public there is one type that seems to have a compulsion to drink or get drunk in the midst of a large group; the tavern provides a setting for this type. The tavern provides a spot for male and female idlers and hangers-on and for those who are in search of company or the possible chance to see something exciting. There are many tavern regulars, and some drinkers regularly make the rounds of all the taverns.

An essential part of the tavern complex is the "juke box" or "piccolo" and its collection of popular hits by colored artists. I did not see a single automatic phonograph in a Negro public place in Kent that had a record by a white artist. This selection is a function in part of tastes of dancers and listeners—a taste that has been stimulated by radio programs and national publicity—and in part it is a function of the white distributor's anticipation of the tastes of this particular segment of the Negro public. There is a characteristic "tavern music" that provides the basis for dancing and listening and tends to become a vogue in the Negro community.

Instrumentation, rhythm, and lyrics fit in with the behavior and sentiments of the tavern clientele. Particular numbers change, but the basic styles and themes are fairly constant: blues of sentiment or pathos ("Rainy Weather Blues"); instrumental "jump" numbers styled for jitterbugging ("The Huckle Buck"); the jazzed-up "gospel songs" of Rosetta Tharpe ("Take My Hand Precious Lord"); rhythmic numbers with topical lyrics ("Chicken Shack Boogie" or "Grandma Plays the Numbers"). Many of these songs have bold sex themes ("I Want a Bow-Legged Woman"); most tend to be pertinent comments on man-woman relationships.

These songs are obviously meaningful; many people adopt a particular song as expressive of their experiences or current sentiments.

Many of these songs tend to be popular among some of the people who are not tavern patrons; they add them to their record collections. The record collection of the lower status person, however, is likely to duplicate in categories, if not in specific numbers, the tavern songs. The tastes of this group were reinforced during this study by two very popular radio programs featuring the latest in tavern music. One of the programs was run by a Negro disc jockey in a nearby city; the other was a late evening program from Nashville, Tennessee, the chief publishing center for American folk music.

The two dominant areas of musical expression are the tavern and the church. Examination indicates certain parallels. The popular songs and the church songs, particularly in the Baptist and rural churches, have heavy overtones of emotion and rhythm. Many of the lyrics in both instances tend to be symbolically appropriate or often topical. The new type of gospel singing has some vogue in each area, and there is a high escapist content and an element of abandon in both art expressions. Each reflects certain features of this subculture and fits in well with it.

Taverns do their greatest volume of business on Fridays and Saturdays. Behavior on week ends is a crude index to status, i.e., whether one is respectable or nonrespectable. The tavern figures in the definition. For a large group of males, the idealized pattern of week-end behavior would involve the following: purchasing a supply of whisky in the whisky store; sharing a drink in the back lot or in Burton's shed; making the rounds of the taverns (or in the case of some, remaining for hours at a time in the favorite tavern); purchasing supplementary whisky from a bootlegger. Contact with or search for a sexual partner is likely to be a goal incident to this round of activity. Some do no more than get drunk with the taken-for-granted risk of getting arrested and fined ten dollars. This risk is part of the pattern and is blandly accepted.

The following describes a Saturday night in one of Kent's taverns:

Zeke's Colored Cafe is the most popular commercial gathering place for Negroes in town, with the possible exception of the colored balcony in the town's one theater. Zeke's occupies one-half of a one-story frame building; the other half houses a barber shop. Zeke's is a combination grocery-cafe-beer parlor; he sells beer and bottled wine, canned and packaged goods, sandwiches— fish, hamburger, hot dogs—and ice cream. Tonight he is helped by two young women clerks who constantly exchange quips with the patrons.

There are five booths and a large multicolored "juke box." On the wall are large lettered signs: "No Cursing"—"No Whisky Drinking"—"$25.00 Fine for Anyone Creating a Disturbance." Dancing couples and solo exhibitionists use a floor space of about 10 by 25 feet.

The fluctuating crowd averages about twenty-five; there are twice as many men as women; as many more men and women are milling around outside. Persons who appear to be in their early twenties predominate. Three small boys of about eleven stand around drinking soda and watching the older groups intently. All the men with the exception of two wear hats or caps; these two have "straight" hair—one natural and the other artificial.

The general pattern is to drink beer from the bottle; however gin and whisky are poured surreptitiously in the booths and mixed with cokes in paper cups. A bootlegger hovers around on the outside selling half-pints of "sealed whisky" for $2.00. A few persons leave, announcing their intentions to get some whisky. Considerable "mooching" and sharing go on.

Two white cops come in twice within a half hour and scan the crowd for about five minutes. The tempo and the noise slacken a bit and the patrons studiously ignore them. On the second visit, one of the cops beckons to a man who is obviously drunk; the man says, "Yes sir, Mr. Brice" and lurches across the floor to him and goes peacefully with him to the car. The group watches impassively until they have gone and then breaks out into laughter and banter. One person laughs and says, "I bet you he'll get out and be back here before Zeke close; he got plenty money; he 'rocked' [drew veteran's unemployment insurance] today."

One man was speaking pidgin-French and talking about his experiences as a soldier; he broke off his comments on segregation in the Army with the announcement that he had to leave to meet his girl who was coming in on a bus. Three youths were trying to make arrangements for transportation to a party out in the country where they could make contacts with some girls. Another man was regaling a group about how he had beaten a man with an axe after the man had cut him; he was bemoaning his luck that he had been fined $75 despite the fact that he had been cut.

The tavern crowd is characteristically a shifting one, made up of small groups that cluster and then fade. There is no constant or common focus of attention except in the case of an argument or a display of exhibitionistic dancing. . . .

The Idling Complex

THE pattern of economic activity is such that it provides a wealth of leisure time: agricultural and associated activities tend to be seasonal, with intermittent periods of peak activity; employment for Negroes in non-agricultural pursuits tends also to be irregular. With the exception of main street crowds —the bulk of the members of which are rural persons in town for the day—public idling is essentially a male pattern that is characteristic of all adult age groups. There are specific idling places, informal idling cliques, a range of conventional idling behavior, and certain days and periods when idling is expected. To some extent, idling places serve as informal labor markets. Employers looking for persons to do odd jobs will frequently seek out persons at these places.

Aside from the idling that is a part of the tavern complex,

the behavior is seen in a number of other locations or settings. For example:

"On the Block" refers in general to the sidewalks, the store steps and store fronts of Kent's main street business center. Within the one-block space there are four main locations where middle-aged and old men in overalls and work clothes cluster to sit, talk, and watch: Max's Corner, at the main intersection where two of the older locally owned department stores are located; the town's two drugstores—Kent Drug and Harper's—on opposite sides of the street; the locally owned Burton's Grocery. All of these places have steps and step-like arrangements in front of the store windows that invite sitting down. On Saturdays, other spots are added: the bus station corner, the movie front, and the five-and-ten-cent store. These clusters are sometimes interracial, but the great majority of the idlers are nearly always Negro. A number of the idlers are unemployed, unemployable, or seasonally idle.

"On the Back Lot" refers to the open spaces immediately behind the business center; these spaces serve as back entrances for the businesses and parking places for cars and trucks. On week ends, in particular, small groups cluster or wait around cars and trucks; some surreptitiously drink whisky. Two of the town's whisky stores face the "back lot." At one end of the "back lot" is Burton's and Burton's Shed. Burton's is a tavern with an interracial patronage; the shed outside has long boards on trestles where mixed groups gather to loaf, drink, argue, and watch the baseball ticker and scoreboard. "Buying a baseball ticket" is a form of lottery that involves guessing the team or teams that make the most runs on any particular day. Many of the idlers here are interested in the results of the baseball games. Burton's is essentially a drinking center; it is patronized by a group of regulars—employed and unemployed, white and colored. The shed is usually strewn with empty whisky bottles, paper cups, coke bottles, and beer bottles. A large percentage of the town's chronic public drinkers make this a regular stopping place, particularly on Mondays, Fridays, Saturdays—and on any rainy day.

"Nunny's Blacksmith Shop" is across the street from Burton's. Nunny is a young Negro, one of the town's three part-time Negro blacksmiths. Nunny's blacksmith shop is a small frame building about fifteen feet square; it contains a forge, an anvil, and a tool bench. There is constant traffic between Nunny's, Burton's, and the two liquor stores in the same block. Nunny's shares with Burton's the distinction of being the chief center for the drinking idlers. Not untypical is the following picture: a cold, rainy Monday morning in the early fall; eighteen men in overalls, windbreakers, and cast-off Army and Navy clothes standing around the forge on which wood has been piled. Nunny refers to them facetiously: "These my helpers; when winter comes, I can't get in for helpers." Groups of two or three share half-pint bottles in paper cups and use cokes as chasers; there is no indiscriminate passing of the bottle. Some are mooching drinks or trying to raise money for a trip to the "little white house" (whisky store). There is a box in the corner with more than twenty empty whisky bottles. Nunny explains: "That's just since Friday; should be more, because some of them took them out." He covers the box and takes it out to a farmer's wagon, explaining that the farmer makes moonshine and can use them. Sample conversation themes and topics: the amount of cotton that has been picked and sold, and the price paid; the persons for whom they work (e.g. "Hear that boy talk about he work for Mr. So-and-So! I don't work for nobody but Mr. Me!"); encounters with the law, with drunkenness the usual charge; prowess in hunting and fishing. . . .

The poolroom is a new feature that has been added to Kent's Negro culture; it is about two years old and is the first poolroom for Negroes in a generation. It is a favorite hangout for boys of high school age and younger adult men. A good cross section of the male community patronizes the poolroom; it has not yet acquired the same aura of non-respectability and danger that the taverns have, so that many persons go to the poolroom who would not go to the taverns. There are usually as many spectators as participants and for that reason it must be considered one of the chief idling centers. Incidentally, it is a place where a number of whites in the community come regularly to play. The winter, rainy days, Wednesday afternoons, and the week ends are peak attendance times.

During the winter, when unemployment among the younger group increases because of layoffs in the mills, completion of construction jobs, and the seasonal lull in agriculture, the regulars include many unemployed who spend the entire day sitting, talking and, infrequently, playing pool. Incidentally, the poolroom is a good place to wait for the daily "number," or to learn what it was and to compare notes on luck and hunches.

A cross section of conversational themes on a day when the idlers were many would be about as follows: "rocking" [unemployment compensation]; the "tightening of the times"; gambling and gamblers; luck with the "numbers"; the merits of different caliber firearms; the propensity of certain individuals to shoot or cut; past fights; contacts with the police; the faithfulness of wives; the delinquency of the younger boys in comparison with the older group; Negroes who talk too much and let whites in on happenings in the Negro community; contrasting patterns of child rearing; the disdain for nuisance drunks.

The filling station is in a triangle that is the center of other Negro businesses, including the poolroom, a barber shop, a cafe, and one of the taverns. The area is a favorite spot for many who "just want to see what is going on." The station is in close proximity to the other popular spots; it provides a meeting place for the exchange of news and a centrally-located base of operations where transportation may be arranged. One can sit there and see a great deal of the town's traffic, as well as the persons leaving and entering the Jackson Street community which is just behind it. For the most part a looking, gossiping, and bantering crowd hangs out here.

The barber shop has important incidental functions. It is a center for the circulation of news and gossip; it provides a forum for the debate and discussion of weighty and trivial matters of interest; it provides an audience for the wit, the "show-off," and the "loudmouth"; it is one place in the community where all males can go and mingle freely without fear of censure. There are two barber shops with a total of six chairs, both of which operate part time.

Among the lower status group (who would also be incidentally the confirmed public drinkers and drunks), Monday is known as "Blue Monday." One person commenting on the group in Burton's shed explained:

Nobody hardly works on Monday; they calls it "Blue Monday." They usually comes around here and around three-thirty to sundown they gits lit.

Another nonrespectable man emphasized his worry about personal problems as causing a departure from his usual week-end behavior:

You knows it must have been something wrong with me whenever you sees me working on Monday. Man, I don't never work on Monday for nobody.

FISHING AND HUNTING COMPLEX

The interest in hunting and fishing is so pervasive and common to all adult groups that it serves as the nucleus of a major complex. Active participation in hunting is essentially a male characteristic, but both men and women participate actively in fishing. The interest in hunting and fishing is characteristic of the South and is not unique with the Negro. The activity fits in well with the cultural situation: relative lack of urbanization, availability of game and fish, the seasonal and intermittent character of economic activity. Hunting and fishing are marked by sincere enthusiasm and pride, plus a disposition to share pleasure with others. Although game and fish have some economic value and satisfy certain dietary tastes, the chief interest in their pursuit is the recreational or sporting one. Combined, hunting and fishing provide year-round outlets. Interest is particularly acute among the middle-aged or maturing adults. The person who cares nothing about fishing or hunting, or doesn't possess the elementary skills, is a deviate and soon becomes the object of playful scoffing.

The shotgun or rifle is practically a universal possession. The gun is for both sport and the protection of person and home. In the town proper, the incidence of hunting dogs is less than in the country. Dogs function as pets, aids to sport, and as protective agents. There is a general willingness to share or lend guns, ammunition, or dogs.

Hunting, like fishing, is a group activity. The lone hunter is rare: companionship and rivalry are as important as the sport. There are several hunters of great experience, skill, and reputation. Ordinarily when persons or groups go hunting, they go with one of these persons who knows the woods and the habits of animals. When two or more of these leaders are in the same party, rivalry and banter increase. The master hunter is usually also the skilled and inveterate fisherman. One of the better known of these masters is commonly referred to as "the man who quit his job as janitor at the schoolhouse because it interfered too much with his hunting and fishing." The animals commonly shot or caught in this area are doves, rabbits, and 'possums.

The "boast" and the "tease" are important parts of the after-hunt experience; this is true of fishing also. The news of the luck, or lack of luck, of individuals or groups circulates rapidly in the community. This whole hunting and fishing complex is an area of good humor, congeniality, and satisfaction for the individual. There is pride in the reference to the Kent locality as "good hunting country," and there is enthusiasm in the expression "I just love to hunt." These activities are marked by a lack of the querulousness and the latent aggression that appear in many other types of leisure-time activities.

Fishing is a year-round activity, diminishing only during the coldest part of the winter and when hunting is at its peak.

"Do you hunt?" "Do you fish?" are standard questions, and "This would be a nice day to go fishing" and "I'd like to go fishing today" express common wishes. The psychological elements and the roles involved in the fishing pattern are essentially the same as those involved in hunting—except that more women participate in fishing. The most popular spots are the bridges and river banks of the Piedmont River and its tributaries. The typical fishing party will travel from eight to fifteen miles unless it has access to one of the private fishing ponds in the vicinity. Some Negroes have permission to use these ponds which are owned by whites. One Negro family has had an artificial pond dug on its farm recently. Occasionally, seining parties are formed. As a rule, both fishing and hunting consume the major portion of the day. Most fishing is static fishing with bamboo-like reed and line, though occasionally rod and reel are used. Equipment is usually shared, since some one person generally owns or has custody of several poles and lines. Preparation involves the digging of the bait or the purchasing of minnows, as well as the fixing of the food and drink that are taken along. Most fishing is an absorbing matter; but, in some instances, the picnic interest and atmosphere dominate. Such occasions come to be open-air parties with the trend of conduct depending upon the composition of the group and the presence or absence of whisky.

Fishing and hunting are taken-for-granted aspects of the life pattern for the Negro in this area; they involve an organization of interests, equipment, and persons that has significance for practically every person in the community.

SCIENCE AND LORE COMPLEX

THERE are three major areas of life marked by a significant admixture of lore and science. They are sickness, agriculture, and sex.

The belief in folk cures and magic is strongest among the

aged, the rural fringe, and recent rural migrants. There is a lingering belief in the efficacy of the old folk remedies. These have not been repudiated; rather, they have been pre-empted by drugstores, patent medicines, and hospitals. Besides, there are very few "root workers" left. The attitude of the older generation is indicated in the following:

There's something in the woods good for everything that ails you. When you goes to the drugstore that's all you gets—some kind of herb something that's diluted and weakened down. It just costs you more that's all.

The dominant and nearly-universal pattern in case of illness is this: if the person is seriously sick, one of the local white doctors is sent for. In the case of minor complaints or old ailments, the advice of the druggist might be asked or some known or recommended patent medicine will be bought. Older informants indicate that the white family doctor has been a typical and taken-for-granted part of the local complex for a long while. Better than average hospital facilities—there are three hospitals within a radius of fifteen miles—tend to be taken for granted also, even by the more remote rural people. There is no question about the general acceptance of scientific medicine. The basic attitude toward the new medicine is probably but an extension of the attitude toward the old—acceptance or rejection on the basis of "results" without understanding or the desire to understand theory or process. The "shot" is almost universally looked upon as the most efficacious of the new medicines. In an urban, sophisticated society, "shots" often have a shameful connotation insofar as they are associated with treatment for venereal diseases; in this somewhat unsophisticated society, "taking shots for bad blood" may be mentioned with some naive pride. On what have come to be increasingly rare occasions, the folk and new therapies may be used together, or one might be discarded for the other. Following are two cases of recent occurrence:

A woman in her mid-thirties, who is literate herself but who has a husband of rural background who can not read or write, became suddenly ill. Her illness was described as "something wrong with her head"; she refused to eat and was extremely lethargic. "The doctor act like he don't know what's wrong with her." One night about 10:30, she was bundled into an automobile and taken about twelve miles down in the country to the "root man" at Ned Legs. The "root man" is said to have told her that one of her friends had "put the root" on her; he described her as a large woman. The inference was that it was someone who was having an affair with her husband or someone who wanted her out of the way in order that she might get to her husband. Close friends expressed no surprise; one person was just curious as to how the person—and she had "a good idea as to who it 'twas—" got in and around the house to "work the root." The informant expressed belief in root practice and said that she consulted magazines for the purpose of ordering such materials through the mail. Subsequent to the visit to the "root man," the patient returned to the doctor regularly for expensive shots; she and her husband described her condition as "bad blood."

The mother of a teen-age girl was committed to the state hospital for the insane. At the insistence of her family and over the protests of one of the physicians, she was removed in an ambulance from the hospital. On the hundred mile trip back to Kent she was accompanied by her husband and the "root man." The "root doctor" worked her into a hysteria by attempting to make her drink some concoctions, including whisky. She was stripped of her clothes and remained in hysteria the entire trip. Part of the "root man's" therapy consisted of an attempt to get her sexually excited. The woman died shortly after returning from the hospital.

It is apparent that the greatest use of the "root man's" magic and potions was in the past, and it was mainly in the area of baffling diseases, mental states, and love or sex problems. The "root man" was called in to take the spell off persons who were in psychotic states; for example, one elderly informant told about her sister who was seized in her youth with a state that caused her to turn around and around. A "root woman" was called in. She said that the informant's sister had stepped on "something" that had poisoned her, whereupon she proceeded to go under the steps and get "it" and destroy "it." The woman is said to have recovered. It should be emphasized that belief in this area is not general nor is it consistent; still, persons who say they don't believe will cite instances with great seriousness or indicate "there might be something to it." Even those who do believe probably use more rational techniques more frequently. In cases where evil magic is supposed to be at work, there is always a counter-magic that can be brought to bear. In some cases, this is the professional secret of the "root man" or "woman"; generally a little salt sprinkled around is recommended as a counteragent.

As a rule, younger people know very little about root magic or herb therapy; even some of the older people find it difficult to remember or are reluctant to indicate too much knowledge or belief. They will refer to persons now dead who were experts, or they will point to the fact that the people in the low country were and are more avid believers and practitioners. Many of the older people make no distinction between the therapeutic and magical qualities of folk medicine; for example, they might explain the use of certain materials in the case of diseases and in the same sequence refer to materials useful in sex problems. When specifics are mentioned by older informants—who actually rarely use them—the usual complaints referred to are fever, dysentery, "bad blood" (a general term that covers a number of complaints), "whites" (leucorrhea), bad luck. Types of materials mentioned are: leaves, herbs, roots, bark, and animal matter. Following are some of the items mentioned and the properties ascribed to them:

Item	*Good for*
blackhall berry, roots, bark	general complaints: back, stomach, liver
sassafras root	dysentery
huckleberry bark	"whites"
wild cherry bark	female troubles
white oak bark	,, ,,
poplar bark	,, ,,
red oak bark	,, ,,
sycamore bark	,, ,,
scurvy weed	dysentery
black sampson snake root	fever
double-jointed snake root	bad luck
"buckeye"	piles
coon root	lack of virility in the older male
boar hog root	,, ,, ,, ,, ,, ,, ,,

Infidelity and impotence are among the chief targets of this folk technique mentioned by older informants. These are some of the specifics mentioned.

Take a snail and a "betty-bug," kill them and rub them on the lower parts of a woman; this will cause impotence in your rival.

Take a "thousand-leg," kill it and after it is dry reduce it to a powder in a cloth; sprinkle it on the lower parts of your husband or lover; he will not be able to perform the sex act with another woman.

The use of alum by a woman will induce impotence in the male.

When a male is unsuccessful in the sex act, he should change the directions in which he is lying until he finds the proper one, i.e., north-south or east-west.

Of greater incidence and practical importance so far as customs are concerned is the general acceptance of the validity of the signs of the Zodiac as guides to certain kinds of behavior. Although there are many who have routines of life which do not encourage a constant sensitivity to "signs" as a basis of choice, there are few who categorically dismiss or question them. Practically everybody takes it for granted that "there is something in the signs of the moon," whether he thinks it necessary to act consistently upon them or not. Those who have agricultural interests—crop planting, hog raising and butchering, etc.—are most keenly sensitive to the signs and tend to follow them faithfully with respect to this phase of activity. *Grier's Almanac*, for the Southeastern States—which advertises itself as being in its 144th year—is distributed by the local drugstores. A current almanac is generally an important—and for some, necessary—household possession. There is, however, the example of one woman who announced that she could dispense with the daily consultation of the almanac because she had discovered that the Burnsville radio station broadcast "the signs" every morning.

The 12 signs of the Zodiac and the parts of the body or qualities—both animal and human—to which they refer and which they are supposed to affect are: Aries (the ram), head and face; Taurus (the bull), neck; Cancer (the crab), breast; Virgo (the virgin), bowels; Scorpio (scorpion), sex organs, Capricornus (the goat), knees; Gemini (the twins), arms; Leo (the lion), heart; Libra (balance), kidneys; Sagittarius (the archer), thighs; Aquarius (the waterman), legs; and Pisces (the fishes), feet.

Many persons will not castrate a pig unless the sign is right. For example, if the sign is in Scorpio (the sex organs), the time would be wrong; if in Taurus (the neck), the time would be all right. In a similar vein, there are persons who will not have operations, such as a tooth extraction, unless the sign is right; that is, not "in the head." A common principle is that planting should be done under the sign of the Twins. Another is that harvesting should be done in the light of the moon or as it approaches full; on the other hand, a hog must be killed in the dark of the moon. There are a number of vague beliefs and expressions as to the relationship between the moon and general physical and mental states and the strength of sex desire, especially in women.

Belief in the Zodiac and moon lore have a regional and occupational character, and, as such, have significant incidence in both the Negro and white—especially mill-village—cultures. The field notes of a colleague working in the mill villages of Kent show almost the identical pattern of belief among these low-income groups with a rural background. The same type of argument was used in both groups to dispel any doubts as to the powers of the moon, that is, if the moon is powerful enough to affect the tides in the ocean, it must be powerful enough to affect other things in life also.

The essentially mixed character of the knowledge of the Negro in Kent is in keeping with the changing character of this small community. The significant fact is that the old and new exist side by side and are used alternately or selectively without apparent conflict or awareness of inconsistency; only in rare instances do changing ways or the contrasts between ways produce crises that are recognized as personal and immediate. This is apparently a subculture which the people themselves think of as relatively stable and, except for the conservatism and nostalgia of the older persons, the people exhibit little sense of loss or acute dislocation when the new is introduced. Very few changes are initiated by the people of this subculture, but changes are accepted and adapted to gracefully, and, in some instances, with moderate enthusiasm. Where objectively there is dislocation or the possibility of it, the new situation is accepted almost fatalistically. The superficially easy incorporation of the new suggests that adaptability as such is a cardinal principle. The way of life of the Kent Negro is changing inexorably, but he does not identify himself actively with the agents or the forces that are producing that change; there is inertia but little active resistance. The significant complexes and institutions of this subculture tend to be, in practice, rather compatible mixtures of the folk and the secular; and, although the folk becomes more and more a vestige, the impact of the urban-secular is neither strong enough nor rapid enough to make for an immediate or acute consciousness of problems or crises. The social psychological character of the Kent Negro's adaptation and the bases of that adjustment in the local cultural situation are examined in the discussion of the orientations and values of the subculture.

Courtship, Marriage, and the Family

CHAPTER 4   INSTITUTIONS ARE THOUGHT of as "small cultural systems"—relatively permanent sets of social habits, values, and equipment "integrated about a generally recognized purpose or purposes which are understood by the members of society." [1] We must know, then, the range and the characteristics of the institutions that have developed to meet the basic demands of living for the Kent Negro.

The Negro society of Kent, viewed alone, lacks a full complement of the institutions necessary for collective existence; it is a dependent segment of the larger society. Some institutions and services are shared or they are parts of the over-all organization of the Kent community, for example, economic and governmental institutions. Other institutions, such as the public school system, are segregated branches of community-wide institutions. The surrogate functionary and the "borrowed" institution or exchanged service are characteristics of this bi-racial society. Considerations of race and the inadequacy of local institutions dictate that, to some extent, the needs or demands of the Kent Negro are serviced by outside communities. Nearby cities like Stone Valley and Metro City, which have larger Negro communities than Kent, provide some economic, professional, and recreational services for the Kent Negro. There are few institutions in Kent that are en-

1. Gillin, *The Ways of Men*, pp. 492-94.

tirely sponsored, controlled, and manned by the Negro—or that exist for him exclusively. In the following sections we will examine some of the institutional fields—both in and out of the Negro community—that operate with respect to basic social purposes: family and sex, economics, religion, education, government, and social control.

Sex Behavior

THE general interest, values, and behavior in the sex area are somewhat similar to—and in fact are related to—the whisky drinking patterns. Unconcealed sex interest and activity are widespread. Among nonrespectable persons this behavior tends to be more frank, unashamed, and public—sex and the values related to it are a prominent feature of the life-way of this category. Sex and sex experiences are important parts of anecdotes, banter, jokes, and boasts. In general, the behavior of respectables tends to be more discreet; however, in a community where one basis of fixing status or typing is the current sex liaison or the recognized propensity or disposition for sex dalliance, references to upper status men such as the following are not uncommon: "He'll play too, if he gets a chance or you let him." Sex dalliance is taken for granted, and there is an enduring interest in the sex status and behavior of others.

Lower status females show a great deal of sex initiative and independence: "I don't have to worry about no one man"; "Anything he can do, I can do." There are some women in all levels of the population who are known as "women who have always done what they want to do." Involved in such behavior or attitudes are the general tendency to take sex and sex experience for granted—as normal and desirable goals; the female assumption—often explicit—that the male is promiscuous; and a rather strong feeling about established claims on the male. Particularly among the nonrespectables, the relative independence and lack of sex passivity on the part of the female,

plus the dalliance tendencies of the male, add up to a considerable amount of tension that seems to underlie many liaisons
and marriages. This situation plays a great part in much of the
husband-wife bickering and violence that is fairly common
and which in many cases is predictable and anticipated with
some humor by neighbors.

Gifts or some degree of support from the male are a constant in nonmarital liaisons; they are taken for granted and
freely discussed. There is some informal ranking of men on
a basis of the regularity and amount of gifts or support. A
woman who "runs out" on a man who has "been good to
her" runs the risk of violent retaliation; she is likely also to
be condemned by other women for committing something of
an ethical breach. In the same vein, a woman who has a man
who is especially "good to her" is considered fortunate and
often receives advice to "hold what you got."

In a culture where the sex interest is an important one and
has major functions aside from reproduction and the husband-
wife relationship, there is a question as to how long sex interest and activity continue. Certainly the evidence indicates that
the interest, at any rate, persists throughout the upper age
groups in both men and women. There are even a few docu-
mented instances of significant activity in the upper age groups
as well. The evidence for the interest appears in the conversation of widows and widowers about marriages and marriage
possibilities; in the good humored mutual joshing and joking
among older people; in the sexual content of reminiscences and
jokes; in allusions to current or recent liaisons of older people;
and in the exchange of gossip and news about the affairs of
younger people. The older men might joke about their current
inactivity, pointing out that it is "all in the mind now"; the
older women never do, although they may point out that they,
in effect, have retired from sex activity. With women, there is
always implicit the idea that they could if they wanted to—
and that they are in fact desirable to some man or men now.

The following documentary material suggests the prevalence of the interest and something of the flavor and range of nonmarital sex activity, particularly among the lower status category.

On the activity of younger girls:

These young girls gets out sooner and does more than we use to do. We never drank whisky and went out with mens that young. . . . Some of these girls ain't nothing but babies; they starts when they's twelve and thirteen years old and before you can turn around they's having babies by some of these old men and having to stop school. . . . I done plenty myself when I used to get around but my mother would have killed me if I had a done what these babies is doing. M - - - ain't but about fifteen or sixteen years old and she done had practically all these men around here; she "burned" K - - - - and M - - - - and they had to take her down to the State Hospital for treatment; I reckon the nurse still goes over there.

High school boy's banter, illustrating social pressures:

Old N - - - - ain't never had none; the girls say he won't do it. Somebody ought to take him out and make him git some; but he wouldn't know what to do if he got it.

Here it is winter coming on and boy, you ain't got no place to go and nobody to keep you warm. . . . I got somebody to keep me warm; you'd better get somebody yourself.

High school girl on personal preferences:

I'd rather fool around with older men and married men than these young boys; they ain't got nothing and they worry you to death.

On female sex aggression and single standard, from a lower status woman:

Why don't he say something to me—he's human, ain't he? Of course, I'm married but my husband do what he want to do and I do what I want to do. . . . Do I have a chance still?

On female sex aggression, from an upper status woman:

I told him: "You come around and pick me up and we'll go and what we do ain't nobody's business but ours. Let me worry about my husband."

An approach by a male:

When can we get together? You just got me so that I don't think about nothing but you. . . . Just about how much would it cost and take for all the arrangements?

On sex jealousy:

He's a fool. He married that woman when she already had three children by other men. Now, he don't allow nobody else to hardly look at her; he'll near kill her if he catch her talking to a man.

On typing and placing:

She's a good girl, but she just can't say no. She just don't know how to say no.

That man there, he got a woman down the street.

He's a good, honest straight man; you don't never hear nobody say nothing about him and no womens. That's hard here in Kent because the womens treats the men nice; but it's a small town and the folks likes to talk. . . . I reckon he must go out of town because all you mens is devils.

On the interest and activity of the aged; a woman in her seventies:

A woman ain't never too old to have a boy friend. . . . I tell you the truth, I wants one to come and see me about once a week and pep me up and unruffle me. That's what God made the men for.

Among the differentiated, or respectable and more stable families, sex behavior lacks the frank, open, and, to some extent, promiscuous character of the relations among their opposites. Public behavior with respect to sex and whisky go far to define respectability. Since pride, respectability and the approach to conventional morals tend to be earmarks of the respectable family, this group tends to frown upon, is ashamed of, and seeks to dissociate itself from "lower class" behavior. The fear of "contamination" of children is not groundless; this is probably the chief parental fear from the "lower class." These respectable parents seek to offset the threat by rigid discipline and supervision as well as by "getting the children out the situation," if possible, by sending them away. Some of the respectable families have not escaped what for them is the acute shame of illegitimacy.

E. Franklin Frazier points out that the social significance of illegitimacy among Negroes becomes apparent only when we view it in relation to the organization of Negro life in the South. In many areas "Negro life follows the folkways that emancipation modified but did not destroy." [2] In Kent as else-where in the South, "in some cases the illegitimacy has taken place during the disorganization following emancipation." [3] More recently, it is related to movement, change, and contact with different ways of life that have resulted in general disorganization of family life. A good portion of Kent's Negroes are marginally rural people in the process of adapting to the demands of a modern culture that has a significant urban and industrial content.

The rate of illegitimacy among Kent Negroes is high; [4] how high is difficult to say with accuracy because much depends on definition, and records are incomplete and unreliable in many instances. Statistics as to illegitimacy make no subtle distinctions, but community gossip and hearsay do. These

2. E. Franklin Frazier, *The Negro Family in the United States* (Chicago: University of Chicago Press, 1939), p. 110.
3. *Ibid.*, p. 113.
4. School records indicate that the rate is around twenty percent.

types of situations are locally recognized and described: (1) conception out of wedlock but marriage before birth of child; (2) conception out of wedlock with no marriage to father of child—although marriage may take place before or after birth to another man; (3) conception out of wedlock with eventual abortion, miscarriage, or stillbirth; (4) birth of child to a married woman with the imputed father other than the husband; (5) the offspring of marriages that are in fact bigamous (divorce has been impossible, yet there are several instances of "divorced" people remarrying and raising a second family).

Given the fact that practically everyone knows everyone else, instances of illegitimacy and alleged illegitimacy are generally known and talked about freely. In most cases, the father or alleged father is identified. Many men admit such facts and openly or tacitly recognize their issue; there is a tendency among some men to boast about the number of children they have "out in the bushes." The mothers of illegitimate children (except those who are married to men other than the father) tend to be frank, almost casual, in their references to the fact— and even to the circumstances of "getting caught." The remarks of Frazier with respect to comparable situations are pertinent for many local women:

The attitude of these women indicates that they regard sex relations as normal behavior during a courtship which may or may not lead to marriage. When it results in the birth of a child, certain obligations are thereby imposed upon the mother. These obligations are the obligations which every mother should feel toward her offspring.[5]

However, there are many girls and many parents whose views are more conventional; once pregnancy ensues—barring abortion or miscarriage—individual, family, and community

5. Frazier, *op. cit.*, p. 115.

pressures begin to operate. It is considered the right thing for the man to marry the girl, and if he does, he is commended. The chances of the man marrying her are high if she has not been promiscuous.

In general, the fact that a girl or a woman has had an illegitimate child does not materially affect her marriage chances. A father in telling a group of men that his son had recently married said: "She's a nice girl, nice family and all—of course, she done had a baby, but that ain't nothing."

The community attitudes toward the illegitimate child are not harsh. It is better, of course, to have been born in wedlock, but the stigma for child and mother, unless they belong to the more stable families, is not great. The sanctions are few, other than mild gossip, which is certain, and possible "churching," i.e., being called before the church and having to express contriteness and to ask forgiveness. In the local Baptist church, when a member has an illegitimate child, the established procedure is for the members of the Deaconess Board or some representative to call on the person and ascertain "if they are sorry and if they will do it again." The emissaries report to the full church, and usually the person who is contrite and asks forgiveness is forgiven and welcomed back into the fellowship of the church. In the last few years this has occurred three times.

There is hardly a family in the community that doesn't have some member or members—in this or the previous generation—who have been touched or are alleged to have been touched by illegitimacy. In some cases where members of the present generation have had a common father but have had different mothers without the father having been married to both, kinship ties are openly recognized.

Indeed, some individuals in the community are known interchangeably by two surnames: by the name of the mother who was unmarried when the individual was born and by the

name of the father, or of the mother's husband, or of the
family that raised him, or even by some name that is chosen
personally. Adoption is likewise a fairly frequent phenomenon;
it is usually taken for granted that the adopted person is the
illegitimate offspring of relatives or friends.

There was not a single male in Kent who by manner or
reputation would fit the stereotype "sissy," nor were specific
references made to individuals in this community as sex deviates, even in jest. Informants can remember but two instances
in recent times of males who were suspect because of their
effeminate manner. However, aberrant sex behavior and types
are not wholly unfamiliar. Younger men, who have been in
the army or to urban centers, in recounting experiences often
make reference to that type of behavior. A suggestion of latent
perversion is seen in the fondling behavior of some men when
drunk; there are one or two who are known as biters and
pinchers when they get drunk.

There was one female nonrespectable, a migrant to the community from a nearby urban center, who was variously referred to as a "woman-lover," "morphodite," "mermaid." An
elderly woman, who is herself viewed as eccentric, reported
rebuffing this person's advances. This one instance was widely
circulated and laughed about, but mixed with the humor there
was considerable indignation and rejection of the deviate. In
general, sex orthodoxy and competence are taken for granted
and are central in the typical personality structure as it is
manifested in public behavior and verbalizations.

It is difficult to gauge the frequency of abortions. Infrequent
references are made to persons who "got rid of it" or to the
individual who "has had five or six abortions." For the most
part, the persons indicated are persons of some sophistication
or status and means. These factors in the general situation
must be considered: the social sanctions against bearing an il-

legitimate child are apparently not severe except among the differentiated, respectable families having significant pride and stability. Thus, in general, the pressure to abort is less, the support of the extended family eliminates much of the economic pressure and also gives some psychological security, the knowledge of efficient methods or techniques is not widespread, there are no generally known specialists in the local community, and the emphasis in the religion upon forgiveness and salvation dwarfs the notion of terrific punishment for transgression.

Older informants in speaking about folk methods and beliefs mention such concoctions as a brew from an unknown root gotten from the woods, brew from the roots of a cotton plant, and a brew from green coffee. One person recalled a woman who was supposed to have used the handle of an umbrella for purposes of opening the womb. They point out that "nowadays these girls when they gets caught sometimes tries to get something from the drugstore." There is a belief in some quarters that it is harder to abort a boy baby than a girl baby.

Older people knew nothing of condoms in their youth. Older women report the use of cotton wadding sprinkled with soda as a contraceptive device. Among the reasons still given in some quarters for eating starch or clay [6] is the belief that menstruation will be assured or eased. Among the younger people, the most common contraceptive devices are the condom and the vaginal douche. Among the unmarried males there appears to be more anxiety about contracting a venereal disease than about conception.

6. Starch eating is more prevalent than clay eating among women. These, plus the smaller amount of soot eating reported, are sex-linked behavior, although young men report having eaten starch as youths. All seem to be related in some way to beliefs about the sex physiology of the female. Random questioning among women indicated that about two-thirds have been or are now starch eaters.

COURTSHIP AND MARRIAGE

COURTSHIP is referred to as "going together" or "courting"; the former expression is heard more frequently and has a slightly different connotation from "courting" or "courting strong," as the expression often goes. "Going together" implies a mutually agreeable stable relationship that will likely lead to marriage and it is tacitly recognized in most instances that intimacy is involved. "Courting" suggests a wooing relationship that is not as fixed or stable as "going together." "Going out" or dating is more casual and catch-as-catch-can; it is a kind of sex game that usually has clandestine or illicit features. An oblique recognition and temporary rejection of some of the accepted values in courtship are seen in the statement of a young man:

I used to go with her. And I was treating her real nice because I wanted to marry her. I was acting like white folks and never tried to "date" her or nothing—I wanted her for my wife. I used to take her to the movies and places and take her right back straight home. But I reckon that wasn't what she wanted; I was too slow and treated her too nice because this other guy came along. . . .

"Acting like white folks" doesn't necessarily mean aping the whites as such; rather it is a recognition that the whites know and are sophisticated about proper conduct. It is a design for proper and conventional conduct rather than the disposition to ape or imitate what are considered *per se* superior ways. The same person who made the above statement in another context referred to whites as being "dirtier" than Negroes in the area of sex morality.

The great bulk of courtship behavior among the young people takes place outside the home: through the movies, automobile rides, and, to a lesser extent, the taverns and the churches. Occasional trips to out-of-town entertainment spots are a part of the pattern. In season, rural lanes, the woods and the fields ("Green's Hotel") are popular. The lack of "nice places to go" is a matter of frustration among some of the younger people. For example: "There ain't no decent place to take a girl in this town. All you can do is take her to the movies, and you gets tired of that. If you ain't got a car, you just ain't nowhere."

The marriage ceremony tends to be a "private affair." The vast majority of the marriages are civil affairs performed by the local probate judge. In general, the couple about to be married take few persons into their confidence; they secure the license with a minimum of publicity, and at a later date— always at night—"slip up to Judge Priest's." After the marriage the news is spread rapidly by word of mouth. Usually they take up residence with one of the parents or some relative.

During this study eight marriages were performed locally in which the principals were local residents; in only three instances were ministers' services used. One was the holiday marriage of the only child of one of the differentiated families to a fiancé of college days; one was the marriage of an elderly deacon to a relative of a minister. Within the past ten years there has been but one full scale wedding. For most persons in Kent, marriage is a matter of "going to the judge's tonight."

THE FAMILY

THE family assumes a number of forms in Kent. Frequently found are such forms or features as the extended family (with or without male head); the multiple family; the family with a skipped generation; the family with half-brothers and half-sisters or adopted children; boarding out; and dual family names (identification and reckoning through both mother and father).

The chances are high that the average Negro child of Kent

gets much of his socialization in a family of orientation that departs from the conventional or ideal forms of the larger American culture. An analysis of the family status of 150 elementary school children based on school records for 1944, the last year in which they were complete, shows the following:

27 or not quite one in five were illegitimate

30 or one in five were only children

70 or slightly more than two in every five lived with both natural parents

31 or one in five lived with a mother as family head

20 or two in every fifteen lived with grandparents or grandparent

13 or one in every eleven had a step-parent

8 or about one in twenty lived with a father but with no mother

The families of this group of children constituted approximately two-thirds of the population. Among them, the median number of children per family was 2.3; the median size of family was slightly less than 4.0. This group is selective in terms of families that had children enrolled in the elementary department of the school. Lacking other precise data, it is reasonable to assume that the size of the average Negro family in Kent is less than three.[7] On the whole there are relatively few children in the Negro population of Kent.

It is a cultural fact, and in the case of the Negro family a matter of record, "that the family may take protean forms as it survives or is reborn in times of cataclysmic change." [8] It is for such reasons that we point out that the Negro family

7. The 1930 Census reported the median size of all families in Kent as 3.38; the median size of the Negro family was 2.99.

8. E. W. Burgess, Editor's Preface to Frazier, *op. cit.*, p. xii.

in Kent, like many other institutions, tends to have an *ad hoc* quality; this is particularly true of the family of orientation, as has been indicated earlier. One of the marks of differentiation is the approach to conventional forms.[9]

In Figures 2 to 8 are diagrammed the kinship relations of sample households illustrative of the varied forms that the family of orientation takes in Kent.

Figure 2 needs little comment. It or some slight variation is probably characteristic of at least half of the Negro families in Kent; it is the family that is marked by the physical presence of both spouses with varying numbers of children. This form is found in all categories but its incidence is undoubtedly higher among the differentiated respectables.

FIGURE 2. Conventional two-generation household

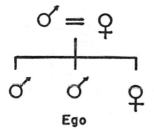

LEGEND

♂   MALE   = MARRIED

♀   FEMALE   — UNMARRIED

⚲   DECEASED, ABSENT OR UNKNOWN MALE

⚲   DECEASED, ABSENT OR UNKNOWN FEMALE

9. Frazier, *op. cit., passim.*

Figure 3 shows an example of a lower-status household of four generations without male adults; it is an example of familial and personal disorganization. Illegitimacy and delinquency occur in two generations in the same household.

FIGURE 3. Multiple generations with maternal dominance

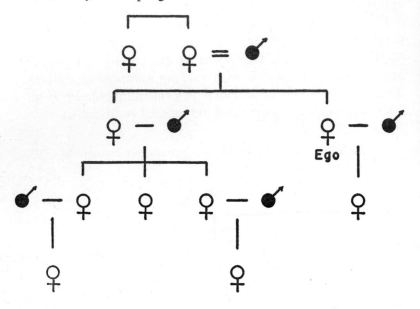

For legend, see Figure 2.

Ego is a girl of eighteen who has a child of three; she is known as an eccentric delinquent who has had several elderly men as lovers. She has been arrested and examined several times after wild outbursts or attacks on members of her family or neighbors. Her sister has three illegitimate children, two of whom in turn have illegitimate children. This is a household of ten persons in which the mother, the mother's sister, and Ego's older sister furnish the main economic support.

In the particular family shown in Figure 4, Ego's mother is dead; the father works in a distant town and does not help support the household; the brother is in the Armed Services and provides some economic help. Ego is fifteen years younger than her nearest sibling. One sister is married and separated from a husband by whom she had a son; she subsequently had a daughter by a man other than her husband. The only adult male in the house is the husband of the other sister; this couple has two children.

FIGURE 4. Multiple-family matrilocal household

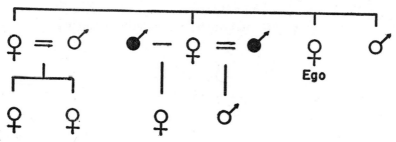

For legend, see Figure 2.

Figure 5 illustrates a family in which the father is away most of the year; the mother works and assumes the major responsibilities for support and rearing, with significant help

FIGURE 5. Two-generation mother-dominated household

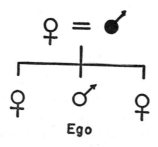

For legend, see Figure 2.

from relatives. In this family both mother and father are members of a large stable kinship group, some of the members of which serve as surrogate-parents for Ego and his siblings.

There are several instances of the type shown in Figure 6 and variations on it, i.e., the fatherless three-generation household. In most instances, Ego is illegitimate, or one of the parents is dead. Responsibility for the child falls heaviest on the grandparents. In this particular instance, Ego's mother died in childbirth and the father's mother informally adopted her and took her into her household.

FIGURE 6. Motherless three-generation household

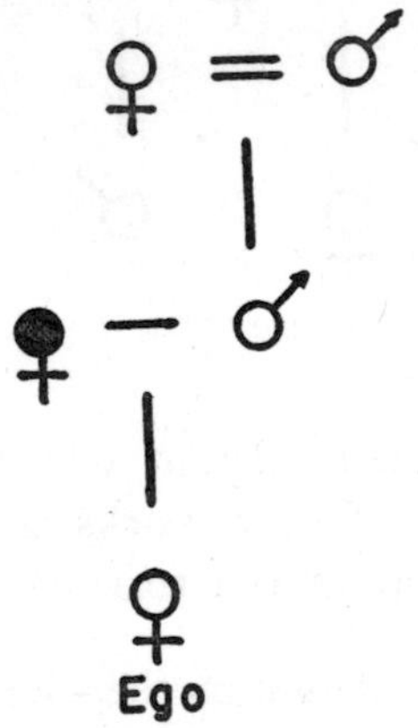

For legend, see Figure 2.

In the particular household indicated in Figure 7 cooperative living enables the participants to maintain a fairly high standard of living. All adults work and share the common board, Ego's mother and grandmother sharing management of the household.

FIGURE 7. The extended family without illegitimacy

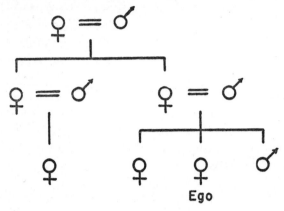

For legend, see Figure 2.

There are a number of such families, as shown in Figure 8, where the mother of a child by one man may later marry another man. The child may retain the mother's name or it may take the stepfather's name. In one instance, a child changed her name while in high school, six or seven years after the marriage of her mother.

FIGURE 8. Household with stepfather and half-brother

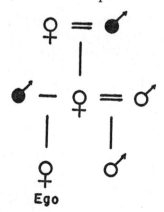

For legend, see Figure 2.

The characteristic structure of the Negro family in Kent is one factor explaining those aspects of the pattern of child care which have to do with who disciplines and who gives rewards. Two facts are clear: first a large number—probably as many as one-half, if autobiographies are a true index—of the children are raised by mothers and/or maternal relatives without significant help from the father for major portions of their lives; and, second, the mother is the more important figure in disciplining and dispensing rewards. The following are excerpts from students' autobiographies indicating a range of types and responses:

My mother raised me in Kent. . . . I was raised with my grandmother, aunt, uncles. . . . I was not punish often but when I was punish it was by either my mother or grandmother. . . . I was praise by my mother. My grandmother and aunt, mother, and uncle are my favorite people. I felt closer to my grandmother because she played after me a lot.

My mother took care of me until I was 24 months, then my maternal grandmother took me. . . . My grandmother said I was troublesome, always wanted someone to play with me or carry me all the time. When I did something wrong my grandmother had that switch waiting for me and she really did use it.

When I was born my father was working on the state highway, and my mother was keeping house. My mother took care of me until I started walking. When she started working my brother took care of me while she was gone. I was never spoiled or troublesome because my brother would leave me in all day while he was playing with his friends. When I was fifteen month old I fell into the fire. We had a swimming pool across the railroad, and one day my brother was swimming, and I was standing on the banks of the pool, and a man came by and my brother ran off and left me. I went to run and fell into the pool. My brother quickly got me out. When I did something wrong my mother would spank me and tell me not to do it again. I was punish often when I was growing because I was in the wrong environment. When my mother whipped me hard I would wish I was dead. To make her feel sorry for what she had done.

I suck my thumb when I was a year old. When I fell into the fire and got better I quit sucking my thumb because I burned my right hand, the one I suck and I couldn't suck it while I was sick, and I quit sucking it when I got better.

Incidentally, the thumb-sucking pattern is widely recurrent in student autobiographies; as a symptom it is suggestive of some of the response problems inherent in the family structure and rearing patterns. The following rather lengthy excerpt, although not necessarily typical, suggests some of these problems, and it also underscores the somewhat ambivalent value placed upon the mother.

I am the 11th child. I have four uncles and six aunts. My father was a farmer until he died, and now my mother is doing domestic work. I was a healthy baby when I was born. Mother said I was the sweetest child she had. . . . My mother said that when my father came home from a hard day of work, I would climb on his knee, and stay there until he would punish me. I had the best of care when I was a baby. I can remember when I was four years old, and father's brother came home with a fuzzy little dog. Father would tease me about the dog. He said that he didn't know which was the fattiest the dog or me. I hated the dog, because he wanted to sleep with me. I was six months old when I was weaned. My father said that I was weaned too early, and that was partly the reason I sucked my finger. . . .

My mother raised me. I was raised with my little sister, and two brothers, and my niece, and playmates. I got along with them fine. . . . There were many children my parents told me not to play with, because they were older than I, and would teach me bad things. I was punished when I did anything bad. Mother would tell me not play in mud, and not to be mean to my playmates. She would punish me every day because I would suck my thumb. Father would punish me because I would go to bed dirty, and without my night cloth on. They would lock me in the room, and wouldn't let me play with the other children. When I was four years old, I would help mother wash dishes and clothes. My father thought I was the best little girl for helping mother, so he gave me extra money.... I was ten years old when my father died. After he died I wanted to die too, because I couldn't go on living with out him. I was his heart. My mother found a way which made me very happy, and it was then that I realized that a mother is more important than the father.... When I was made mad I wished that I was dead, that is when mother or my sisters made me mad. I wanted to be dead, but alive the same time to see them cry over me. I was 11 yrs. old and still suck my thumb, I still suck my thumb now and have night mares. There were many things that I wanted very much, such as jewelry, a piano and a bike. Mother wouldn't get them because she thought that I didn't need them. I will cry and stop speaking to her, and my playmates. I had many fights with my friends. Mother disapproved of them and she would punish me.... Mother is very interested in my school work, she feels that I can do better every six weeks. All through life I have considered myself as a follower, because I am a little timid, and if someone will start I will take a part in what is being discussed. I am not satisfied with myself, if I had the power I would change myself. I want to be a nurse. I think I can if I try hard. I have always wanted to do something good for the people that will help them probably save their lives.

To a great degree, the child finds himself either deprived of balanced bi-parental care in a family situation marked by the total or frequent absence of one or both parents, or he finds himself in a large or extended family situation—which itself may be lacking one or both parents—competing with a number of siblings and relatives for care and desired responses. The significant amount of childhood accidents, sadism, thumb-sucking, bedwetting, and trouble-giving recalled and reported in the autobiographies of youths is probably related to these facts. The lesser part played by the male parent in these autobiographies is striking and suggests a lack of appreciation for the father, and even implicit rejection of him: when the father is mentioned significantly there is a tendency to idealize him, particularly among the girls. Similarly, the psychological implications of the fact that the mother is characteristically the most stable element, and at the same time the chief dispenser of punishment, could be speculated upon. As suggested, there is some apparent ambivalence. It may also be that what appears to be a lack of a truly confident and aggressive approach to life problems might be related to the lack of the male's influence that would counteract the emotional dependence upon the mother and the absorption of some of the aura of patience and tolerance that surrounds the mother or grandmother. Also suggestive is the recurrent expression of youths of the desire to "do something" for people or for the world. This could be significant in view of an awareness of what their mothers have done for them.[10]

Aside from providing a setting and the means for rearing and nurturing, the more obvious functions of the Kent Negro family are these: crisis aid and protection, transmission of work skills, support in design for upward mobility via education, limited ascription of status, definition of role vis-a-vis whites and provision of techniques of survival and getting along.

Innumerable crisis situations are a part of the normal routine of life for most Kent families. Whether prepared for or not, these situations tend to be parts of the normal expectancy in this setting and they usually involve some mobilization of relatives. The type of aid ranges from sympathy and moral

10. Again, we are dealing here with differences of emphasis rather than differences of kind because the picture here is but an exaggerated one of the role of the mother in the kinship system of "Western Society." Talcott Parsons' analysis of the kinship system in relation to sources and patterns of aggression supports this point and is highly suggestive. See Talcott Parsons, *Essays in Sociological Theory* (Glencoe, Illinois: The Free Press, 1949), Chap. XII.

support through various degrees of material or physical support. In many cases a most significant function is that of intercession with whites or with the white agents of law and power. The following account illustrates some features:

Mr. and Mrs. Strong have four boys and one girl. The four boys are married and all except one live away from home. One of the boys and the daughter who has three illegitimate children live at home. One of the sons in particular is addicted to week-end drunks and frequent fights and to scrapes with the law. On such occasions there is usually an immediate rallying of family members around the mother who proceeds to furnish the necessary bail or fine and to intercede with the law or whites with influence. On a recent occasion she referred to her childern and her role as follows: "Our children, you know they will do wrong but they is still our children. I tries to help them out as much as I can. When I goes uptown and tells the Chief that I will stand for something, they takes my word for it; it all depends upon how you lives. I don't try to put on no airs like dicty people who thinks they so much but when I needs money for my children— one hundred or two hundred dollars—I got it and I ain't got to ask them for nothing. All those white people knows me and they knows I will do what I says. I can go to them and get things no other colored woman in this town can get. I works hard and I tries to mind my business; I tried to raise my children right but it seems like they just will do wrong no matter what you does. They's mine and I ain't ashamed of them. . . . I had to lay Miss A____ out about talking about my daughter and her three babies. I told her that although she had got them babies, that not nary one was got in my house; she got them away from the house; nobody, I mean nobody, can accuse me of letting some man lie up in my house with my daughter. That's more than some other peoples I knows can say. I keeps my house decent. What they does outside, I can't help that. I'm going to take care of them as long as I is able."

Even in the most loosely organized or disorganized families, there tends to be some recognition of the support and protection demands of kinship. There is particular sensitivity to the outside attack or the supposed insult. This ties in with the oft-expressed creed: "I minds my own business; other folks is supposed to mind theirs." These factors enter the situation: there is a great leveling tendency; people tend to be sensitive to persons or families that they think are "trying to be better than somebody else" or "dicty"; the situation is such that every family has its "skeleton" or "black sheep"; and there is disposition to circulate or talk about these things despite the expressed creed.

The transmission of work skills from father to sons is particularly noticeable. A great premium is placed upon the male's being able to do something with his hands, and the average male possesses a mechanical skill or ability. The fact that many of the Negro's jobs are of the odd-job utility character helps to explain a certain necessary versatility and the wide dispersion of elementary skills.

There is an oft-expressed belief that there is a demand for the person who can do something. The elite workers of previous generations and of this generation are the carpenters, bricklayers, and painters. To a large extent the older men trained their sons and insisted upon their acquiring some mechanical skill; there tends to be a family monopoly in the bricklaying and plastering area; there are a number of families with two generations of carpenters or painters. A student wrote: "I wanted to be a bricklayer. Because my uncle said there wasn't one in my family, and that you make a good piece for the work."

In this setting, a greater premium has been placed on the higher education of girls than boys. In the past, this was probably due to the fact that the most significant tradition of success locally involved the ability to do something with one's hands and property-getting for the male and school teaching for the female. These are the ways in which independence—

working for one's self in the case of the male and "getting out of the white folks' kitchen" in the case of the female—has been defined in practical terms.

Training, or the wish to be trained, for professional callings (other than teaching for girls) has been relatively rare. The means and the disposition to pursue training beyond the high school are more prevalent among the stable, differentiated families, but even among them there is some ambivalence about a college education. As indicated, this is due in part to the fact that the successful males of the older generation secured what they have with a minimum of education and to a large extent by their own efforts. It also reflects the very important fact that there is little for a college-trained Negro to do in Kent except teach. In other words, to reach the maximum security or status in this community, a pattern is prescribed for the Negro in which higher education for the male would be, on the surface, superfluous, wasteful, and undoubtedly frustrating. This is reflected in ambitions and family designs for education.

Among the relatively undifferentiated families and among a considerable number of the differentiated and more secure, there is a strong drive to provide for children the minimum amount of education necessary to cope with problems and to make "a good living": this by its nature is a flexible and pragmatic goal. A mill worker explained:

I got four children down there in school. I'm going to give them as much as they can take or want. I didn't have the opportunity myself; and it takes more to get by with nowadays. I want them to be able to take care of themselves and I don't mean in somebody's kitchen.

On the other hand, a member of one of the differentiated families pointed out:

My old man taught all of us boys to do a little carpentering and he thought that was enough. My mother had to scuffle like the dickens in the white folks' kitchen and washing and ironing their clothes to see that all of us got a college education. My father just couldn't see it.

It is only among a small core of the differentiated families that higher education as such has practical and prestige values sufficient to make it a must or a taken for granted aspect of their way of life.

It is only at the two extremes of the status or prestige scale that the family acts significantly to ascribe status. Members of the few families who are differentiated by property, enterprise or artisanry, education of children, public morality, and the symbols of family unity and loyalty, are designated by family name and ascribed a certain place in the status or success hierarchy: "He's one of those Thorpes" or "She's a Roberts, you know." There are certain power connotations involved here also; these are usually people who are recognized as "respectable" and solid by whites and who can get things done. The personal characteristics and behavior of individual family members is often set apart from the general position given them by the community. Individuals retain the ascribed status and the aura of the family name despite their personal nonrespectable behavior. Family name and family support offer a degree of protection and insulation against some of the risks of lower status individuals. Although there is some intermarriage among these top families, there is a minimum of social commingling, and there is no evidence of clique behavior among them. They tend to be proud isolates, each with a certain amount of disdain for the other. They, in turn, are outstanding targets for status-starved groups in the community who both respect and envy them, and who show both deference and deprecation. A part of this ambivalent regard flows from the general sensitivity to behavior of members of one's own group: one must not act as if he were better than another; one should always know "how to treat people";

education doesn't necessarily make a man better than others. This latent resentment appears on occasion:

I takes a delight in beating [at pool] "Chick" Thorpe; he thinks just like all them Thorpes he can do everything better than anybody else.

Just because she's "Buck" Roberts' daughter she thinks she can do anything she wants in this town and get away with it.

There is acute awareness on the part of differentiated families of their anomalous position, and there is a conscious ordering of behavior to prevent arousing sensitivity of Negroes and whites. With little or no consensus existing among the various upper families, and with a gulf of family pride and respectability between them and much of the community, they tend to be lonely groups. A member of one of these families pointed out rather philosophically:

A lot of these Negroes around here don't like me because I don't go around and get drunk with them. If you go around and get drunk with them, then they think they got something on you —they get too familiar and try to take advantage of you. That's a nigger. . . . I don't bother with them. I just try to go about my business; I go home and I go to church. I don't hang around none of these taverns or nothing.

At the other end of the scale, lowest status is imputed to member of families who live under the worst conditions or whose records for public morality and conduct are poor. A member of one of these families, who is generally well liked and spoken of usually as "the best of these Strongs," told bitterly of an experience:

I was taking this girl home—she was staying out at "Buck" Roberts'—and I was standing on the porch and wasn't doing nothing when old man "Buck" hollered out and asked who I was. When I told him, he cussed me and told me I was one of them bad Strong boys and for me to never come around to his house to see nobody. He made me so mad I wanted to cry. I ain't never got over that to this day.

The Redmonds live under very squalid conditions. The family history is marked by alleged incest, multiple illegitimacies, delinquencies and brushes with the law. To say that a person is "one of these Redmonds" is to ascribe him the lowest possible status; yet it is admitted that particular ones are "not so bad" or are "pretty nice persons." In this connection, one person points out:

They're mean as the dickens and tough and hard to get along with. But all of them are just as nice if you recognize them or say something nice to them. They seem like they appreciate it more than anything in the world.

As pointed out before, with the exception of these extremes of the status scale, family names tend to have a neutral connotation and are used for placing and identifying rather than ascribing differential status.

One of the important functions of the Negro family in a bi-racial community is to define the role of the child in relation to whites and to provide techniques for "getting along" and for lessening tension and frustration. There are two mental patterns which early become a part of the adaptive equipment of every Negro in Kent: the concept that "white folks is white folks," and a concept of "how far to go with white folks." The first involves a feeling that there is a wall between the two groups and that there are certain things that are intrinsically true of persons in the white category. For example: in crucial situations, white loyalty to white ("white folks stick together") will over-ride considerations of justice or sentiment. It means, too, that a white can never be thoroughly trusted or incorporated into the intimate ways of Negro society. There is always a measure of reserve in any relationship no matter how cordial or benevolent. The second pattern suggests the sensitivity that every Negro has to the limits of approved or permitted behavior in relation to whites; it is a set of restrictions or reservations. These basic, controlling patterns are acquired early by the child in the family, the play group, and to a lesser extent the school. For the growing child, they constitute a life view that has the effect of temporarily reducing tensions and traumatic experiences involving race. Illustrative is the comment of a thirteen year old student: "I do not feel resentful against no one because I feel that I can get along with both white and colored."

When 136 school children between the ages of 13 and 18 were asked about their first awareness of the fact that they were Negroes, the majority (77 percent) indicated that awareness had come gradually or that they had always known "ever since they were big enough." Those who recalled specific instances were in the minority; none commented on the fact with bitterness. The range and quality of responses is indicated in the following excerpts:

I have been fully aware of my being a Negro ever since I knew myself as a human being; so it made absolutely no difference to me.

I remember when I was about 2 years old; I was walking with my mother when I noticed a group of people in the store. The white was waiting on the colored.... I asked mother to explain to me why the colored wasn't waiting on people; then she told me the story. After that I begun to realize; and now I am glad I am an honorable colored citizen.

Whether it dawned on me or came natural, I have always realized I was a Negro.... Knowing that I was a Negro did not make me feel cheap or inferior. I am more or less proud to be a part of such a great race. I want to see and will help it to progress.

...the time when color, race, and religion had a specific bearing on me was about the time I was about fourteen. This is what dawned upon me, one day a white lady asked me to rake her yard for her, and when I had finished she called me to say it was time for dinner, the daughter was called to eat by their sides while she fixed my dinner in the kitchen where I was to eat alone. But, being very sensitive and easy to catch a hint, she came into the room where I was to keep me entertained while I ate.

It was the white family across the railroad I was told not to play with because they was bad and told story on colored people.

I realized I was colored when some person of the other race called me out of my race's name.

Student autobiographies show little overt and direct resentment with respect to race—or at least, a reluctance to verbalize about it. (There is also the possibility that much of it is not at the conscious level.) This suggests that the family and Negro community function early to develop awareness and cushion shock through providing ready rationalizations. Adult bitterness and dissatisfaction about racial matters are rarely directly indoctrinated. Family and school seem to act as "race shelters" for the child and teen-ager. To some extent the mere fact of being a dependent youth in the family and in school imparts some sense of security, worth, and optimism that counteract the direct impact of race at that stage. A comparison of youths who are in school with those who are out of school, and of the same approximate ages, indicates that the incidence of disorganization and bitterness is greater among those who are "on their own."

Supporting the hypothesis that the Negro family imparts protective values and rationalizations about race is the fact that school children's *explicit* objects of aggression tend to be nearby and personal rather than removed and abstract—ingroup rather than outgroup. They tend to be the individual who does one harm or segments of one's own group who behave in unapproved ways. Fifty percent of the children wrote that they felt resentment against no one, and about one in four did not comment at all. Of the one-fourth who mentioned specific objects, more than twice as many mentioned the Negro than mentioned the white group: 18 percent to 8 percent. Those who expressed ingroup aggression mentioned "bad types," embarrassing types, and those who try to appear better than they are.

To cushion the effects of ethnic and social status there is a tendency among families to emphasize to the child that he is as good as anybody else, that one is judged by his conduct, and the inevitability—if not the correctness—of segregation.[11] The emphasis upon individual responsibility and respectability has the paradoxical effect of internalizing aggressions and guilt feelings. The Kent Negro family tends to have the child seek satisfactions and goals within the framework of the local situation. The typical family is no organ of frontal attack on discrimination; the imparting of resentment and bitterness is indirect and incidental; it is not a part of child-rearing doctrine and practice.

Following are some student answers to the question "Do you feel resentful toward anyone, white or colored?":

I don't feel resentful against neither race. No one hurt me or my feelings.

I do not feel resentful toward neither white nor black because we all can't have the same luck.

In some ways I feel resentful toward colored because some try to be more than they really are, and the white I don't have the least idea to worry about them in any respect.

There are some people I feel resentful against; they are Negroes of course and its the way they act and they make me angry.

11. A few parents foster career ambitions for children that will permit escape or emancipation. An extreme example is the parent who has musical ambitions for her eight-year old son and refuses to permit him to use his hands for chores. Somewhat similar is the parent who is obsessed with the idea of "sending my son to New York to school if it ain't for no more than one year."

... because a white person word will go farther than a colored person word will go.

Because a white man will hire a colored man and he'll do anything he say do. Then the colored man say yes sir captain I'll do it. It would be alright if he wouldn't be saying yes sir.

One thing I feel resentful against is the white people because they have many more privileges than we do. They have better schools but our race have come a long distance. I hope they will continue to strive upward.

I feel resentful against both white and colored because the white act Jim Crow and the colored don't have respect.

I do not feel resentful now—but maybe in later life.

I could answer that question but when you put something down in black and white that can be held against you.

A man who has been married nearly fifty years and who has raised a family of ten children—nine of whom are in northern cities—explained his design for living and rearing children. He said that he and his wife had never had a cross word; that they had never called each other a liar; that he had never allowed his wife or his children to hear him utter a profane word or see him take a drink. He had tried to teach all of his children "good citizenship," i.e., not to bother anybody and to take care of their own business. Although this epitomizes the creed of the respectables, the emphasis on not bothering anyone and taking care of one's own business is a recurrent and expressed theme among families of all categories. He who doesn't bother anyone doesn't get in trouble; nor does he get hurt. In this way, withdrawal and a certain passivity with respect to whites are rationalized as virtues in this subculture.

The Economics of Negro Life

CHAPTER 5   THE KENT NEGRO's chief economic roles
may be summarized as producer of raw
materials, provider of auxiliary services, and as consumer of
goods and services. Economic institutions for the most part
are controlled by persons or groups not identified with the
Negro. There is no Kent Negro economy, nor is there a significant elaboration of economic activities with specific reference to the needs or demand of the Negro community. The
Kent Negro's economic activity and interest are geared into
national and world economic activity. Neither larger Kent
nor the Kent Negro community constitutes an economic system in itself; yet there is a much greater elaboration of economic activities and agents in the white community than there
is in the Negro community. The economic activities of the
local Negro must be seen in the context of the economic
functions and characteristics of the local community.

It is difficult to classify precisely the characteristics and
components of the local economy because so many strands
come together in it, and because it is influenced by so many
factors external to it. Although the wage system dominates
and production is capitalistic, some subsistence features linger
and even become stronger in periods of economic crisis. The
total Kent is all these things: a producer of raw materials in
the form of cotton and agricultural products; a trade center
for a small rural hinterland, though in this respect it is dwarfed

by larger nearby centers; a point of exchange and shipment of raw materials; and a producer of finished goods that enter a world market. The ebb and flow of economic activity have a customary and traditional charcter to be sure, but in the final analysis the economic health of Kent tends to be a function of factors beyond the control of the local resident.

The local producers, processors, distributors, owners of capital goods, promoters, and financial workers are agents in a larger system of economic activity and organization. Only to a limited extent do Negroes of Kent participate directly or act as prime agents in this process. They are significant at the first stage—but not always as their own agents—in the production of raw materials, and as consumers with significant demand; however, their economic functions tend to be mainly secondary or supplementary—to a large extent servicing the prime agents or the major purveyors of goods and services in the community.

Among cotton brokers and warehouse owners, mill owners and supervisory personnel, and bank owners and managerial staff there are no Negroes; some Negroes are attached to all of these as service agents or in secondary occupations. Similarly, among the retail and service establishments that supply the bulk of the population, Negroes figure only as auxiliaries. Of course, there are a limited number of retail and service establishments owned and manned by Negroes that operate with particular reference to the Negro community. These and their functions will be described later.

The general picture is this: the Negro does not figure significantly in either the ownership or managerial functions of the economic institutions that directly or indirectly furnish him with the means of livelihood and supply his wants; what economic authority he has is manifested in the demand for his labor as a producer of raw materials or as a supplier of necessary but essentially menial services, and in the demand his purchasing power exercises as a consumer. His patterns of economic behavior are dictated by the general market situation of which Kent is a part and by local employment patterns. The few Negro enterprises have more of a symbolic than practical effect insofar as employment and capital accumulation are concerned. The net effect is that the Negro of Kent is relatively lacking in power and status as an economic agent. A large amount of the male's time is necessarily spent in uneconomic activity or in random economic activity. This situation is due to several factors: the seasonal character of agricultural activity, restricted employment opportunities due to custom or the limited volume of work, and possibly lack of incentive. The pattern of employment for the female domestic tends to be more constant or stable than the general male pattern.

The basic employment pattern for the Negro (as well as the white) worker is a mixed one that is marked by the more or less successful adaptation of agricultural habits and attitudes of the rural area to the commercial-industrial pattern of the town. The two types of economic activity go on simultaneously or supplement each other with significant recruiting of workers from each. On the one hand, there is the cycle of planting, hoeing, and picking cotton; on the other hand, there is the pattern of fluctuating employment in the mills which affects the Negro both directly and indirectly.

Types of Work

In both practical and psychological terms, labor tends to be something that is done for the white man in exchange for money and/or necessities. There are several types of characteristic work activity. There is, first, the basic, personal pattern involving work for "Mr. Dick" or "Captain Tom" or "Miss Alice" or "Miss Rose." Except in the case of female domestic servants, this pattern is apparently on the decline; or at best it represents a relationship marked by intermittent or seasonal employment. The going wage for the domestic is seven to ten dollars a week.

Second, there is employment by a locally-owned concern like Field's Drug Store, Kent Furniture, or Stacy Motors, with the relationship retaining some personal and informal features. Such small concerns have lagged in adopting the impersonal efficiency methods of larger concerns or of concerns owned by outsiders. In some instances, a Negro employee may achieve a position of trust and responsibility; some of these employees are like old retainers or sentimental fixtures. A recent change in a benevolent relationship will illustrate this type: the Negro employees of Kent Furnture were until recently free to use the company's trucks after hours and on weekends; they used them freely for personal purposes. The practice was stopped, ostensibly because the insurance company disapproved. Incidentally, some Negroes thought otherwise, and some who were apparently envious were glad the "gravy train" was stopped.

A third type of employment pattern involves the impersonal, large corporation as employer, for example, Maximum in Stone Valley or "the mill," locally. Rates of pay are generally higher in these establishments, and the workers—when working— constitute something of an elite because good-paying, regular jobs are normally rare. This is true despite the fact that Negro mill workers work exclusively as maintenance workers or janitors or, in the case of the two females who were working, as maids. Employment security in both the mills and at Maximum has not been high. During the last stage of this study there were about twenty-five Negroes working in the mills; this represented a drop of nearly fifty percent within a four month period. During peak production, the total number of Negroes employed in all the local mills never went above fifty; in 1947 the seven mills reported to the state a total of 1225 persons employed. Several of the men who were laid off in the mills' reductions in force started part-time farming as a cushion against unemployment and to supplement income from odd jobs. Most of the work at Maximum in Stone Valley involved the construction phase rather than production; during the peak period as many as fifty local Negroes commuted; during the study there were but five local Negroes working there. The bulk of the Negro workers who worked during the construction phase at Maximum have not worked regularly since. The reasons for this vary: jobs are not available; some have welcomed the opportunity to draw "social security" or, as they colloquially put it, "to rock" (from "rocking chair money"); and some express bitter unwillingness to accept low-paying jobs in view of their conception of their worth and of their previous dignity achieved in a good-paying job. For example:

I'll be goddam if I will take a job paying me fifty cents an hour doing hard labor when I been making eighty-five and ninety. How they expect me to take care of my family. I'd rather "rock" and pick me up some odd jobs around.

The fourth type of employment pattern concerns the independent skilled artisan. (Incidentally, nearly all bricklaying, plastering, paper hanging and a good bit of the carpentry work in Kent are done by Negro artisans.) In some instances, the skilled worker or master craftsman does not enter a contract or subcontract in the full technical sense. Rather he goes to perform certain services at a stipulated rate for himself and probably a key helper. He will also furnish a crew of less skilled helpers who will be paid by the person wanting the job done at the going rate, which is usually much less than that for the skilled artisan. In this way, some responsibility is avoided. It means that there are several informal work bands who periodically "go out on jobs."

There are eight independent full-time farmers in the community, about twenty part-time farmers, and a fluctuating number of farm laborers.

A fifth employment pattern includes entrepreneurial and service workers who function with particular reference to the Negro community—"Negro business." At the time of the study there were these establishments or functions manned by Negroes:

- 5 taverns
- 2 tavern-stores

- 8 groceries or sidewalk stands
- 1 store-cafe

- 4 beauty operators (3 of whom work in homes)
- 2 barber shops

- 1 gasoline service station

- 1 poolroom

- 1 passenger bus for hire

- 1 taxicab owner and driver

- 1 insurance agent

- 1 commission salesman of beauty preparations

These constitute a limited range of economic activity; almost without exception, the volume of business is small and the stock or equipment meager. There are but eleven Negroes in Kent whose chief source of income is their own business or service function; altogether they hire but two full-time employees. Even these owners or operators tend to have other interests, mainly in real estate and agriculture. For the rest, business activity has a part-time, supplementary, even make-shift character. "Putting me up a store" or "going into some kind of business" is a frequently heard expression that suggests the quest for the satisfactions of ownership plus an interest in or a need for supplementary income. A grocery store or sandwich stand is relatively easy to put up; the capital requirement is low; business can be started with a small stock; and operation can be left to the women or children in the family. With few exceptions, these activities are essentially noncompetitive with whites; they are protected service functions; and with the exception of insurance they have a purely local Negro sponsorship.

The sixth type of gainful economic activity is the professional and quasi-professional: preaching, teaching, funeral directing, and midwifery. Seven of the eleven teachers in the local school are "outsiders" who participate only to a limited extent in local activities. One of the male teachers is the only paper hanger in the community and his services are much in demand; there have been periods when his supplementary income was significantly greater than his teaching income. There are ten local residents who commute daily to teaching jobs in the rural areas during school season. There are two former teachers who are now inactive as teachers.

There are nine local residents who bear the honorific title of reverend or minister, even if they are not full-time professionals; only two serve regularly in the local community. Of the total number, two are full-time pastors with one or more churches; five are pastors with at least one regular church who have other jobs as prime sources of income; four are part-time pastors (including one woman who occasionally preaches at the "sanctified" church but is not known as "Reverend") without regular charges who do fill-in jobs. The two full-time pastors and one of the part-time pastors are college or seminary graduates.

There is one Negro funeral home that also provides ambulance service for Negroes in the area. Four persons are involved in its operations. The funeral home services a much wider area than Kent proper.

There are four active licensed midwives in the community. There are also four Negro women who serve as nurse's aids at the local St. Mary's Hospital.

The seventh type is made up by a group of part-time, odd-jobs workers who are a cut above the unemployables and the chronic "won't works." They are apparently not clever enough, or not energetic enough, to have a "racket" or to engage in illegal or extra-legal activities. They are few in number and include the town's eccentrics and the physically and mentally handicapped.

The eighth type includes the less than half a dozen persons who get the bulk of their income from shady activities, mainly selling whisky and gambling. These persons work occasionally as a "front" or have vocations at which they can make livings. This group reflects to some extent one type of practical pursuit of "quick money" or "easy money"—a recurrent interest in the local culture.

There are a few employment patterns that are deviate in a sense. A Negro man had achieved a position of prestige and responsibility in one of the local drugstores before he was beaten and run out of town for violating a racial taboo two years prior to this study. Although unlicensed, he filled prescriptions and in general was the key employee; in the Negro community, he was referred to as "Doc." The other drugstore still has a trusted Negro employee of nearly thirty years' service who doubles in brass as clerk and porter; he rings the cash register and waits on all customers. The chief projectionist in the local segregated movie house is a young Negro of twenty-one. For a period, both projectionists were Negro youths—until one quit because of the conflict of work with basketball practice.

The average income for working Negro females in Kent is less than ten dollars per week. The average weekly income of males who are steadily employed is less than thirty dollars per week. The average is pulled up by the independent and semi-independent artisans, the bricklayers, carpenters, and painters; by the few workers at Maximum in Stone Valley; and by the few workers on the railroad. Employment for

women is more steady on the whole, and the average income
of a woman working 52 weeks a year is something less than
five hundred dollars. During the study, because of significant
unemployment and lay-offs, the average annual income for
the working male was less than one thousand dollars per year.[1]
This income was supplemented by garden crops and in a few
cases the return from small scale cotton cultivation. In the
latter part of 1949, there were signs of real economic anxiety
which would have been more acute if it had not been for the
monies many drew as unemployment compensation. Among
the signs of anxiety were the frequency with which the expression "times is getting tough" was heard; the rush of many
laid off workers to secure land for the planting of cash and
garden crops; the feverish attempts of veterans to sign up for
courses under the veterans' program which would assure them
of a monthly income while learning bricklaying or farming;
the concern about how the periodic interviews with the "social
security lady" would turn out; an increase in idling; an increasing willingness to accept odd jobs; and a decrease in
tavern business.

Although there are many persons and families in the community on the bare subsistence level, cases of acute need that
are striking enough to arouse public sentiment and mutual aid
gestures outside of the church and fraternal orders are few.
There is a certain amount of spot charity and philanthropy that
goes along with "Miss Phoebe" Thorpe's role as leading Negro
citizen and businesswoman. The three cases during the study
which involved some degree of mobilization of parts of the
Negro community were a non-native who was involved in a
serious accident; an ill and destitute female resident of Ox
Row; and the wife of a feebleminded tenant who lived in a
remote spot on the edge of the town and who died of malnu-

---

1. This judgment is based on knowledge of salaries and estimates of time
worked plus an examination of a number of income tax returns while helping persons to fill them out.

trition. The last of these cases shocked some of the leaders of the community into an effort to assure the woman a decent burial and to ease the situation of the feebleminded children. In the other two cases, volunteers sponsored collections for the assistance of the handicapped but the movement to help them never reached large proportions. Although there was widespread sympathy and discussion, identification in this scattered community was not sufficient to elicit spontaneous support of the sort that would be expected in a close-knit small community.

With the exception of those persons who are obviously in relatively good circumstances, reserves in the form of savings or property that can be converted into cash are few. To some extent the need for reserves is lessened for some by pensions and insurance—some form of the latter being a universal. Among those who save and use the banks, women—particularly older women—are relatively more numerous.

ECONOMIC ATTITUDES

As IN other aspects of life, the Negro who remains in Kent tends to adjust overtly or "make peace" with the economic pattern—the ways of making a living and spending money. Some who refer to Kent as a "good little town" emphasize that one can get by easily or cheaply there. Among others, there is a degree of wistful thinking about former conditions or about future possibilities. Among some of the ex-G.I.'s there is evident bitterness, but for the most part there is no attack upon the prevailing economic patterns unless we conclude that a certain diffidence and lack of enthusiasm are forms of aggression or rejection. For example, some young men tell now of the period just after the war when they were "flush" and given to idling in groups: whites would approach them with offers of odd jobs and they would jeer "How much you pay?" "That ain't enough!" "I'll take the job if you bring it down here!" The attitude toward social security benefits fits in: benefits act as a salve, the attitude being that this is something that is due, and there is little overt compunction or shame about accepting it. It is a case of getting something, or of having a valid claim to something that cannot be effectively denied, as other claims might be. As one person put it: "I takes everything I can get from white folks; they don't pay you nothing, anyway; don't refuse nothing they give me." Or there is the attitude that the government gives it and it is right to take it.

The normal distribution of wealth, services, and economic opportunity tends to make the Negro skeptical, cynical, and opportunistic. Among those who have not "made peace" with the situation—those who are obviously restless or dissatisfied—there is a striking interest in "quick money," even if actions are not always consistent with the desire. For the most part these are talented people who appear to be—and often express themselves as—frustrated by the barriers erected by size of town and race. For those who are active in pursuing this interest,[2] the chief goal is not basic economic security, because many of them have this security or could obtain the local version of it easily. Such people tend to be opportunistic and calloused; their choices of economic careers tend to be dictated by the amount of time involved and the existence of a local market for talents or services. They show a tendency to pass up or be diverted from what they really want to do and to restlessly seek the power and balm of quick money. There are these types in all segments of the population. The point is, that for such people quick money has been projected into dominant position as a goal, thus suppressing other career wishes. Important in this situation is the fact that the means of getting quick money in Kent are limited. In the main these

2. A selective factor operates inasmuch as undoubtedly a large number of the younger people who left for other centers were drawn by greater economic opportunities among other factors.

means are confined to exploitation of one's own people, or at least capitalizing on enduring interests or needs: real estate transactions, small enterprise, shady activities—whisky, gambling, numbers. Incidentally, the general interest in playing the numbers is consistent with this mental pattern.

A young man who has two regular jobs—one full-time and the other part-time—explained his hustling activities:

Of course you know I sells whisky. But I'm going to stop this business pretty soon; the onliest reason I got into it was because I wanted me some quick money. I know for certain that if I wasn't a Negro that I could be somewhere and somebody in this town. I know lots of white men who got plenty but I know they ain't got no more on the ball than I got.

A young man about to finish a northern college was speculating about future training and expressed uncertainty. When asked why, he blurted, "Man, I'm interested in quick money!" Another person who is keenly alert to "business opportunities" points out that one compensation for being "stuck in this town" is that he is better off financially than he has ever been; he expresses the feeling that since he is here he will make the most of it and capitalize on every legitimate opportunity.

One characteristic of this type of person is activity in many and diverse fields. The economic career of one such person includes the following: several small legitimate enterprises, a tavern and after-hours spot, concert and sport promoter, maintenance contractor, and local agent for national sales companies. He is known as a person who is "always in everything that has a dollar attached to it." In general, the activities of this person and some others like him are marked by a certain amount of inconsistency and impulsiveness, as well as by shoe-string and makeshift operations.

The Negro business man of Kent is typically a small operator who tends to think in immediate short-range terms. A criticism that is often voiced is that "The Negro don't know he got to spend money to make money; just as soon as he makes a nickel, he takes it right out." A person who himself is in business wryly remarked: "Negroes bury their business." When asked to explain, he pointed to the death or decline of a business with the death of the founder as a consequence of the businessman's failure to expand or to build a strong business for the future.

The closest approach to a corporate business venture is the Kent County Colored Fair Association. A tightly-knit group—including some but not all of the prominent farmers, property holders, and lodge and church leaders—control and benefit financially from the annual fair. They tend to be a "closed corporation," and it is difficult to buy shares. Education and recreation are ostensible purposes, but the dominant motive as revealed in practice is making a return on investment. Members of the community, including some Fair Association members, point out wryly that the first inquiries after the close of the fair are: "How much did we make?" and "When are we going to divide the money?" There is no disposition to re-invest funds or to expand activities or membership; physical properties are allowed to deteriorate. The exhibitional and educational features of the fair have diminished to the per-functory point; it is in fact an economic operation that benefits a few.

There is a widespread feeling among Negroes of Kent that Negroes do not like to work for Negroes. In practical terms this is not entirely true, but there are enough supporting in-stances to give it some credence. It is significant that ideas such as the following have a general circulation:

One Negro won't work for another; he'd rather work for the white. It takes an intelligent Negro to work for another one.

Negroes don't like for other Negroes to act business with them. When the white man is strict on them, it's all right; but when the Negro gets tough, they don't like it.

The reasons behind this reluctance when it does occur are probably not economic, because many Negroes point out that they pay or offer to pay as much or more than whites for comparable work. The fact that some Negroes will stress "I'll work for you as quick as I will for the white man and won't charge you no more neither" suggests some deviation from a pattern. As a possible explanation, it should be stated again that in the traditional economic situation work has been something that is done for the white man and certain associated attitudes and status implications carry over. In the second place, status-sensitive Negroes are over-sensitive to each other's roles and would tend to resent indications of status differences implicit in the employer-employee relationship.

Further, there is no general evaluation of work itself as intrinsically good, nor affirmation of the "dignity of labor." These values are important in the community, but they are the middle-class values of the differentiated who associate work with property accumulation and respectability. For other segments of the population, work, as such, lacks value. This lack is consistent with much of the idling and random behavior that characterizes a section of the population. An older resident criticized this segment in these terms:

People today are not like old times. Too many don't want to do work with their hands—clearing, building, and so on. There's so much land in the country going idle, while folks who can't or won't do anything going to the north and the city.... Some people don't have no venture about them...; they are not progressive.

Contrary to the above opinion, the chances are that the more restless and ambitious who "want to work," or who want the things—money, prestige, comforts, and a sense of personal importance—that are ideally associated with work, tend to leave Kent because the economic base and social atmosphere of Kent do not afford these consistently for a large part of the population, white or black. As indicated earlier, those who remain in Kent apparently adjust to an economic pattern that puts little premium on incentive and initiative, or, if they are restless and have a sense of being trapped, seek "quick money." Of course, there is a solid core of the Negro population for whom work and thrift are traditional parts of their design for respectability.

Religion and Salvation

CHAPTER 6   THE VALUES and virtues of having religion or of acknowledging God are generally taken for granted and are not matters of dispute or discussion. But religion means different things to different individuals and categories of the population, and the action patterns related to religious experience or belief vary markedly. For example, the worship form, going to church, is a complex that involves a variety of activities and meanings. In Negro Kent it is centered around three active local churches—the Field's Street Methodist Episcopal, the Mount Prospect African Methodist Episcopal Zion, the Union Baptist—and around nearby churches in the rural community and adjoining towns.

If the Negro community of Kent were defined in terms of church attendance, it would form a rough circle with a radius of about twelve miles: in addition to the three major local churches, there are six churches in the surrounding rural area which attract regular members and visitors from Kent. Nearly two hundred Negroes remain loyal to the rural churches in the communities in which they were born. They attend these churches rather regularly, give financial support, and are buried in the churchyard cemetery when they die. The churches of Kent proper list about four hundred active members on their rolls. This means that about three in every five Negroes in Kent have some active church connection, and that about one in three of the active church members is identified with a church outside Kent.

Attendance at regular Sunday morning services averages less than one-third [1] of total membership enrolled; attendance at prayer meetings and night services is less. Actually, the Negro churches of Kent are filled only on special occasions: funerals, rallies, communions, and homecomings.

During the course of the year, practically everybody in the community will attend some church one or more times; there are some who attend only once: the annual homecoming, which is as much a social event as a religious one. It is a small minority of regulars who constitute the core of the church-going population. Using as a base the estimated Negro population of one thousand, along with available figures on church membership and attendance, the following general picture is obtained:

(1)   more than ninety percent of the population have been affiliated with some church at some time or another;

(2)   less than sixty percent of the population are considered active church members or carried on church rolls;

(3)   approximately one-fifth of the total population and one-third of the active church members retain affiliations with churches outside the community; and

(4)   on any Sunday morning that is not a special occasion, only one-sixth of the total population and approximately one-third of the active church members will be found in church.

The relatively small regular attendance at church does not measure its impact on the community, however. In the first place, going to church is highly approved behavior and even the chronic non-churchgoer will indicate that he should go more often—and goes occasionally; in the second place, there are special church events such as the "annual meeting," com-

1. This figure is based upon an analysis of the attendance records of two of the major local churches for comparable 35-week periods, and upon personal observation of all churches over an extended period.

munion and homecoming which are more fully attended and
which loom large in the anticipation—and memory—of most
people. Traditional values involved in the church and the
minister are recognized if not fully supported, and the pro-
liferation of church activities and influences throughout the
community makes it an important institutional complex.

Going to church involves many values and functions other
than those related directly to worship and religion. There is
the display and conspicuous consumption factor: in general
the best and special clothes are worn; special occasions such
as the annual meetings involve new clothes and elaborate
preparations. Public recognition and personal satisfactions
come to those with special duties and powers—the deacons or
trustees, the white-clad and beribboned ushers, choir members and choir leaders, the prayer and collection experts. On
those occasions when church attendance is high, the spectator
interest is high; many go to see and be seen, to socialize and
make and renew contacts. The size of the church area and
the pattern of church attendance are dependent upon access
to transportation: this involves use of personally-owned cars
and trucks, ride-sharing, and the hiring of vehicles.

The Meaning of Religion

To merely say "the Negro is deeply religious" is to be guilty
of a bland over-simplification that obscures a wide variety of
meanings and activities. Also, it tells little about the content
of that religion in the Kent setting.

Salvation and forgiveness—the rewards of the Christian or of
the "saved"—are the central themes in local religion. Even
among the most "religious," it is rare that the Christian implications of the many acts and decisions involved in everyday
behavior are reflected upon or cited. True, moral injunctions
and condemnations of certain aspects of secular life are a part

of the content of sermons, but these tend to be secondary or incidental to "living like a Christian" or "putting my Jesus first." These latter tend to be in the nature of self-assuring slogans. In ongoing behavior it is the folkways and the mores and individual preferences and predilections that guide and control; of course, the Christian ethic permeates or colors many of the ideal patterns of the society.

Sermons, songs, and prayers, with but few exceptions, stress the reward and salvation features of religion; the punishment feature is often secondary or implied. The positive promise and expectation of salvation from a forgiving God outweigh fear of hell as a punishment for un-Christian conduct. The idea that "the greatest value in life is working to meet your Maker" is reiterated, but religion is otherwordly only in the sense of projection and promise. It is not otherwordly in the sense that it forces or preaches withdrawal from worldly concerns—although it says that these are unimportant. Religion does, however, stress that forgiveness and salvation are possible at but a small price: prayer and belief loom larger than actual modification of conduct. The following incident illustrates the point:

Several persons were discussing the great religious singers and performers in the community. One person referred to some of the better known ones: "As much whisky as they drinks and the hell they raises, I don't have confidence in none of them." The person's mother answered: "That's where you is wrong. God forgive everything except self-murder; He forgive 'from the stirrup to the ground.' All you got to do is pray. Good thing God ain't like man."

When a definition of a Christian is sought, these themes are stressed: living among the people but living above them (in a moral sense); kindness to one's fellowman—"treating people right"; living like Christ said; following the Bible; and having the spirit of the Holy Ghost. In this connection, it is important to note the emphasis that the most overly devout and confident Christians place upon the individual, and his responsibility for himself alone in terms of salvation. There is a tendency among these confident Christians to stress the fact that they have nothing to do with others, that they must answer for themselves, and that this is the only thing that concerns them.

Religion is something of a reservoir; it is individually tapped and allowed to flow when needed or when ritual or the customary rhythm of life so demand. References to the Bible—which are frequent—are verbal props used to prove, document, underscore, or just to display a kind of erudition. "The Bible says . . ." is an expression used by even the most profane and secular when occasion demands.

Within this general framework there are many belief and action patterns; characteristic variations are related to age, sex, denominations, and individual differences. In religious worship and ritual some persons and groups are active and highly emotional; others are restrained and passive. Likewise, varying amounts of energy and time are devoted to religious activity.

Religion appears to be a much more important aspect of the thought and behavior of older people; religious references sprinkle much of their conversation and they tend to be more numerous and constant in following worship forms and ritual. To a large extent, church activities are oriented around the interests, support, and participation of these older people; effective control of the church is in their hands. Identification with the church is a personal and emotional thing with them. Characteristically, they are aware of the imminence of death.

A widow in her seventies pointed out that she was through working; she was saving herself to meet Jesus. She knew that Jesus doesn't want any tired and broken bodies; she wanted to be fresh so that she can enjoy herself when she gets to heaven. She had been reading Revelations and its description of Judgment Day recently; the way she understood it, all the people who had died were not in heaven yet; they are somewhere in between waiting, and when the day comes all will arise and be judged. She wasn't worried because she had the faith. Although she hadn't been perfect, once she had accepted she had never turned back. She was always going forward; she was certain of her wings.

Expressions like "The Lord will provide," "I'm putting my trust in the Lord," and "I'm ready when my time comes" are characteristically the expressions of elder, mature people. Older people are more likely also to provide the vocal support and "encouragement"—"Amen!" "Preach!" "Ain't it so!" "Yes, Lord!"—for the pastor; they, too, tend to be the public prayer-experts. The person who displays marked religious emotionalism is an object of admiration or sympathetic identification among the older persons; among younger persons he may be an object of amusement or curiosity. Emotionalism and overt spirituality are the marks of the "old time religion" with which the elders identify themselves. Many deplore the diminution of religious fervor:

All the spiritual done gone from the church; money done driven it out.... Once you could get a revival anytime, but no more.... The preachers is different; I ain't got no respect for preachers now.

In the local Baptist church and in the rural regions, the clash between old and new expressions of worship is to some extent crystalized in the conflict over singing styles. The conflict is not as acute among the more sophisticated groups or congregations where worship tends to be more passive. In the Baptist church there are two choirs: the "vocal choir" and the junior choir. In the former, the group is led by the "leader"—who establishes the beat and sometimes lines the numbers—and the singers enthusiastically shout, chant, hum, and at times almost moan songs according to the announced meter and without benefit of instrumental accompaniment. The songs may be spirituals, old-time gospel hymns, or published hymns from the hymnal that have been lined out by the pastor or leader. This kind of singing lends itself to audience participation and mass emotionalism. These are the songs and this the type of singing that developed in a period when many people were illiterate and the piano or organ and the trained musician were rare. These are the songs and this is the style which the older people tend to like; they fit in with their concept of an active, emotional religion.

On the other hand, there is an approach to the more formal choir which sings conventionally-arranged numbers to the accompaniment of a piano and under the direction of a musician leader. The formation of the new choir in the local Baptist church met significant opposition; even the introduction of printed hymnals was opposed. This new junior choir is not the official choir and, when it sings, it sings as if by special dispensation. Although the opposition or resentment comes from the older group and others with vested or sentimental interests in the old form, there develops even among them some pride in the new choir; but full peace has not been made because this new style is essentially vicarious worship. One ex-choir leader criticized modern trends in singing:

You got to git ugly to sing. Some folks wants to look all pretty —keep a smile—and sing; you can't do that.

Another leader in announcing a song, said:

I like the new songs and the new ways they has of singing them. But I likes the old songs too; I likes them best. I wants to sing this song just like my old mother used to sing it. The first time I heard this song, my father sang it.

A younger member of the church commented on the conservatism of the older members:

They're hard to change; some of them been with the church forty years and feel they own it. Some change but most of them hold fast.

The control of religious instruments and ritual by older people is explained by two facts: they participate more and they hold the majority of the church offices. Spot checks over a 9-month period indicate that upwards of sixty percent of those in attendance at any of the three local churches are persons over forty; the proportion of younger people at the sparsely-attended Sunday night meetings, the prayer meetings, and church meetings is much less. Of the six deacons in the Union Baptist Church, four are over sixty-five; six of the eight deaconesses are over fifty. The Field's Street Methodist Episcopal Church deviates slightly from the pattern, mainly because, as one officer put it, "all the older men died off"; but every older man who is active is an officer. The situation in the Mount Prospect African Methodist Episcopal Zion Church—the best organized of the three—reveals the general pattern: up until a few years ago the church had a trustee board of eight men; the youngest was in the early fifties, the average for the group was over sixty-five. The move to reorganize the board by introducing younger members nearly precipitated a split in the church. The newly organized board, that has three members under forty, averages about fifty-two. None of the seven deaconesses is under fifty.

Women outnumber men in attendance and membership at all three churches.[2] The membership figures:

	Men	Women	Total
Union Baptist	34	82	116
Field's Street M.E.	42	64	106
Mount Prospect A.M.E.Z.	56	97	153

2. The figures used throughout this section are as of June 1949.

Despite the fact that nominal control and direction are in the hands of the men, women apparently contribute a larger share of the financial and moral support. Church politics is primarily a man's game, but the women wield great indirect power. In a recent, prolonged dispute in one of the churches, the women staged a coup and temporarily assumed authority as a means of forcing a truce between factions in the church.

As a general rule, older people show a greater disposition to active and emotional religious expression; in these age groups sex differences in amount and intensity of expression are less great than among younger groups. If a person is given to overt religious expression in the younger group, the chances are greater that the party will be a female.

DIFFERENTIAL RELIGIOUS BEHAVIOR AND CHANGE

RELIGIOUS expression in the three churches [3] varies in quality and quantity. These are not necessarily denominational differences because rural churches of the same denominations show less variability.

The most restrained and passive type of religious behavior is seen in the Field's Street Methodist Episcopal Church. This church has the smallest membership of the three major churches and, on the average, a smaller percentage of its membership attends church regularly. This is the oldest Negro church in the town; it tends to be a "family" church with a relatively few families dominating its membership rolls: one-fourth of the membership—and possibly a larger proportion of the support—comes from two families, the Thorpes and the Roberts. Members of this church tend to look upon it as some-

3. The "sanctified" churches and the Presbyterian Church are left out of this analysis: the former were not active during the period of the study, and the latter had but five members.

thing of a responsibility that they are duty-bound to discharge, as well as to attend occasionally. It is a taken-for-granted aspect of their way of life rather than the fountainhead of salvation and the place of active religious experience. This is a "sophisticated" congregation. It is the only one of the three churches where the active emotional display known as "shouting" does not occur. "Encouragement" for the minister is meager and restrained. The members tend to be proud of their restrained patterns and particular denominational affiliation; with reference to some of the practices of other churches, members have been heard to say, "We just don't do things that way." They will explain: "We're just plain Methodists—no African, no Colored, no Zion—just straight Methodist." In some quarters, they have been termed "stuck up" or "proud folks." A member of another church referred to them facetiously as the "Black Presbyterians" of Kent (the local white Presbyterian church is probably the most prestige-laden church of the community).

The Mount Prospect African Methodist Episcopal Zion Church is the largest local Negro church. With a membership of slightly over one hundred and fifty, its attendance averages less than fifty. The Mount Prospect members exhibit a liveliness and self-confidence that is not matched by the other congregations: they tend to be something of a we'll-show-them group whose drive to excel is reflected in successful church programs. Their aggressiveness is in part the answer to what they consider the smug pride of the Field's Street group: "Whatever we set out to do, we're more than likely to do it," or "We're all colored; they have had white bishops over them; we ain't never had nothing but colored from the very first beginning." Their public religious behavior is less restrained than that of the Field's Street church and not quite as active and emotional as the Baptists' tends to be. In the middle class sense, this congregation tends to be progressive and aggressive and the church is one of their vehicles of expression. Their energies incline toward diversion into works incidental to the operation of the church rather than into pure religious expression, as such.

The Union Baptist Church is the only one of the three that has services on alternate Sundays. It is the only local church with a pastor who does not live in the community. The Baptists have a membership list of 116 persons; average attendance for Sunday morning services is between forty and fifty. On the whole, the level of sophistication of this congregation is lower than that of the other two churches. This church is closer to the rural church in ritual and membership than the other two. Its organization is looser, there is greater informality, and religious behavior on the average is more active and emotional. The greater tendency to cling to the old-fashioned ways—which makes some of the members refer to the church as "backward"—and the strength of the conviction that total immersion is the only Biblically approved means of salvation, give the Baptists a more sect-like character than is possessed by any other local group, with the possible exception of the six unorganized members of the "sanctified" group. Incidentally, there are but two Negro Catholics in the community; they worship with the sisters in the chapel of the local Catholic hospital.

Church differences tend to extend to such other forms of religious expression as prayers, communion, revivals, and burials; this is true despite the fact that a basic pattern is present in each. For example, the basic pattern and content of public prayers tend to be the same: humble address to the Deity, expression of thanks for past protection and favors, request for blessings on selves and sundry, and conclusion in the name of the Trinity. In keeping with differences in the churches and subject to the skill of the person praying, prayers and the congregational responses to them are likely to be longer and more emotional in the Baptist and African Methodist Episcopal Zion churches.

The responses of the Baptists to communion are greater and more enthusiastic. In all churches, Communion Sunday is a special occasion for which the turnout is large, but the turnout for the Baptists is relatively larger. It tends, in fact, to be a cooperative affair in which members of other churches in the area come to share the fellowship and the ritual. It is a "big turnout day" and one can anticipate that the emotional peak will be high. It is a day on which the more expert and constant religious performers can be expected to perform; these performers are people who are well known and who, at the same time, are conscious of their roles and of what is expected in singing and shouting. Despite the over-all emotional atmostphere and tendency to overt religious expression, it must be remembered that, even in the Baptist church, the bulk of the audience is passive and spectator-like, with the exception of general participation in songs.

It is generally agreed that the effect of revival services on the Kent community has waned. They are held regularly in the local churches, but attendance is small and during the year of the study the number of converts was negligible. The stonghold of the revival is in surrounding rural areas where more of its former force remains. It is significant that the Baptist meetings were the most successful during a year that was poor generally for revivals; at the same time, older participants pointed out that even these meetings did not compare with former times. Revivals for the other two churches were perfunctory and poorly attended. Local churches also have the annual custom of homecoming—a day on which all persons who are able are supposed to return to their home church for all-day reunion services. The ceremonies are topped off with a basket dinner. Enthusiasm and attendance have waned here also.

An essential feature of religion and church membership is the expectation of a church funeral; indeed, it is one of the motives for maintaining church membership. Among the first

questions asked after death are "To which church did the
deceased belong?" and "Whom do you want to preach the
funeral?" In many cases persons indicate long before their
deaths the minister they want to preach the funeral. As in
the case of other practices, there tends to be a basic pattern
within which variations occur. The basic pattern combines
these essential steps: return of corpse to the home the evening
before the funeral; on the day of the funeral, body and funeral
party are driven to the church. (For all exits and entrances,
the corpse is borne between parallel rows of women "flower
girls" who are usually dressed in white.) The corpse is borne
into the church while the church bell tolls and the choir sings
or the minister utters an incantation; a song is sung by the
choir and audience; a Scripture reading and/or prayer is
delivered by assisting minister or prominent church member;
obituary, acknowledgment of flowers, messages, and testi-
monies by friends and neighbors are delivered; a eulogy is
rendered by the pastor; final view of the remains is taken by
the audience; interment follows, with male volunteers filling
the grave after final rites.

The quality and the length of each of the above steps depends upon such factors as the importance of the deceased,
community reputation, family wishes, and his relation to the
church. There are other important variations that are related
to custom and denominational or church practice. At the local
Baptist church and at rural churches, the casket is opened and
the audience files by in sections for a last view. At the other
two Kent churches, the corpse will be wheeled to the door-
way of the church and members will view the remains as
they file out. This is an important distinction that involves
taste and sophistication. There are a few who would like to
eliminate the viewing of the remains entirely and "do like
the white folks."

The chances are high at the Baptist and rural churches, particularly if the relatives of the deceased are persons of limited

means, that a collection will be taken as the mourners file by the corpse. It is significant that the "Methodists don't do it that way; they'd rather reach down in their pockets and help out in a case where needed." This practice probably had its beginning as a form of mutual aid—and it undoubtedly still serves such functions—but the interests of the family are not always paramount; the ministers and church officers often insist on this collection. One church officer stopped a group on the way to view the remains and said: "Now the family has not requested this, but the church and the pastor have their expenses; will you please drop in an offering as you pass by?"

The practice is for the pastor to receive $10.00 or one-half of the collection, whichever is more. Occasionally, the family and the church get a portion, and sometimes the undertaker. Instances are cited where a pastor has wanted to take a collection despite the expressed wishes of the family to the contrary.

Some indication of a changing attitude toward the church as a source of mutual aid comes from the reaction of an elderly woman to the practice described above; she referred to the traditional dependence upon the church and said:

When some of them gits in trouble, the first thing they do is run to the church. That ain't right and it ain't necessary now 'cause they got societies, pensions and Social Security. The government can take care of them better than the church can; the government can afford it.

The prayer band and the all-night meeting constitute one form of religious worship and expression that lingers and engages the active interest of some members of the population. The two phenomena are significant because they incorporate the most active and expressive features of a type of religious behavior that, despite its prevalence, is on the defensive and will eventually disappear as the young gain control and sophistication increases. The all-night prayer meeting is an institution that survives and has its greatest force in the rural periphery and among the rural migrants to nearby urban centers. Specialists in song and prayer operate with respect to it, giving it continuity and direction. As a "prayer band" or "prayer union" these specialists will travel from church to church. This group constitutes one of the strongholds of the "old time religion," and the chief participants are mature men and women. Whenever there is an all-night prayer meeting, members of prayer bands within a radius of fifty or more miles gather by bus and car. They wear badges indicating their local band and the number of the band in cases where there are two or more bands in the community. Each local group is organized and has a president or leader; the group has a lodge character. Many husbands and wives participate together.

All-night meetings usually start on Saturday nights and last until dawn Sunday morning. There is an economic aspect to these gatherings, for the collection is usually shared with the local church. The economic aspect explains why the only all-night meeting held during the study in Kent proper was held at one of the minor churches—a denomination which normally would frown upon such activity. The pastor of a congregation of five invited the group in order to get some financial help on his building and maintenance fund. A description of the proceedings and participants follows:

Members of the prayer band came by bus, truck, and car from eight different communities, including Kent. There were about sixty persons—an equal number of men and women—who were the core performers; the age range appeared to be between thirty-five and sixty-five with over half beyond forty. There were about thirty-five spectator-participants.

The schedule and round of activity—praying, singing, testifying, and "shouting"—started at 9.00 p.m. and continued until 2:30 a.m., when a recess was called to permit participants to eat the food and drink hot coffee. Activities were resumed at 3:00 a.m. and continued until 6:00 a.m.

The president of the local band, a man in his sixties and an accomplished singer, prayer, and shouter, acted as a roving master of ceremonies who set the pitch and kept things moving. The members of the band proper sat in an irregular circle facing each other. The program consisted of successive cycles of prayer, song, and testimony interspersed with shouting. Representatives from each of the groups and the audience took turns. The general and recurrent theme in words, songs, and actions was joy and satisfaction in the knowledge that one is a child of God. Standard patterns were: reference to past troubles, sins, and dramatic experiences; indication of the awareness of the imminence of death, and an expression of a lack of fear in view of certain salvation as a child of God.

Prayers, songs, and movements were mixed in a rhythmic pattern: as the prayer was said or chanted, a song was sung in obligato fashion and a moving pattern of exhortation was woven. Under such influences, there seemed a real compulsion to participate actively in some one of the approved ways.

Both men and women "shouted." There were three main types of behavior, each stylized: the "exploder" broke out suddenly in a violent paroxysm accompanied by shrieks, tears, or moans; such persons usually had to be restrained and often "passed out"; the "jumping jack" jumped up and down excitedly as if on a pogo stick, singing or talking all the while; if there were other jumpers in another section of the church, the "jumping jack" usually proceeded by jumps to join the group; and the "strider" moved quickly across the floor in somewhat agitated strides, singing, shaking hands, waving arms, and patting bystanders. Any one person may go through all three phases in a session; all three types can be seen in action at the same time.

Two of the "star" performers struck themes in their testimony suggestive of the meaning of religion and of this behavior to them. The first, a man, spoke of his troubles during the wartime rationing period; he continued and said: "White folks can ration gas, food, and the something t'eat—but they can't ration Grace!" The other, a woman, said: "I works all day for the white folks—in their kitchen and taking care of their children, and I just skips around all day because I'm so happy. . . . I've got Jesus."

It must be emphasized that much of this type of active religious expression which marks some features of the Kent Negro's religious behavior is highly stylized and predictable. In the meeting described above, the prayer band members constitute a team of skilled performers; they are expected to perform and they expect to perform; many of them, in fact, have wide reputations. In this style of religious expression a premium is placed upon emotion and action. In this setting freedom of expression and movement are maximized—everyone is moved to some extent by the deeply accented rhythm of the topical songs and hymns that are sung, by the soulful prayers, and by the contagion of "the spirit." One person who is a member of a non-shouting congregation observed: "I came to watch the shouting—and to have something done for my spirit too." The comments by the participants and spectators on the days following such a meeting were to the effect that "We sure had a good time down there," "I really enjoyed myself," "You don't want to miss the next one; it's going to be a big one down at ————."

This pattern of expressive religion reveals many of the basic values and functions of religion on the local scene: personal balm and release, self-expression, recognition, sublimation, recreation—all are demonstrably involved. These meanings become all the more clear when we realize that many of the chief "actors" and most constant performers in religious activities are persons who in their extra-church behavior are not the most religious persons in the common meaning of the term.

Auxiliaries operate with respect to church and religious functions in all three churches; they seek to organize the activities of all age groups and of both sexes through such organizations as Sunday Schools, usher boards, choral clubs, and "aid" clubs for men and women. These groups represent to some extent training and recruitment devices, but, more importantly, they constitute designs for church control and sponsorship of much social and economic activity; they are important financial arms of the church. There is imitation and some rivalry among comparable groups of the three churches. The duplication and rivalry, particularly in the men's and women's clubs which have important social functions, foster divisiveness and cleavage along church or denominational lines.

Despite certain basic similarities, the differences among the respective clubs are suggestive of the differences in the meaning and functions of religion among the different church groups and to some extent between the sexes. The men's groups have been organized more recently and in the respective churches they parallel and imitate the expressed purposes and programs of the female organizations. The nominal core functions in all groups are church and community aid and uplift. These are well stated in a review of accomplishments of one of the groups:

The Helpful Ladies Club could as well be called a goodwill organization. The club is not only willing to work but is constantly spreading happiness and goodwill in the church and community, whenever and wherever opportunity presents itself....

These are the accomplishments of the club for the past year: we donated $50.00 to the church's furnace drive, bought plastic tablecloths and curtains to beautify the basement for the annual conference. We purchased a collection table for the offering in the church auditorium. We purchased twenty-five more chairs for the basement making a total of seventy-five chairs by the club. At each rally sponsored by the church, our club made liberal donations. This club also paid on the first Sunday in each month its assessments of $2.00.

We have sent get well cards to the sick, cards of confidence to the bereaved and flowers in some cases. We sent Xmas greeting to all of our out of town members and to the boys of our church in the service.

Xmas day, the Helpful Ladies sent out thirty or more baskets of fruit, candy and nuts to the sick, shut-ins and aged people of this town of all denominations.

We have worked hard to live up to our success, and credit what we have accomplished to the sisterly love that exists among us, and our ability to work together agreeably.

These might be stated as typical aims and functions, but the groups vary as to the extent of activity and quality of organization and leadership. The statement above is a report from what is recognized as the most active group in the community. The incidental functions involving considerations of prestige, display, status, and fraternizing loom importantly among all groups.

The paired groups of the three major churches are:

Women	*Men*
Helpful Ladies	Young Men's Betterment League
Excelsior Guild	Fraternal League
Missionary Ladies	Fraternal League

In the case of each group, meetings are held every two weeks in members' homes in round-robin fashion. "Having the club" or the "society" is a significant event for the host or hostess, involving as it does some preparation and expenditure for the usual repast; this feature of the club serves a social function and is the source of some little rivalry.

Certain elements are common to all meetings: the formal religious tone and the ritual of prayers, songs, and Bible verses prior to the business session and formal program; the collection of dues and a decided emphasis upon money matters. Characteristically, the religious tone is stronger and more persistent in the Baptist clubs. Their programs are almost wholly devoted to religious and church problems. Each group has its "lesson" at each session; the lesson is a discussion, led by some member, of a religious or church problem, and is obtained from books that the members purchase. The almost exclusive religious and church interest goes far to explain the relative stability of the Baptist men's group, in contrast to the other two men's groups. The other groups—although they operate under the aegis of the church and in their meetings and activities give symbolic and material support to the church—have ambitions for community-wide influence and a larger degree of independence from the church. The indecision that results from these conflicting purposes makes for ineffectiveness and lack of member interest. The women's clubs do not have the same problem because they are to a large extent controlled by social and status considerations. The only group that has restrictions on membership other than that of church membership is the Helpful Ladies. These ladies vote to admit members and strive to be a prestige group.

The church sponsorship of what, in fact, are social clubs has this effect: the chief forms of non-commercial entertaining are church-related or church-oriented. Teas, suppers, and similar affairs are either sponsored by some auxiliary of the church or are given for the benefit of the church.

RELIGION AND MONEY

A LARGE portion of the time, energy, and inventiveness invested in religious or church matters is devoted to money raising. The prominence of this aspect of religious behavior makes for a considerable body of criticism and sardonic humor. Pastors recognize this criticism and resistance and defensively apologize for or rationalize the money-raising activity. Whether understood or not, there are good grounds

for the church's need of money from the participating individual: a smaller number of participating individuals than
formerly, higher maintenance costs, expanded church services, and changing patterns of support for the pastor. The significant clash in values is reflected in the statement of the old
lady who said, "All the spiritual done gone out of the church;
money drove it out." The usual multiple collections and appeals that are a part of the normal service probably prompted
the reaction of a convert to the Jehovah's Witnesses' sect. He
said about the sect meetings: "You goes in there and you stays
an hour exactly—none of this all-day stuff. And when they's
over, you comes out and nobody tries to pick your pocket."

The extremist—but rare—position questions or tries to dis-
credit the entire church institution. This rarely heard position
was stated to an appreciative group of idlers in Burton's shed.
The opponent of the speaker was defending regular contributions to the church and pastor. The speaker answered:

What's the point of telling a poor man he might go to hell?
He done had hell here; if he gets hell, it'll just be hell all the way
through for him. Ain't no point in paying a preacher; ain't
nothing he can do for you. What you gets, you got to work for
yourself.

You can travel from here to California or to New York, and
wherever you go, you'll find the biggest thing the nigger is got
is a church. They lives in shacks and the finest thing they's got
is a church. . . . The trouble is, they pays the preacher, he educates
his children to be something; while the nappy head's children eating corn meal and picking cotton.

Resistance and criticism are diffused and have not crystallized. In general, among church goers "having my money" is
accepted as a necessary part of the pattern. For some it is a
matter of competitive pride and prestige; status in the church
is often equated with faithfulness of contribution—and to
some extent with the amount. A woman leader remarked at
one of the innumerable rallies:

We's here to sing and pray and give money. Some folks says that when you talks about money so much you kills the spirit. That ain't so when you love Jesus; you got to love to give.

I's got my money ... what I got, I got. What you got, you got.

In general, the devices used for raising money are standardized; frequently, however, some ingenious person or group will develop or import a novel method that is soon imitated. Each of the auxiliaries of the church has a money-raising function. The usual devices used, aside from regular collections and special appeals, are: special assessments, envelopes for soliciting, special programs, food selling, and rallies. The favorite and most effective device is the rally using the theme of the Twelve Tribes or the Twelve Apostles. This device was introduced into the Kent area by a professional fund raiser from a nearby town who organized the rallies for a fee; the professional is no longer used. The basic pattern is this: twelve groups are organized under captains and given the names of Biblical tribes or apostles. Quotas are set and the groups report at a meeting that is marked by the marching of the tribes, other church members and visitors as a final appeal is made and the monies collected are turned in. Local people refer to these as "the rally," or they say such and such a church is having the "Twelve Tribes" tonight. Other churches and other choirs are invited; the usual practice is for the groups to help each other. The following describes a rally at a nearby church that was participated in by many persons from Kent:

The crowd of more than 300 persons gathered early. While waiting they were led in prayer and song by one of the experts who is one of the more active and fervent leaders in the community. Eventually, fourteen women dressed in white robes appeared; each carried a small stick to which was attached a piece of white cardboard with an Old Testament Biblical name printed on it in large letters: Benjamin, Levi, Zebulun, Asher, Dan, Napthali, Manaseh, Joseph, Issachar, Judah, Simeon, Reuben.

The leader of the group made a fluent and folksy appeal and explanation: "Some folks wants to know why we always has the 'Twelve Tribes' every year, over and over. We has it to raise money so we can fix up things. Look all around you, you can see what we's been doing. And then some folks ain't never seen the 'Twelve Tribes'; we wants them to see it. We wants them to help us: and when they needs us, we'll help them."

Four persons were called upon to help count and check the money. Then the groups were called in order. As each leader got up to lead the march, she would indicate if she had asked a particular choir or church group to march with her; if she had asked a group, she led them around the church singing. If she had not asked a particular choir or church group, she would request one of the song leaders to sing a song for her and invite the entire congregation to join the march and help on her quota. The procession was always led by a man who carried the placard with the name of the tribe; as he approached the table, he would kneel before the minister and would recite a Bible verse. The group leader would place a handkerchief full of money on the table and other members of the congregation who wished to help this particular person followed with their contributions.

This rally raised $505.00; this plus $335.00 raised in a special day session made a total of $840.00.

Earlier, the Baptist church had used a variation on the "Twelve Tribes." "Twelve Gates," all leading to Heaven, were substituted for the tribes. Those who had their quotas could pass by "St. Peter," who was guarding the gate with a sword. All this was not without a point of humor: one lady was too fat to go through the gate; she had to go around. Quotas for the groups were first set at $144.00 per group; protest resulted in lowering the quota finally to $25.00. Participants showed anxiety about raising assigned quotas and getting through the gate. They succeeded in raising a total of $918. The Baptists were proud that they had raised more money in their rally than the Methodists had.

The most significant example of inter-church co-operation

centered around a competitive rally involving all three major churches. This came on the heels of earlier rallies and heightened criticism of the "money-mad" churches. Each church was to use its own devices to raise $1000.00 to be used for its own purposes; the church that raised the largest amount was to have its representative crowned "Miss Kent." Each church used the basic rally pattern, only this time leaders representing the 48 states were chosen. Over a 2-month period, the leaders set up a variety of fund raising projects. The most notable of these was a banquet given "for our white friends" by one of the groups. This was a coup not without some unfavorable reactions in the Negro community, including a fight between two men over the propriety of the event.

There was some resistance to the almost continuous money-raising activities of the churches. The least enthusiastic were the people of the Field's Street Church: they are the smallest church and "we just don't do things in that way." The rivalry between Mount Prospect and Union and the respective pastors provided the chief spark of interest. Mount Prospect won the rally with a total of $1001.00; Union raised $697.00; and Field's Street, $490.00. There were whispered recriminations after the rally about the "unfair tactics" of Mount Prospect.

Aside from underscoring the constant interest in money-raising and the fact that a major portion of church energy is diverted into this channel, this event represents a distortion of the community fund idea—an idea which is a rational answer to the problems of fund raising but that is unlikely of adoption because of rivalries. And it is one of the few intimations of real church cooperation on the local scene. The Presiding Elder called for more such examples and said pointedly: "You folks always talking about getting ready to live in Heaven; you've got to learn to live together in the mud and dirt streets of Kent."

Religion and Needs

Religious conduct appears to be primarily a means of affirming faith and belief in individual salvation. The quality of the expression ranges from the most passive and perfunctory to the highly active and emotional. Going to church and having religion are highly approved patterns, and thus social pressure and prestige are important factors in religious behavior in a community where the status of everyone is known. The restrained behavior of the more sophisticated is in keeping with their conceptions of themselves and their emotional demands. Similarly, the active, emotional behavior of older, less sophisticated, and marginal persons has meaning in terms of their traditions, statuses, and needs. Emotional behavior is a link with a more congenial way of life; it supplies balm, security and a sense of personal worth. The following expressions are illustrative:

Somebody ought to say something! You done heard this fine Christian message—and aint nobody said nothing. I'm going to say something! That's what I came here for—to say something! I wants to let folks know I got Jesus!

Sometimes you gets gypped here—but Jesus will make it up to you.

You can't ration Grace!

Assuming that the Negro of Kent lives in a relatively "tough culture"—one marked by significant blocking of wish goals— the free-expression aspects of his religious behavior parallel the patterned indulgence in whisky, sex, and tavern behavior, and they serve something of the same function. Religious expression is a function of social and personal needs as well as tradition: its manifestations vary roughly with the indices of sophistication, status, and security. In a Kent that is neither wholly rural nor urban, the old "old time religion" persists; but it tends to be on the defensive as educational and urban influences increase. Some leaders seek to "bring out" the more "backward," but there is understandable resistance and inertia. There is still significant "need" for this kind of religion.

Teaching the Children

CHAPTER 7 THE EMPHASIS IN this chapter will be upon the chief formal embodiment of the educational function—the public school. Something of the educational role of the family has been indicated in a previous chapter. Like the church, the school touches in a significant way every family and person in the community. It is a focal point of many interests and activities and of some conflict. The school for Negroes is a segregated branch of a community-wide institution. A description of its functions, support, and control reveals the ancillary character of some Negro institutions. The Negro school and the Negro teacher are products of a racial division of labor in the distribution of services and equipment; they are agents with restricted and limited prestige who are carrying out a phase of the whole community's educational functions and purposes. A description of the Negro's school reveals, among other things, the sources of effective power and influence in the subculture, the channels between Negro agents and white policy makers, and the values involved.

The Jackson consolidated school has an enrollment of a little over three hundred, approximately two-thirds of whom are residents of Kent proper. Classes are taught in three buildings: a 4-room frame building for high school classes and home economics training; a brick Rosenwald building with six rooms and a small auditorium that doubles as a gymnasium during basketball season; and a recently-built 2-room frame building to house the increased population due to the addition of the twelfth grade to the curriculum. The buildings lack a central heating system and at the time of the study were in poor repair. A member of the school board, on one of the rare visits of school officials, was led to remark: "You folks don't have a goddammed thing down here; how in the hell can you do anything at all?"

During this study extensive repairs and improvements for the Negro school were projected or under way. The background, procedure, and reactions of this movement are illustrative of attitudes and of the nature of intergroup mechanisms. A bond issue of $650,000.00 had recently been voted upon for the prime purpose of erecting a new white high school. Negroes were asked to vote favorably with the understanding that some of the funds were to be used for improvement in the Negro school. In the early stages, there were no definite understandings, but the attitudes seemed to be, "What have we got to lose? We're going to have to pay increased taxes anyway. Anything we get will be more than we had." After passage of the bond issue, a report, supposedly coming from a school official, stated that $150,000.00 had been earmarked for improvements on the Negro school. Negroes were hopeful, but intensely cynical and skeptical. The following comments were typical:

They might have the money, but I bet you they don't put it down here; most of it will wind up over there [in the white school] or in their pockets.

They'll come down here at the last minute and throw a little paint and plaster around and that'll be all that's to it. That way they think they'll pacify the Negroes.

I won't believe it until I see it.

Whether true or not, these reactions and allegations reveal basic attitudes. They are fostered and fed by the lack of information in the Negro community and the lack of direct participation in policy making. Here, as in other areas, there are no systematic or patterned lines of communication between the informed policy makers of the larger community and the functionaries and clients of the Negro community.[1] Communication is on a sort of haphazard, informal basis; among the persons directly involved and charged with certain responsibilities, there is uncertainty as to whether—and how—representations might be made. Without power and knowledge, Negro officials are ancillary to the community's educational functions and operations. In this matter, as in others, comments and "advice" were elicited from—and bits of information relayed through—a few Negroes in the community. All of this was done in an informal and casual manner. These persons—cooks, servants, idlers, "responsible Negroes"—constitute "pipelines" between the white and Negro communities

The personnel of the local school is composed of a principal, ten teachers, and a janitor. The teachers constitute the bulk of the professional group in the local community. As "educated people" they are objects of respect; their roles, as defined by the community, require them to be circumspect in behavior and not too aloof in manner. The fact that the community is small and that they are prime gossip targets shows in their restraint and general public behavior. With few exceptions, the teachers are isolated persons with some indications of fear and insecurity; outside of the school room and public appearances at churches they participate in a minimum of community activities. The grade of teaching certificate and salary depend upon performance in a state-sponsored examination; thus the teachers tend to be certificate and salary conscious. Contracts are for one year and, in practice, tenure depends upon pleasing the students, influential parents or mem-

---

1. Since writing this, the word was given that a new "gymtorium" (combination gymnasium and auditorium) was to be built immediately. Preliminary steps to build were taken—but they were stopped abruptly, leaving the Negro community puzzled and speculative.

bers of the community who can transmit displeasure to influential whites, the principal, and the superintendent. Other possible factors explaining their behavior: differential tastes and interests related to college training and teacher status (e.g., "There's nothing to do around here; I have to go out of town to have my fun and see my friends. Kent is a terrible little town."), the operation of selective factors in choice of teachers (salary scale, size, and reputation of the community), knowledge of unfortunate experiences of previous teachers in the community (turnover has been rapid).

One commentary on persons, roles, and the situation is the fact that consistent use of the formal respect and deference titles—"Mister," "Missus" and "Miss"—occurs in the relations of teachers among themselves. Of the 11 teachers, none, with the exception of the members of the two family combinations, addressed each other or referred to each other in familiar terms. This somewhat exaggerated use of titles indicates that, in a relatively undifferentiated community without many honorific callings, the teachers constitute something of an elite; their status is respect-laden. The situation here is that the functionaries themselves follow the rule rigidly. This is of the same order as the practice of physicians calling each other "Doctor" in a variety of formal and informal situations. There is added significance to this behavior in this status-poor and status-starved society: there are few points at which the Negro is accorded the conventional symbols and gestures of respect in the larger local community. With the teacher, who presumably has differential self-conceptions, sensitivity to respect-starvation may be more acute; hence, the exaggerated usage of respect and deference symbols among themselves.

The principal of the school, who is a college graduate, has one of the more important roles in the Negro community. He "runs" the school under the loose supervision of the white superintendent to whom he is directly responsible. He is an agent of the dominant white community, inasmuch as he is designated "in charge" and is expected to follow a program that is congenial to those who have the power and make policy. On the other hand, the fact that he is the top public official in the Negro community gives him considerable status within the community, and also imposes upon him certain leadership and interpretive functions. His is a strategic role with respect to both the white and Negro communities, and he is peculiarly exposed in both areas. The later discussion of "who runs the school" will indicate something of the dual character of the Negro teacher's role and the general power situation in the Negro community.

The minimum course of study and the textbooks for all public schools are standardized by the state. The Jackson Street School is not on the state list of accredited high schools; it doesn't meet requirements as to library facilities and physical equipment. The only course offered with direct vocational emphasis is domestic science for girls in the ninth, tenth, and eleventh grades. Manual training for boys was dropped during the war period. There was some desire to have the shop course for boys reinstated, but by the end of this study there had been no direct or organized effort from the Negro community to accomplish this, although some persons decried the fact that "our boys are not being taught now to do something they can make a living with."

The following formal courses were taught in the high school during the school year 1948-49:

Ninth Grade
    Literature and Life
    Algebra
    English Composition
    Everyday Science
    Building Citizenship
    Home Economics (girls)
    Economics (boys)

Tenth Grade
    Literature and Life
    Algebra
    Correct English
    Biology
    Home Economics (girls)
    Economics (boys)

Eleventh Grade
  Literature and Life
  High School English
  Development of America
  Everyday Problems of
    American Democracy
  Home Economics (girls)
  Economics (boys)

Twelfth Grade
  American Literature
  French
  Living Chemistry
  Plane Geometry
  World History

Outside of a few families, the school is the only agency in the Negro community that fosters "cultural" activities which are essentially non-religious and non-commercial. Its contribution consists, in the main, of providing limited opportunities for students to take part in musical, dramatic, and intellectual activities that have a content and emphasis different from the church-centered and religion-oriented art forms, and the popular art of the movies, radio, newspaper, tavern and idling places of Kent. There is apparently no attempt to combat these other forms of expression. Certainly the religious and folk-song emphasis is carried over into the school, because these play a part in such school rituals as devotions and assemblies. Aside from textbooks and a few scattered periodicals, the school is not equipped to compete in reading matter and tastes with comic books and the popular magazines. The school library consists of about three hundred miscellaneous old volumes which are neither catalogued nor classified, nor are they used by students to any significant degree.

Some musical training and acquaintance with some of the "classical and better" music comes through the efforts of an elementary school teacher who doubles as "musical director." She teaches piano and voice to individual students, most of whom have pianos at home, and she trains choral groups for public appearances. Her students are presented to parents and the community in an annual recital. In a similar fashion, other teachers train students in the dances and recitations for the annual May Day, for the annual play in the school auditorium, and for participation in commencement activities at the end of the school year.

Expectations of the community are geared to a certain cycle of cultural events, entertainment, and ritual at the schoolhouse; for the most part, these events occur in the Spring and climax a considerable period of preparation and anticipation for students, staff, and parents. These events are important because of the significant sense of pride in individual and group achievement involved, and they are also important because they constitute for many the only "cultural" and intellectual experience obtainable outside of the church. Performances are judged critically, particularly by those who don't have immediate and close ties with the participants. One way of indicating disapproval of school personnel or policy is to boycott school activities and to make invidious comparisons between what goes on now and what went on formerly.

During the fall and winter, the athletic teams are central interests. During the fall about twenty-five boys are directly engaged in football; during the winter the boys' and girls' basketball teams involve about twelve persons each. Around these teams and their fortunes—and the exploits of individual members—clusters a great deal of the community's recreational interest and activity; in fact, some of the interest spills over into the white community. The athletic teams are objects of great pride, support, and criticism. The most significant community-wide celebration and mobilization of the year was centered around the Homecoming Day during the football season.

Preparation began two weeks ahead for a celebration that was to include a parade and a football game with a nearby rival. There were to be floats, a borrowed band, and a Miss Homecoming. Parents bought special outfits for the smaller children—red sweaters and blue skirts for girls in grades 5-7 and blue skirts and blue sweaters for girls in grades 8-9; the hairdressers did rush business, straightening and curling hair. Committees worked on the floats for the better part of a day; cars and trucks were borrowed for the parade from both white and colored friends or merchants. For two hours before the parade was scheduled to begin, a large portion of the student body, teachers, parents, and other townfolk roamed or worked in the schoolyard.

Led by the Chief of Police, the parade proceeded through the main streets of the town to the athletic field of the white high school where the game was to be played. The parade was watched by small clusters of Negroes and whites; some persons waited more than an hour for the parade to appear.

The game was witnessed by nearly five hundred people, about one-tenth of them white. Players reported that they had an added incentive to make a good showing before the home town crowd; with sadistic humor they pointed to the fact that the white high school had lost the game it played the night before to its arch-rival.

Older residents spoke of the round of events as the biggest day Negroes had had in Kent in many a year; some were reminded of the long-abandoned Emancipation Day parades. For younger persons it was the only parade and public celebration that the Negroes of Kent had had in their lifetime. One older person pointed out that he knew nothing about football but that he came along because the school and the colored people were doing something and he wanted to support it. This school-sponsored event touched in some way practically every segment of the Negro population—and some whites; and it elicited great group pride and satisfaction.

The chief auxiliary of the school is the Parent-Teachers Association. Composed of 51 members, it was reorganized during the study after having been inactive several years. Informants report that the former organization in its later stages was marked by small attendance at meetings and the lack of a definite program. The leaders and much of the membership were persons of the older group; a portion of the members had no children of school age. Personal rule, favoritism, and lack of program are given as causes of its ineffectiveness and decline. One story is cited to indicate its diffused character and lack of directed program: an officer is alleged to have paid for a load of wood for an indigent person (who happened to be a relative of the officer) out of association funds; some persons refused to pay dues after this incident. At one of the early meetings of the reorganized group, the president of the former group expressed pleasure at the fact that the majority of the new group consists of persons who actually have children in school.

The 13 persons—11 of them women—who reorganized the association include persons who were generally conceded to be "smart" and aggressive.[2] The officers were well-poised and articulate, and they kept the movement of the business meetings brisk. They represented a new stirring in the community; they condemned the previous indifference of the Negro community to sub-standard school facilities. Their activities for the year indicated determination and some skill at mobilizing community support.

The group set as its first goal the establishment of a school lunch program "so that our children can get free lunch like the white children." It was too late in the school year to get the program started, so the group set up another objective: the equipping of a library for the school in order that minimum accreditation standards might be met. The group pledged itself to raise the necessary $1500.00. They initiated a 3 weeks drive to raise the initial $500.00. A canvassing of the Negro and white communities brought $445.00. The drive was climaxed at a community-wide mass meeting that was notable for the themes stressed by the main speaker, a local minister. Among his emphases and allusions were:

2. Prior to the reorganization of the group, one person pointed out that what the group needed was "some of those Mount Prospect people to take an active interest; they could make it go." Six of the original 13 are members of the Mount Prospect Church; three of the five officers are Mount Prospect members. The Mount Prospect Church is generally credited with having a group of "smart" women who will work to put over programs.

The Negro as a race doesn't read enough. You take the Jew, he reads a lot and doesn't say much; the Negro says a lot and doesn't read. . . . Parents should pay attention to the education of the boys as well as the girls. When the girls marry, they should be able to reach across rather than reach down. . . . Books are highways to the world; the Negro needs more of them. . . . If the people would get together and stick together like they have shown they can do in this drive, we can get any kind of school we want down there.

The traditional role of parent-teachers associations and similar auxiliaries of the Negro school in this community and others reveals one of the dilemmas of the Negro community. The dilemma is indicated in the negative reaction of a few persons to the fund-raising activities. One person reported himself opposed to such self-help measures on the part of the Negro, particularly when these measures are born out of the pattern of discrimination. He points out that they represent a kind of double taxation: "If the Negro had the power or the sense he would ask for or demand from the general funds such things as these which are his rightful due."

It is a commentary on the community and on the personal dilemmas that confront some individuals that this older man felt that it was not wise to state such a position publicly; few people would understand and he would be accused of obstructionist tactics. Though opposed in principle, he admittedly takes the easy way out. He contributes when solicited: "it's easier that way."

The operations of the Parent-Teachers Association reveal, among other things, the Negro's lack of access to normal institutional devices and services and the necessity of incidental adjustments and indirect methods to achieve desired goals.

CAREER WISHES OF HIGH SCHOOL SENIORS

THERE is little in the formal public school curriculum that relates to the customary ways of making a living among Kent Negroes. The career wishes of high school seniors are influenced by school experience only in a general and informal way. This influence usually is in the direction of getting a college education as a basis for career and self-improvement. Guidance and counseling by the teachers are on an informal basis and are confined for the most part to the senior year. They consist of informal talks and encouragement to students who are talented in classwork, athletics, or music. Among the senior class of 16 students—which incidentally was the first 4-year high school class in the history of the school and contained 11 students of the original 34 first grade students—the interest in college was primarily a contagious interest among the students themselves. It stemmed from clique and friendship association in which the key members had significant parental support and were practically certain of going to college. Out of the class of 16, there were five students—the son and daughter of the principal; a son of a prosperous farmer who has another son in college; the son of a cook for a prominent white family who has a college graduate daughter; the daughter of an old upper status family, a number of whose members have attended college—who were certain of going to college. Only in these cases did the wishes and expectations of the children coincide with the willingness and the ability of parents to support them. Acute interest and anxiety appeared in the cases of girls who were uncertain about going to college. The summary on the following page shows a tabulation of career choices of the members of a senior class:

CAREER CHOICES OF HIGH SCHOOL SENIORS

| | Male | | Female | |
| | First | Second | First | Second |
Careers	Choice	Choice	Choice	Choice
Athletic coach-teacher	3	2		1
Teacher		1	1	
Social worker		1	2	
Dietician			2	
Dentist	2			
Business	1			
Secretarial			1	1
Nurse			2	
Beautician				2
Interior decorator				2
Music			1	2
Tailor		1		
Electrical engineer		1		
Pharmacist			1	
Housewife				1

Models for only a few of these callings exist on the local scene; in no case was the first career preference the same as the occupation of either parent. The general wish for upward mobility was matched by manifestations of confidence only in the cases of those students who, because of family support, were certain of going to college. The following excerpts from autobiographies of seniors indicate confidence:

After completing my college course I plan to work to obtain enough money to go to medical school to take up pharmacy. I think I will succeed in doing this since I have the desire to make this my field and I can attain success by striving hard to accomplish what I want.

My hope for later life is to become a successful teacher and successful housewife, wife and mother. I intend to become these

in the best way I can. My chances seem to be good to fulfill my
desires.

Uncertainty and resignation are seen in the following excerpts:

When I was very young I wanted to be a school teacher so I
could whip kids. As I grew a little older I wanted to be a doctor
and I still do. Doctors do so much for humanity. . . . At present I
am not satisfied with myself, I want to be and do better. I still
want to be a doctor but I don't think I have a chance.[3]

In later life I think I would like to be a stenographer or either a
private secretary. But it seems dark at the present of securing this
ambition because of the disadvantages we have. Typing isn't even
exercised at school.

I always wanted to be a doctor or a lawyer when I grew but
now I have changed from that, because there is more to it than
just wanting to be different things. . . . In general I'm not satisfied
because I wish I could afford the many different things that I
want or need, especially a college education and others. I have
planned many things to do in later life such as teaching, coaching,
or being a lawyer or something that I would enjoy in later life.
My chances of becoming some of the things are fairly well, in
fact it depends on me.

The ambition and wish patterns of Kent Negro youths have
a markedly wider range than the actual career patterns of
Kent Negroes, and they are in general on a different level.
Despite this, there is undoubtedly in actual practice a high
rate of regression to the career patterns of fathers and mothers,
particularly for those young people who remain in Kent.
Youth's design for upward mobility is not always compatible
with some of the mental patterns and "realities" of the local
subculture, such as: the suspicion and lack of respect which
some local whites accord the educated Negro; the low in-

3. When this person was asked later for career choices, she indicated
social work.

come level of Negroes; the lack of a basis of support and effective demand for diversified activities and services; and, to some extent, the incomplete acceptance of the need for advanced training within the Negro community.

EFFECTIVE POWER IN SCHOOL POLICY

AN examination of the circumstances related to the dismissal and resignation of some of the school personnel at the end of the school year 1948-49 shows some of the types and bases of power in the Negro community, as well as the channels of communication between the Negro and white groups. Three main facts appear.

First, crucial for the maintenance of position in the Negro community is a favorable or neutral relationship with strategic whites. A person may "rub" Negroes the wrong way and escape censure or sanctions for a considerable period, although the feelings of the Negroes will be informally transmitted to strategic whites and have a cumulative effect.

Second, the Negro is without *direct effective* power; his power is indirect because it is always channeled through a white intermediary or friend, and the resulting action stems from a personal relationship. This is the reason why the cook who has intimate access to whites is looked upon as being one of the more influential persons in the community. ("You can get along all right just so you don't cross one of these white folks' cooks.")

Third, the pattern that involves nearly every Negro having access to some white intermediary or friend works against effective Negro group organization or mobilization and the development of formal channels. There is a preference for handling matters individually and informally where the claims of a personal relationship can be made and the symbols of racial difference in status maintained. This lends some support to the pervasive in-group condemnation: "Negroes don't stick together."

Two female teachers were dismissed after serving but one year, despite recommendations from the Negro school officer responsible for them that they be re-hired. A white school official indicated that their contracts were not renewed because he didn't like their manner: they didn't say "Yes sir" and "No sir" in conversations with him. Their dismissal caused little overt concern in the Negro community beyond speculation of the curious.

The male teacher who was dismissed was a "local boy," and consequently his leaving brought different reactions. There were those among his friends who sought to intercede for him via the usual channels. One person said: "If he still wants his job, all he's got to do is let me know and I can do something for him. This thing ain't through with yet." The fact that the speaker was probably over-estimating his power is not as important as the indications of the channels by which he might seek to wield influence or make wishes known.

The resignation of the principal was a more complex and, at the same time, revealing incident. Immediately prior to the resignation, the school situation was externally quiet; the great bulk of the people were apparently neutral or indifferent to the principal and the school situation; a number of persons in the community were critical—but they had been for some time, and now they didn't appear too active or organized in their opposition. A new element in the situation was the revitalized PTA: some of the members were either direct critics of the principal or indirect ones in the sense that they decried the backwardness of the school. For personal reasons, the principal was undecided as to whether he planned to come back or not, and there was some speculation as to whether he would resign voluntarily.

Two weeks prior to his resignation, the principal was told by a friend that a white school official had asked how the principal was getting along and had volunteered that he had been getting a lot of complaints. The principal's friend defended him vigorously and said that if proof were wanted of the attitude of the Negro community that he should try taking a poll. The rumor was abroad that some "Negroes who called themselves 'big shots' had the ear of the superintendent." Later, when the white school official called the principal in, he informed him that there was dissatisfaction with him in both the white and Negro communities; he told him that he wasn't forcing him to resign, but that he [the principal] would run into opposition when the Board considered his re-election. The official expressed an unwillingness to go into the reasons at that time.

The school official gave the news of the resignation letter almost as soon as it was received to several Negroes, among them the women who worked in the cafeteria of the local white high school. There were those who held no brief for the principal but who felt strongly over the manner in which the school official had let the news out.

There was much speculation in the Negro community as to the circumstances and causes of the resignation. Negro "pipelines" into the white community soon brought back some of the answers: retention of the principal for another year had been highly questionable, but all questions were erased by a crystallizing incident: the principal had made the "mistake" of sending a letter to a school official suggesting an athletic contest between teams of the Negro and white schools as a means of raising money for a benefit drive then current in the community—and, incidentally, improving race relations. The school official did not answer but passed the letter on to a member of the school board; the member exploded: "The nigger must be crazy wanting those niggers to play with our children." (The interesting point is that the idea for the suggestion came from white high school students who had informally expressed a willingness to play the Negro school teams.) Negroes themselves were critical on this score: "He ought to know you can't do nothing like that down here." The school official indicated that his candidate for the vacated position was a person from another part of the state whom he had never seen but who had been highly recommended by a "white man." Support developed among the Negroes for a local candidate, and the pattern was repeated: several Negroes spoke to influential whites on his behalf. Since this appeared to be what the Negroes wanted, the school official reluctantly yielded. The attitude of some whites was typified in the remarks of one: "I guess your preachers are satisfied now with the appointment."

Ironically enough—yet understandable in the local context—townspeople and school teachers prefer the present system of complete white control to the system of having Negro trustees. This latter system by which white-appointed Negroes served as an unofficial "Negro school board" with limited powers was discarded several years ago. Many say that that system was marked by too much favoritism, nepotism, and meddling, that "things was always in a mess then": "We don't ever want them in here again."

Government and Social Control

CHAPTER 8   IT IS HIGHLY probable that when the average Negro in Kent refers to the government, he is thinking about the Federal government; when he speaks of the law, he is referring to the local police and court machinery. Identification tends to be a matter of personal experience and meaning: the government gives in the form of unemployment compensation, pensions, crop loans and subsidies; the government takes in the form of taxes and payroll deductions. The police are always in evidence, and involvement with them is always possible for everybody and highly probable for those who consciously accept such risks as normal parts of their way of life.

To Cast the Ballot

PRIOR to 1948, few Negroes had voted in this state since before the turn of the century. For nearly three generations active participation in governmental affairs had been almost nil. Identification with local and state government tends to be vicarious and small. Literally and figuratively, local and state government and governmental functions have belonged to the whites and have been instruments of dominance. The fact that many Negroes refer directly to a former period when relatives held local offices or participated in state politics underscores the current lack of identification. It is apparent—even now with the vote—that the sense of really being an integral part of the governing process comes slowly; for many, particularly those of the older generation, the vote is a symbol of increasing status and respect, and, secondarily, an instrument to achieve ends. Even among those who realize or anticipate the practical effects of participating in local politics to secure such things as paved streets and better school facilities, the chief expectation is that a voting Negro will receive a larger measure of public respect. A young veteran said:

I hate to go up in that courthouse, those lawyers just say "nigger" like the Negro is the lowest thing on earth. They going to stop that though: that's one of the first things that's going to change. When the Negro gets to voting they going to cut out that nigger stuff; they might not call you mister but they won't say nigger so much.

Public officials and candidates are adjudged primarily in terms of their treatment of the Negro and their conception of fair play, but even with reference to the best liked persons, Negroes apply the rule "white folks is white folks." A frequent expression is "He's a good man, as white folks go."

Negroes voted in considerable number for the first time in the elections of 1948. Seventy-nine were registered for the municipal election, and an official estimated that seventy, or nearly ninety percent, cast ballots. A few Negroes had been exercising the privilege for several years. An election official pointed out:

We've had a few niggers voting in Kent for years. They are good niggers—know their place. And there has never been any trouble about their voting. On election day, they always come to the polls as soon as they open, vote and leave.

Negroes have voted in elections subsequent to 1948 without incident beyond minor embarrassments at the hands of reluctant officials. A white observer reported:

The Negroes were standing in line to register—just as quiet and orderly as they could be—along with the white people. When a white person came to the registrar, his attitude was all politeness. But when a Negro came up the whole atmosphere changed. The Negroes were permitted to register, but the attitude of the registrar was surly and begrudging. They were perfectly rude to the Negroes, but still the Negroes behaved properly and did not raise any commotion.

The local move to register and vote in large numbers was led by the Reverend Sampson, a minister who showed persistence and personal courage in seeking out officials and pushing the matter. He was armed with a recent court decision that he constantly cited. In the background was a loosely organized branch of a state political club—The Fair Deal Democratic Club of Kent—that served as a means of educating and mobilizing the Negro voter. Although designed as a permanent organization with regular meetings, the club has had an *ad hoc* quality: it was most active just prior to elections and conventions and met on call of the leader. In the summer of 1948, just prior to the elections, there were 59 persons, 49 from the town of Kent, enrolled. During the summer of 1949, there were about fifteen active members, nine from Kent. Recent meetings have shown these features: significant religious influence in leadership, proceedings, and ideological justification; lack of participation by younger adults; greater representation of persons from the surrounding community than from Kent proper; the tendency of leaders to denounce the indifference and lack of aggressiveness of Negroes: "I tell you, it's hard to help a Negro"; "Some folks act just like some Negroes did after surrender. They're free but still don't want to leave the white folks."

At a caucus of voters just prior to an election of local significance, the 20 people attending were advised to "support the candidate that will do most for the group, not the one who will do most for the individual. Old Captain Tom might have been very nice to you and your mother who cooks for him—but ask yourself, is he best for the race?" With the understanding that there was no coercion and that voting was a matter between a person and his conscience, an informal agreement was reached to support two candidates. One was a woman related to "Huck" Berry, a leading political figure in the state whose prestige was at stake. Arguments advanced for her were: "She's a woman and our women can go up to her and talk with her"; "She can get up and say things for you that a man can't"; "She's a woman and a foreigner and she ain't got some of the same ideas that these people here have." The other candidate was a young veteran who had commanded Negro troops during the war and was reported to have treated his men just a little better than the average white officer; in addition, he had charge of the armory and through him Negroes could get access to it for benefit programs.

Both candidates lost, the woman by a small margin. There was a feeling in some quarters the next day that her loss was due to Negroes switching votes. Whether the allegation is true or not, it is clear that many of the Negroes voted in terms of personal preferences and personal identification rather than in terms of rational considerations of what was best for the group. The situation also revealed the speedy operation of the informal "pipelines" between the two communities: by the day after the elections, Negroes had told whites, and whites had told Negroes, their respective versions and interpretations of what had happened, and a number of recriminations had appeared. Negroes, in fact, had been caught up in a skirmish of a larger political battle the main stakes of which they were not aware—could not, in fact, have been aware—and they were in danger of being made scapegoats.

One good measure of local political strength and participation is whether one lives on a paved street or not. The Negroes, with the exception of those who live on arterial streets leading to white communities, uniformly live on unpaved streets. The vast majority of whites live on paved streets. In a recent election one of the candidates appealed to a group of whites by reminding them of his services in getting a road paved; "Remember who got our road paved" became an effective byword of his supporters. Negroes anticipated some such rewards after their recent participation. Streets were improved by the addition of tons of rock and grading but they have not been hard-surfaced nor have pavements been provided. No candidate has made direct appeals to the Negro voter; communication here as elsewhere is informal, indirect, unpatterned, and dominated by personal relations. Despite this, candidates have been charged with soliciting the Negro vote by white opponents. One white said, "I didn't vote for "Huck" Berry, and I'll tell you why. It was because he canvassed every nigger house in Kent County, and he got all of their votes too."

White officials estimate that a total of 1,500 Negroes in Kent County voted in the last primary; there are approximately 20,000 Negroes in the county. Roughly the same proportion of Negroes to Negro population voted in Kent as voted in the county. The revival of Negro voting in Kent is a part of the general trend now apparent in the state and the South.

The only Negroes in Kent on the public payroll are the five who work on the town's garbage and maintenance trucks and the janitor at the county courthouse. One official commented with respect to the maintenance crew of two whites and five Negroes, "We pay them (the whites) more than we do the niggers, but they are no more intelligent; and their jobs don't require more sense."

"The Law"

As already indicated, the Negro knows and experiences local government and law as symbols and reality of white dominance and control. On the local level these facts are important: the police watch carefully and constantly almost every phase of public behavior of the Negro; few Negroes or families of Negroes have escaped some incident involving "the law," and for a number of persons involvement in relatively minor difficulties is a recurrent and expected thing; Negroes expect discriminatory treatment by the police and the courts, even if it is no more than the matter of lack of respect for the dignity of their persons; there is pervasive interest in the doings of the law, i.e., the police and the courts; and the design for respectability has as one of its components an exaggerated avoidance of the law and its agents.

The taverns and idling places where many Negroes spend much of their leisure, and which are places of recreation or relaxation for many, are patrolled regularly by the police: the Negro gets to feel that a good deal of his "relaxing" behavior is under constant surveillance. The uneasy stiffening of behavior is noticeable when the word is given "Here come the boys" or sardonically, "Here come the head-whippers." Some Negroes have been heard to mutter resentfully:

I bet you they don't go round to the white folks' places like that. Them folks tell them when they wants them, they'll send for them.

A young veteran was commenting on the propensity for Negroes to get in trouble and he said:

Me and Jake is the only boys who came back from the army and ain't never been in no trouble and had to pay a fine or go to jail. I guess we's just lucky.

The high incidence of "trouble," plus the fact that family lines are so intertwined, means that practically every Negro (especially the males) or someone close to him has had some brush with the law. For the respectable families this is a source of some embarrassment; but these involvements—direct or indirect—can not be kept secret, and there is little effort to do so. For the nonrespectables—the public drunks and brawlers—involvement with the law is a normal and expected risk. The theme of this type is expressed crudely and defiantly:

Call the law! I don't give a good goddam. I got money; I can get out.

A man in his middle forties who is a regular weekend drunk explained why he does not own an automobile and, in doing so, indicated a philosophy of calculated risk:

I gets drunk and it don't cost me no more than ten dollars; but if they catches me driving a car while I's drunk, they'll fine me $100.00 and take my license away for six months. And if that happens it would hurt me on my job because I have to have a license to drive a truck. I can spare them ten dollars but I'd be ruined by the other. I likes to drink and I drinks a whole lot of whisky. I knows that if I gits drunk and wants to go somewhere, I'd git in a car and do it; and there I'd be. I might kill somebody; I might run into you. They says, "If you's drunk, don't drive; if you's driving don't drink." Last Saturday, I was going home drunk and the cop comes up alongside of me and he said, "Boy you might git killed before you git home." (I had a cousin who was killed by an auto while he was drunk.) "Don't you want me to take you in and have it just cost you ten dollars and not take the chance of getting hurt? You ain't so drunk; of course, I could take you home." I said, "White folks, do with me what you wants to do. Just don't hit me. . . ." These cats 'round here talking about the cops beating you and that they so much different up North and 'round. Man, they beats you everywhere; and much more than they does here sometimes. 'Course they gonna hit you if you

talks back to them. You wouldn't like nobody be impudent to
you, now would you? These cats don't know what they's talking
about. You better talk low when you's wrong and save yourself.
...I used to do a little bit of everything—make whisky, sell
whisky....

Lawlessness in this case involves something different from
mere lack of respect for the law; it involves the recognition of—and the resignation to—a hazard or risk that is accepted as part of a chosen way of life. Bitterness arises from
differential treatment, brutality, and the lack of respect for
the dignity of the individual.

Police classify Negroes in three categories: (1) those who
have given minor trouble; (2) those who have given considerable trouble or "bad niggers"; and (3) those who have
not given trouble or been in trouble. Generally speaking, the
police can be expected to treat persons in these categories
with some slight degree of difference; for instance, they'll say
a good word for the person who has not been in trouble, or
will "give him a break." Negroes recognize these differences,
also, and the possibility of differential treatment within limits.
However, all Negroes are concerned about the possibility of
arbitrary and capricious acts or of incurring disfavor for incidental reasons. And they expect no "breaks" when the other
person involved is white.[1] Negroes themselves tend to be
sardonically amused when some person who is relatively "respectable" and had thought himself immune from the usual
brusque treatment is given the normal treatment. A veteran
who has none of the traits of the trouble-makers commented
bitterly:

These police will bother anybody; it don't make no difference
who you is. I ain't never bothered nobody in this town; I don't

1. For example, in cases of automobile collisions where the white is
obviously at fault, instances are cited where the investigating officer said,
"Why don't each of you folks fix his own car?"

get drunk and I ain't never been to jail. One evening I was driving Steve's car and it had a bad tail light. The cops pulled up beside me and asked me whose car it was and who I was; and before I could explain and tell them I had just gotten out of the Army, he pulled his blackjack out and said, "Don't you tell me no goddam lie, nigger! Get out of that car." I told him I'd get out and go with them but just don't hit me up side the head. . . . They do just what they want to do when it comes to a colored man.

All police are well known and ranked in terms of their treatment of Negroes and the public in general. All Negroes tend to agree that Jim Banks, the current Chief of Police, is a decent and fair man and that they are fortunate in having "Mr. Jim" as a restraining influence.

With the police constituting such an ever-present aspect of Negro community life, it is understandable that there should be great interest in their actions. They are an important conversational theme. Police Court is the clearing house for the weekly quota of arrests, the bulk of which are for public drunkenness. Most persons are arrested on the weekend and most of the arrested are Negroes. The city jail is familiar to many people and there are those who will willingly admit that they have been there but will add emphatically that they have never been to the "big jail" (county jail) or chain gang. The capacity of the city jail is supposed to be four—two whites and two Negroes. An official points out, however, that "on some Saturdays I've seen as many as a dozen in each cell." He said further, "Most of our lock-ups are drunks, and of course most of them are niggers. But some Saturdays we get almost as many white people as niggers."

Police Court is usually held late Monday afternoons in a small auditorium and is presided over by "Dink" Berry, the mayor of the town. The following describes a session of Police Court:

The mayor is presiding; four officers are present to testify; one serves as clerk of court. The chief of police is also present. In a courtroom that is not rigidly segregated there are eleven Negro men and one woman, and six white men—some are spectators. The mayor disposed in rapid-fire fashion of twenty-two drunk or disorderly cases; most of the defendants were not present and they were invariably fined the amount of bond that had been posted. Good humor marked the comments of the mayor and arresting officers. Fines were reduced or suspended in the cases of two defendants who testified that the charge was their first offense. When the mayor asked one: "Is this your first offense—and your last?" the room rocked with laughter. When the defendant said that he would try to keep out of drinking trouble, the Chief interjected: "Yeh, he'll try, but he'll be back." One defendant had his fine reduced when the Chief gave the name of the white man under whom he worked and said that the defendant had given the police no trouble.

Another Negro was charged with drunkenness and the use of profanity. The arresting officer testified that he had driven by Zeke's Saturday night and observed the defendant standing by a tree with a beer bottle in his hand; "relieving himself." The officer flashed the light and the defendant cursed, "Goddamit, turn that light out." The officer made it clear that the defendant did not know that he was an officer. When the defendant recognized the officer, he ran—and, as the officer put it, he ran out of his shoe before he was caught. The officer testified laughingly that (1) the defendant did not know that he was an officer and (2) the defendant was not very drunk; the fact that he ran so fast he lost a shoe would indicate that. The man's fine was reduced amid much laughter.

A local white bondsman and money lender held whispered conferences with the clerk and two youths; the youths pleaded guilty with the understanding that the fine was to be sixteen dollars. The money lender paid the fines. One of the youths had been fretting earlier about cotton that he wanted to get out of the field before it rained.

The most serious case called was that of a Negro man charged

with "drunk driving." The Chief and the arresting officer remembered that the same person had been caught for the same
offense exactly a year previously. The officer testified that he had
been at a road intersection watching the cars returning from the
colored fair when the defendant's car appeared, weaving from
side to side. The defendant had no permit. The case was remanded
to the higher court.

Interest in the quarterly "high court" sessions is general although selective factors tend to operate in the attendance.
There is interest in the disposition of the cases of persons who
are relatives or are members of the Negro community; there
is avid interest in murder trials; and the performances of the
judges and the lawyers are followed closely. Among those
who attend court sessions, a general comment is that "You
can learn a lot by listening to court." By this is meant that
one can learn a lot about the intricacies of the law and human
nature, and, incidentally, about the seamy ways of whites.
"Respectable," "sensitive," and "sensible" Negroes do not attend as a rule. This is due to these factors: customary avoidance of all contact with the law and its agents and instruments,
along with resentment and embarrassment at the court agents'
free use of "nigger," "darky," "Nigra." Psychologically, there
is also a kind of group guilt feeling, or shame, that results
from the inevitable identification with law-breaking members
of one's own group: law-breaking Negroes harm the race.

Proportionately, more Negroes are tried than whites and
relatively more Negroes attend sessions than whites; over
one week's session, the ratio of Negro women to Negro men
in attendance ranged between 1:3 and 1:4. The bulk of the
Negroes in attendance were in work clothes—a source of
embarrassment to some Negroes:

Those Negroes go there looking so bad. It seems as if the least
they could do would be to decent themselves up. They ain't got
nothing else to do; if they was working, they wouldn't be there.

The courtroom has a seating capacity of three hundred; Negroes are normally allotted the entire left side of the auditorium—or half the seating capacity. Court proceedings are followed with great interest (the writer has heard one person recapitulate an entire trial for the benefit of a barbershop audience, with verbatim quotations from all participants); some persons are wont to identify and characterize court officers or pass comments on proceedings in undertones; others sit silently with passive faces. Some of the pattern of the proceedings is indicated in the following descriptive excerpts:

The judge had been accepting guilty pleas; his attitude toward Negro defendants was humorously benign—but strict. One Negro defendant had an odd name; the judge asked him where he was from, saying that he must be from the lower part of the state because he didn't know any Lomaxes in this part of the country. A white mother from New York appeared on behalf of her two teen-age sons. The judge said, "The people up North are always condemning the South; now what do you think a judge in New York would do if he had two South Carolina boys before him?" He inquired about the woman's political affiliations and, after showing leniency in the case of her sons, told her to go back North and tell how she had been treated. Later when trying two Negroes for bootlegging, he said, "I wish that woman from New York was here so she could see how we help our colored folks down here. See all these men up here are trying to help these boys; they know they aren't anything but country boys." In passing sentence on another Negro man, he explained that he had had a white man before him on the same charge and had given him the same thing that he was going to give the Negro.[2]

2. The judge's remarks are symptomatic of guilt feelings and a recurrent disposition among whites to justify and rationalize local and regional practices. The pattern which the judge—as the representative of authority—follows here is analogous to that of a father with a son who is considered to be different or subnormal and toward whom he has marked ambivalence. His conception of father's responsibility for discipline on the one hand and of the ward-like character of the son on the other are alternate bases of judgment and action. When the control or dominance of the rest of the family is threatened, discipline for the son who is different is harsh and

The first case after a holiday recess involved two young white
sailors charged with assault with intent to ravish, and assault of
a high and aggravated nature. All white principals were involved,
and Negroes in the courtroom followed the testimony intently.
Some would mumble approval of telling points made by the prosecution or defense depending upon whether they felt the "virtuous
housewife" had been wronged, as the prosecution tried to show,
or whether the "woman of loose morals" had led the boys on,
as the defense tried to show. The judge threatened to clear the
Negro side of the courtroom unless the whispering and giggling
ceased. During recess, the dominant theme of the conversation
among Negroes was what would have happened if the boys had
been colored. There was sympathy but there was also bitter satisfaction over the airing of white misery and seaminess. The trial
lasted the entire court day and a large number of Negroes stayed
until 6:30 p.m. to hear the jury's verdict: not guilty on the more
serious charge; guilty of the lesser charge. Before sentence was
passed, the defendants' attorney sought to point out extenuating
circumstances and asked for a light sentence. The judge replied
that the boys were lucky and that he had known many a man to
go to the electric chair in this state for less than they had done.
He cited a case where a man had entered a room where a woman
was and closed the door; the man was charged with a capital
offense. The attorney, "Rocky" Rhodes, interjected quickly:
"But he was a nigger!" The judge replied that it made no difference; he was convicted on the evidence and under the same law.
The judge went on to state that he hated to think what would
have happened if the defendants had been colored. The Negroes
listened in intense silence; later these words were to be repeated
(and garbled) in the Negro community with bitter satisfaction.

At the trial of two murder cases involving Negro principals
from Kent County, seats on the Negro side were at a premium.
The defense attorney was "Rocky" Rhodes in both cases; he was

strict; when no direct threat is involved, discipline is tempered with tolerance—and even humor—and a specious understanding of the deviate. In
neither case is the son looked upon as mature or normal; and so it is with
the Negro.

free in the use of "nigger." The court engaged in a certain amount
of levity, revolving around the names of the principals and "Negro
morality." Many Negroes would snicker at these references. Both
cases were particularly brutal. In one, a man used a hammer to
crush the skull of another; in the other, a young man had used a
shotgun to blow off the top of his wife's head. The first case was
presented to the jury and was fought, in part, over the question
whether the killer's wife had been out with the deceased, thereby
providing provocation. The argument of the defense combined
in a peculiar fashion disparaging and patronizing references to
"niggers" and "Negro morality" with references to what a human
being, "be he white or black, or of any clime or continent," would
do. The prosecution stressed the brutal character of the act and
the duty of the jury to protect society and deter criminals. Despite a certain superciliousness and discriminatory language and
manner, in questions of law or legal machinery the rules were
followed or announced scrupulously. The defendant was adjudged
guilty and received thirty years.

The second defendant pleaded guilty to a lesser charge of manslaughter and the judge sentenced him to 21 years. Before passing
sentence, the judge listened to testimony of attorneys, officers,
and witnesses. The evidence indicated that the man had shot his
wife after a period of bickering that had climaxed a day that had
been marked by going to church, visiting relatives, and the drinking of home brew. The last words of the wife were: "Pull it,
goddammit! Goddammit, pull it!" Her husband shot her from a
range of five feet and then cried, "My poor Ruth!" The judge
remarked that the pictures of the corpse introduced in evidence
were the worst he had ever seen. He sought by questioning to
verify his assumption that sex immorality or jealousy were involved. The officers testified that there was no evidence to that
effect. The introduction of a woman's name, Jezebel, brought
amusement. The defense attorney made constant reference to the
"white folks" for whom the man worked and who vouched for
him. He explained that he hadn't subpoenaed them because it was
useless to subpoena a white man who was busy ginning wet cotton. The evidence indicated that the man's wife was contentious

and uncooperative. The judge asked the defendant where he had found her, mentioning an adjoining state. The defendant replied hopefully that that was where she had come from and emphasized that he was a local boy.

For the Negro spectators the operations of the courts seem to foster a kind of grim ambivalence; there are overtones of both sadism and masochism in the apparent satisfactions that are gained.

AGGRESSION AND COUNTER-AGGRESSION

THE infrequency with which in recent years extra-legal violence and terror have been applied to Negroes [3] is one of the features that recommends the town to the more loyal Negroes. A lynching has not occurred in the town over the last half-century. Older people remember lynchings here and a lynching in a nearby town, but they are quick to add that times have changed: "We don't have none of that now; things is different. The onliest places that is uncivilized now is Georgia and Mississippi." Although dramatic violence as a sanction is infrequently used, the threat of violence and the possibility of terror are ever present and are, in effect, controls. More frequent than expressed fear of mob or individual violence for violation of laws or taboos is the matter-of-fact recognition of the certainty of swift and extreme legal punishment. "They'll put you in the electric chair for that" is heard more frequently than "They'll lynch you" or "They'll string you up."

There is some feeling that "times are not like they used to be," both in terms of individual whites using violence on Negroes, and in terms of Negroes' disposition to take such treatment without retaliation. A young Navy veteran said resolutely:

3. This excludes the slapping and "head whipping" that are frequently a part of police procedure.

I ain't gonna do nothing to them as long as they don't bother me; but if they corners me, I'm going to try to mess them up. I means that.

An older man frowned upon Negroes fraternizing with whites:

If you plays with them, pretty soon they's gonna be wanting to kick your ass. That time done went out. Now, if you kicks ass, you've got to bring ass. Used to be they could do that and wouldn't nothing happen. We kicks each other's asses now.

There are certain rules or principles that the average Negro knows and follows, and realistically accepts: "the law is the law; don't buck it; you can't win"; use the formal respect titles when dealing with whites; avoid controversies with whites, if possible. It is probably true that the great bulk of the Negro's aggression is repressed or diverted into other channels—against his own group, for example, but there is a twilight zone of touchiness wherein "out of bounds" behavior by whites tends to elicit overt and direct aggression on the part of some Negroes. The average Negro will pick his spots; he will "give the white man (or selected white persons) hell" when he gets the opportunity. "Hell" is highly variable; it may be a short, curt answer or the refusal to answer; the refusal to cooperate; some type of major or minor sabotage; and even overt challenge on occasions. The following are some examples of overt challenge:

A young white businessman jovially referred to a Negro who was in a group of Negroes: "What is this nigger here doing? Is he any good?" The Negro immediately went over to the white man and shaking his finger told him that he didn't play that kind of business, that he was a man and didn't have to take it from anybody; he wanted to tell him emphatically that he didn't like it. The white man apologized but failed to fully satisfy the Negro man and the Negro bystanders who muttered long after he left.

A Negro man tells the story of one Mack who loaned money to Negroes; when the Negroes would not pay on time, Mack would take a stick that he carried and beat the Negroes. The man relating the incident said that he owed Mack fifteen dollars right now, but that Mack had never beaten him. He said that Mack called him and waved a stick at him, telling him that he was going to beat him. The Negro drew a pistol from his shirt and told him to come on, that nothing stood between them except the pistol. Mack didn't bother him.

A Negro was discussing the brutality of police; "I hope God may kill me, I done made up my mind that if they ever puts a stick up side my head, I'm going to die right there; especially if there ain't but one.

Don't think every colored man is scared of white men; there's many a one who won't bother you but'll kill a white man. . . . I'm harder on them than on my own color because I thinks they wants to do something to me just because they's white."

Reports of mob violence against Negroes in other sections bring a sort of quiet, hard-bitten bitterness among the individuals who comment. In the case of the men, it is usually coupled with a statement indicating what they would do in a similar situation or what more Negroes should do, i.e., meet violence with violence. The theme is that, if the flogging or other molestation is inevitable, strike boldly (shoot) and take several along with you. This is seen as a deterrent to violence as well as vindication of person. It is likely that the universal possession of a shotgun, pistol or rifle has some meaning in terms of these sentiments and potentialities.

All told, these things seem to be true: the incidence of extra-legal force and violence against the Negro in Kent has diminished significantly in the past two generations, and currently there is less of a pattern and expectation of its use here than in certain other areas in the state and region; the Negro of Kent tends to have a greater awareness of the possibility

of legal sanctions unevenly applied than of extra-legal sanctions; some disposition of the Negro to meet aggression with
aggression has always been present but the probability is
greater now, although a considerable amount of aggression
remains masked; there is a considerable quota of violence-
tinged fatalism that operates when the individual is pushed
too far; the limits of tolerance, or "taking it," tend on the one
hand to be traditional or customary but on the other hand
there are significant individual differences.

The only major instance in the five years preceding this
study that was marked by the application of extra-legal sanctions to a Negro was the Jack Poe case. The factors and values
involved were many, but the events and the reactions in different segments of the community were consistent with the
setting. Because they adjudge the Negro victim as "not having
been smart" and of knowing better, the Negroes in the main
hold no brief for him. The violent act itself was not in keeping with the particular idea of justice that many whites have
in the community, and consequently there were some protests.

Jack Poe, familiarly called "Doc" by many Negroes, was
prominent in church and fraternal circles. He was a native of
Kent and he began to work in one of the local drugstores as a
youth. He became a trusted and efficient employee who had the
run of the store, waiting on customers, and it is said that he filled
prescriptions although he did not have a license. He kept the
keys to the drugstore. In emergency calls for medicine, one called
on "Doc" Poe. He was well liked by Negroes and whites.

He was suspected of being unduly familiar with a "foreign"
woman—a northern white woman whose husband worked at a
nearby establishment. Various stories are told of the extent of
the familiarity. Some persons allege that the woman was being
supplied narcotics by "Doc"; others tacitly admit that sex was
probably involved. "The whole story ain't never been told" is
the usual feeling.

The police trailed the woman's car one night and watched

"Doc" get in; they stopped the car, took "Doc" out despite his protestations, carried him near the state line and beat him severely. "Doc" has never returned to his home.

A white Presbyterian church group sent resolutions to the city government protesting the brutality and asking that justice be done. It is said that the police officer chiefly responsible for the beating was discharged. Negroes were shocked that this should have happened to one of their "best boys." There was condemnation of the white woman and disappointment that " 'Doc' wasn't smart and lost his head"; the beating was an event to be expected in the circumstances and was not necessarily viewed as an outrage.

A generalized estimate of "Doc": " 'Doc' was shocked because his white folks just loved him; and he loved them. He had gotten too big. He still loves Kent." There is a feeling that "Doc's" violation of one of the most elementary of mores in this situation did the Negro group considerable harm. Other Negroes will find it difficult to get the same breaks he got.

Control Within the Subculture

Among the social controls, other than the family, that operate within the Negro group itself are the churches, the fraternal groups, the leveling tendency, and gossip.

The control powers of the churches tend to be nominal; there is no question that they are considerably weaker than in former times. Rarely is the weapon of dropping a person from church rolls used, and when used it is likely to be the climax of an issue that is more political than moral. Even when used, it is not a serious hardship, because the person can easily join another church. There have been instances in the past of pastors being forced to resign, churches splitting, and members being dropped but nothing like this has happened in the recent past. The "churching" of delinquent girls in the Baptist church is a perfunctory gesture. "Love feasts" and the "examinations" of members tend to be perfunctory also. Pastors willingly admit that, if the written or traditional church rules were to be applied, their churches would break up, and among the persons who would be hit hardest by strict application of the code would be some of the officers and hardest workers in the church. There isn't a single pastor in the community who is strong enough to apply sanctions or to speak in more than general terms about the personal conduct of members.

The sanctions applied by fraternal groups such as the Elks or the Masons are apparently more feared than those of the church. These groups hold "trials" of members and impose fines and punishments. Among men, the fraternal creed and code are spoken of with a degree of pride and awe that the often taken-for-granted or ignored church can not boast of. The possible effectiveness of the fraternal groups is dissipated by loose organization, bickering, and infrequent meetings. One person characterized the gap between code and behavior that marks both church and fraternal groups by saying, "The rules is in the book, that's the onliest place they is; they sure ain't in their heads."

Those who show signs of group status deviation—i.e., acting as if they are better than someone else, or displaying too conspicuously education or prosperity are subject to a kind of group pressure marked by resentment and criticism. Great emphasis is placed upon friendliness and the courteous gesture as ideal patterns; this combines with a great sensitivity to the slight. Leveling is achieved by two sets of sanctions (they may or may not reinforce each other): both the Negro and the white community react negatively to ostentatious behavior, conspicuous consumption, or the social slight when the subject is a Negro; but the social psychological reasons operative in each type of group behavior are probably different. In the case of the Negro, it appears that a status-hungry or status-deprived group is oversensitive to the deference behavior of its own members: resentment and envy are accentuated by intimacy and the low availability of status positions. Enforced and defensive group consciousness makes exaggerated demands of loyalty and identification upon the individual. Examples of these pressures are seen in the following expressions:

These Negroes in Kent are damn funny. They seem to resent success or any Negro getting ahead too fast.

He's a nice fellow; there ain't nothing dicty about him. He can get out with the people and he know how to treat them. He don't have certain ones that he just bothers with.

Now education is all right—and I know I ain't got but a little bit—but it seems to me that sometimes our people who are in a position to help us, do us the most harm. They harder on you than somebody way out there.

He ain't in my race. I don't consider him as being a colored man. He ain't never done nothing for the colored man. All he does is hang around the white folks—kissing their ass and telling them things. . . . I tell you somebody else I don't like: The Negro who always come back and talk about what the white folks is doing, like that is the authority for everything. The Negro ain't got enough pride.

It is difficult to estimate the social-control functions of gossip because it serves so many other functions as well. Gossip is rife and one gets the impression that by far the greatest part of it has to do with sex, whisky, and the course of marital and extra-marital relationships. The pervasiveness of sex-tinged gossip ties in with other aspects of the culture: the basic interest in sex; the desire to "get something on somebody" which is an aspect of the leveling tendency; the vulnerability of practically every family group; susceptibility to rumor and a basic streak of suspiciousness; random talk as a means of dissipating loneliness, establishing rapport with fellows, and maintaining status. Gossip is rarely vicious in tone; those who have the most to fear from it are persons or groups with relatively high status or status-pretensions. Gossiping is expected behavior and to be gossiped about is also expected; few persons eschew the activity or escape some of its impact. A resident of the community for more than twenty years said that during this time there were but two women in the community about whom he had never heard something snide or derogatory. Since status reputation is not a prime concern of the nonrespectable category, the behavior of persons in this category is not affected by gossip as is that of the members of the category for which reputation and respectability are important. There is no question that gossip, or the possibility of gossip, gives a few persons pause and makes them more careful of their behavior.

Orientations and Values

CHAPTER 9   IN OBSERVING and living in the Negro culture of Kent, one notes characteristic group "leanings" and emphases. Organized customs tend to be "pointed"—consciously or unconsciously—in a desirable direction or directions. The desired ends of behavior and the activities and qualities that seem to occupy people most are elements that help to characterize a culture in social psychological terms.

This is no attempt to idealize, or to oversimplify, complex and ever-changing behavior; nor is this a search for a "folk soul" or "folk spirit." Our interest is in the demonstrable value-emphases of this subculture. The clues taken from the examination of customs and institutions indicate that there is no single orientation or value which will adequately explain everything, nor is there necessarily any logical consistency among the many that are to be found.

The significant things that concern and occupy people most in the Kent Negro subculture involve considerations of race; religion; self-expression and release as measured in whisky, sex, and leisure-time activity; touchiness of the ego as measured in querulousness and ingroup aggression and violence; and a desire for appreciation of the person and for respect. Many of these emphases are functionally linked, and they conceivably are colored significantly by the same situational factors, the most important of which is, of course, the color line.

The Race-Ridden Character of Life

In general, life for the Negro in Kent tends to be race-ridden: considerations of ethnic role and status pervade every aspect of the life-death cycle and color a great deal of the minutiae of everyday life; much of life consists of adjusting to, rationalizing, making consistent, or combatting the force and implications of ethnic role and status. Group consciousness, and a not-always-too-comfortable identification with one's own, derive from the facts of minority status. Invidious inter-group comparisons are frequent, and there are elements of defensiveness, pride, defiance, individuation, and sharp criticism, condemnation, and rejection of one's own.

An implicit and explicit dominating theme is "white folks is white folks." [1] It can be said in different ways, in different contexts, or in tones ranging from awe and respect through sardonic humor to disgust and bitterness. As indicated earlier, it bespeaks a feeling that there is a gulf or wall between the groups; that there are certain things that are categorically true of the white group: in a crucial situation, loyalty to one's own will over-ride considerations of fair play, sentiment, and personal relationships. It means that a white man can never be thoroughly trusted or incorporated into the intimate on-going life of the Negro community. It means that there tends to be an item of reservation in any relationship, no matter how cordial or benevolent.

A corollary of the above is the map that every Negro carries around in his head of "how far to go with white folks." It is marked by a sensitivity that every Negro has in his re-

1. This does not mean the qualitative differences are not recognized among Negroes; for instance, there is a general disposition to "look down upon" the poor white mill villagers as a different breed of whites who do not get—and often cannot demand—the same deference and respect accorded upper class "town whites." The taken-for-granted "low-class" behavior of "Mill Hill" folks is a matter of amusement and gives some sense of superiority. Still there is recognition of the stubborn fact that they too are white.

lations with whites, along with a set of reservations and restrictions on free expression and behavior with whites. "I ain't going to do that"; "I know better than to go too far," typify expressions of restraint. The line separating that which is permitted and that which is "too far" is not a straight and consistent line, nor is it absolute, as it is broken on occasions and by special persons. Part of this sensitivity flows from a knowledge of the stereotypes that whites have about Negroes. In this way, the stereotype serves a social-control function. A case in point is cited by a colleague:

We had told the Negro grocery delivery boy to pick up and take back to the store any empty Coca-Cola bottles that might be in the kitchen when he delivered groceries. He never took them however. The owner of the grocery store said that he does not like to take anything from a kitchen, even though he has been told to do so, for fear he will be accused of stealing. This Negro man enters the kitchens of white people whether or not they are at home and delivers groceries. Due to the prevalence of the belief that "all Negroes steal," he probably has to avoid anything that would give the slightest grounds for suspicion. His job no doubt hangs on his avoidance of any such suspicions.

In another category was the wry but facetious comment of a young man who works in the business section:

Man, the cops is after me because I don't get drunk. They think that because I don't get drunk like these other cats that I'm a smart nigger. They talk around sometime and try to trick me into a smart answer; but I'm too wise for them.

Another illustration of the mental restraints on normal behavior that race imposes is the case of an elderly man who told of losing a wallet. In retracing his steps immediately he met a white woman and saw what appeared to be his wallet in her hand; he asked her if she had found a wallet; after some hesitation she said she had not. The man said that he started to go back and approach the woman but "something told me not to, for you see, that woman was a white woman, and I figured I would get in some kind of trouble that would cost me more than was in the wallet. . . . But I am as sure as anything that she found it."

A Negro man reports that in his early manhood he made enough from a cotton crop and odd jobs to purchase a particular brand of car that he wanted; he asked his father about it. His father consulted with a white friend to see "if it would be all right." The white friend advised: "Moe, go on and get the car; if anybody says anything to you, come and see me." This incident illustrates also the white patron-intermediary-friend pattern that is almost a necessary adjunct to successful adjustment on the local scene.

The role of the race factor in establishing status is shown in the following; there are also indications of ingroup criticism:

I know practically everybody in town—white and colored—and they all know me. When I walk down the street, they all call me by name, and I don't mean no nickname. I can get favors out of any of them—and I don't "Charlie" to them either. These white people are generally decent; they treat you much more decent than some of those whites up North. . . . Some Negroes don't know that you don't have to "Charlie" white folks; they really don't like it, and they respect you when you talk straight to them. They know them; white folks can tell you every respected Negro in this town. I kept my uniform on ninety days after I returned. One old peckerwood down there in front of the ten cent store told the Chief that I was impersonating. The Chief told him, "You're a damn liar. Don't start that stuff. I've known that boy all his life. He ain't never got in trouble; what he's got, that's what he is."

Condemnation of one's own and rationalization of the implications of ethnic status are indicated in the following comments which are not necessarily typical in content but tend to be in tone. A middle-aged Negro businessman said:

Negro been petted in the North. They brought on themselves a lot of trouble and discrimination. That Chicago riot was their fault, or at least a good part of it. They don't keep and know their place. I like to know my place.

A middle-aged Negro mill worker:

I thinks the Negroes knows they's free but they's got so much cowardism in them, they don't act like it. . . . These white folks is funny; if you acts like a man, you can talk up to them like a man. They appreciates it and don't do nothing about it. I believes a man's a man.

An elderly Negro widow of the "old school":

Hoover had the nigger down to fifty cents a day. I reckon if he had kept on he'd had 'em all in county home. Roosevelt straightened all that out. . . . This man Truman's trying to carry all that out that Roosevelt started. I'd like to see him continue but I fear he gonna lose out. But he didn't have to do all he did. . . . We's got so many bad niggers don't need no rights. If they could just give the rights to the good niggers would be all right. Leastwise till you could bring the bad niggers up. I tell you, we's got a heap of bad niggers; they'd get in there and ruin everything. . . . Whites don't want to change. . . . Niggers ain't had enough experience. Niggers ain't got equipment and stuff; they can't run the courthouse. Whites feared they'd git up with them and be looking at their women. . . . Better not do that; you gits kilt.

More nearly typical of the younger group is this Navy veteran's statement on civil rights:

They don't know what they're talking about. All I want for them to do is just give me room on the streets—and don't try to brush me out of the way. I don't want to socialize with them.

As indicated, invidious ethnic comparisons are frequent; all indicate group consciousness although all are not self-critical.

The disposition to compare Negro and white ways is a constant one. Comments may be streaked with bitterness, disgust, or shame; or they may show a tolerant sardonic humor. Some miscellaneous examples: "That's a spook [Negro] for you!" "Negroes don't stick together." "You can never trust a Negro with your business; he'll put it in the street every time." "Negroes haven't learned to respect their own women." "Anything happens the first thing the Negro will do is run to the white man." "My Negro (or nigger) came out." However, all comparisons are not unfavorable, and there is a legitimate question as to whether these verbalizations are indications of true feelings: some of them have a catchword quality and others are family-like outbursts indicating annoyance and frustration as much as anger and hatred.

Actually, in many generalizations and categorical statements there is significant pride and a feeling that Negro ways are superior. Here are four generalizations expressing criticism or disdain of the ways of whites; these were all made at the same poolroom "bull-session" devoted to comparisons and reminiscences.

When a Negro can really do something, he can do it better than a white man.

The white man knows when you're right; he sees but acts like he don't.

A white man will recognize a smart Negro but he won't tell the Negro; he'll tell some other white man.

A white man never says he let a Negro go, or fired him; he'll always say "I had to run that nigger off the place."

One of the most constant generalizations critical of whites is that the Negro in many ways is morally superior to the white; it is usually stated in the form, "The Negro ain't as 'dirty' as the white man." For example, a trusted Negro em-

ployee of a fairly large business just outside of Kent explained
why his boss preferred Negro employees:

White man'll take it all. A Negro'll take a little bit for himself
and leave you a little bit. A Negro ain't like a peckerwood.

These feelings are often linked up with a comparison of opportunities; for example, the feeling that whites are "dirtier"
in terms of sex morals, taking advantage of the weaker, large-
scale larceny, and lack of loyalty to country, is sometimes
related to the notion that whites have more opportunity to
commit such acts.

Ain't white folks dirty? A Negro ain't as dirty as a white man.
... One thing, they don't give the Negro the opportunity to get
up in them big places and positions.

A veteran commented on one of the federal spy trials:

Ain't it a damn shame that white woman doing like that—be-
traying her country. There ain't never been a Negro was a traitor
to his country. And yet a foreigner can come here and be anything he want and a poor Negro can't get nothing.

These expressions indicate, among other things, the Negro's
observation of the white from his vantage point as servant, his
one-sided relationships with whites, and an acute interest in
newspaper accounts of tragedies and crises, successes and fail-
ures. They are a part of an attitude of detachment—a process
of dissociation—that comes from observing rather than participating and feeling fully a part of the local and larger
world. "The white folks are doing" or "the white folks have
done" become almost standard ways of introducing accounts
of happenings that are remote because of a lack of participation and identification. To say this is not to deny that there
are some employee-employer relationships where the Negro
for a variety of reasons may speak of "we" or "our place";
but the few such Negroes are likely to be laughed at or looked

down upon. Locally, there is one Negro of mixed background who is a sort of man-of-all-duties for "Rocky" Rhodes, a prominent white; the Negro is looked upon for this and other reasons as something of a renegade—a traitor to his group; this Negro speaks of "me and 'Rocky' " doing many things— to the amusement and disgust of other Negroes. An older woman refers to them as "two bad niggers together."

Reports from Negro servants and workers as to the sex and drinking behavior of whites are common. They are usually told with an air of amused superiority, with emphasis upon the low-down or dirty aspects of the behavior. There is one young woman who has a minor obsession about Caldwell's *Tobacco Road*. She reports having read it several times and seeing the picture six times. When asked if the reason were the off-color language she replied:

No, I just likes to have those white folks see how bad some white folks lives. I used to have me a job and I would carry the book to work and talk about it every chance I would get. Once the lady sent me up the street and she said, "Mary, leave *Tobacco Road* here; you'll stop on every street corner and sit down and read it." I just likes that book.

The race orientation as seen in the race-ridden character of all phases of life is probably the closest approach to a universal emphasis; race is something that colors a considerable portion of the behavior of everyone. It is at once a factor making for group consciousness and a factor making for ingroup tensions and divisiveness.

The value correlate of this pervasive orientation is related to survival and getting along—adaptability—in a society where "white folks is white folks" and "colored folks is colored folks." This is the closest approach to an over-all unifying value; it reflects a kind of folk realism and opportunism. This doesn't mean that there is absolute resignation to *status quo*, because there are other values that operate also. For instance,

the democratic value involving opportunity and equality before the law has some force; there is also considerable belief
in all areas that things will get better—a belief spurred by
recent happenings on the national and world scene. Patience
comes to be an important subsidiary value.

The Salvation Myth

The earlier treatment of religion and the church gave an estimate of the strength of the religious orientation. Like race, it
colors a significant part of behavior and thinking, albeit verbal
and ritualistic. Religion in this society is a sort of talisman, a
magical guarantee giving assurance about salvation. Salvation
is the meaningful goal; religious behavior to some extent gives
reassurance and a sense of security. The projected goal of
salvation ties in with the immediate value of survival and
getting along. Salvation is one of the chief myths of this society: "Sometimes you get gypped here—but Jesus will make
it up to you"; "Everything is going to be all right." A local
minister sketched the recurrent theme in this fashion:

Man's earthly treasure is liable to be destroyed at any time;
worldly riches have in themselves a principle of corruption and
decay. They will wither away themselves. Jesus points out to us
the different forces that will destroy the earthly treasures. There
are some whose treasure is fine clothes, but it is not to put your
highest joy in them. For they breed moths and moths will eat
holes in your clothes. . . . There are others who cherish their food,
but it is not wise to put your trust solely in food for the mice will
eat your wheat, and you will be left hungry. And there are others
whose treasure is their bank account; don't treasure that too
highly. Because gold and silver canker and will become less even
if we don't use them. . . . During World War I, the people of this
country laid up treasures upon the earth for themselves. Most
everybody had a large bank account and they glorified it. But it
was not long before the moths and rust corrupted it; and thieves
broke through and stole all they had.

But lay up for yourselves treasures in Heaven, there where moths cannot eat it, the rust cannot canker it, and thieves cannot break through the Pearly gates and steal them. If you want treasures in Heaven, you must send something up there. Send up good counseling, good will for all mankind, and send up prayer. Send up truth and righteousness and not anything will be lost or forgotten. In Heaven there is a book of remembrance and we will be paid according to the book. Down here in this world, unfortunately some of us cannot read books, but that book that is called the Book of Life—every child of God can read it for himself. Yes, lay not up for yourselves treasures upon earth. . . .

SELF-INDULGENCE AND SELF-EXPRESSION

WHISKY drinking is a central pattern among men of all strata, and concern over male drinking is a common anxiety among wives and mothers. It is an admitted type of self-indulgence, and, as such, it ties in with a general design for self-indulgence and release that would include much of the nonmarital sex activity, much of the idling, and much of the tavern behavior of the nonrespectable. Whisky is also an essential ingredient in a pattern of behavior that is marked by individual touchiness and ingroup aggression. The people tend to think of themselves as drinkers of large quantities of whisky. That much of the drinking is sectional or situational—and not unique to the Negro community—is shown by the fact that comments and behavior in both the white and Negro communities parallel each other. Here are two statements typifying the local person's assessment of the community; the first is from the Negro community and the second from the white community:

There's more whisky drunk here than any other little town in the country.

You'll find more old drunks in Kent than any town of its size around here. . . . Kent is a town of drunks and old maids.

It is theoretically possible that the behavior here might be the same in both communities but that the basic motivations might differ. The chances are, however, that drinking is a pattern available to all that has become widely diffused here; any different meaning that it may have in the Negro community would come from the fact that it fits into a slightly different social and value situation.

Although no systematic probing of the motives behind whisky drinking has been undertaken here, some of the factors involved can be inferred from observation and comments. There is a basic distinction between respectable and non-respectable drinking. The respectables—those who are concerned about reputation and status—choose their drinking companions and tend to confine drinking to homes; the non-respectables drink publicly with anyone, are likely to have an arrest record for drunkenness, and are prone to "make fools of themselves." Among the types of drinkers are these:

(1) the ritualistic drinker: this is the drinker who has the habit of drinking at regularly spaced intervals or on special occasions. The time and the procedure can be pretty well predicted: he may be the week-end drinker who begins Friday or Saturday evening and spends the greater portion of the period until Monday drinking or "booted." He expects to do it and is expected to do it.

The philosophy of the extremists in this group is well stated in the remark of a young married man: "I'll tell anybody; I works hard all the week and I drinks my liquor and gets booted on Friday and Saturday." A variant is the person who has a habit of taking a drink in the morning "to get started" and/or a drink before bed.

(2) The constant drinker: these are usually persons who have a large amount of leisure time or who do not work regularly. Drinking for them fills a void of idleness and tends to create more idleness. They drink regularly and at all times and are always ready to drink or seeking a drink.

(3) the spasmodic drinker: there are three types: (a) the confirmed drinker who has been ill or who has sought to stop but who breaks out once in a while in a rash of drinking; (b) the person who is known to or who admits to getting drunk once in a while for the purge-like effect; and (c) the infrequent drinker who lacks compulsive features but who likes to "take a little drink once in a while."

As already mentioned, there is a dividing line that runs through all these types distinguishing the public drinker from the home drinker. The etiquette of drinking is roughly this: the bottle is usually shared among persons who are close acquaintances and have some kind of informal reciprocity pattern, or persons who have contributed to the price of the whisky. Under conditions other than these, the offer of a drink is a gesture of hospitality or good will and a sign of acceptance. When drinking among casual acquaintances, rather than thoroughly trusted intimates, the person who owns or offers the whisky must always take the first drink to allay suspicion. The great bulk of drinking is group drinking, i.e., two or more persons. "Let's get one!" or "I don't enjoy drinking by myself" are recurrent statements. An older man who has stopped drinking because of the doctor's orders said:

I tell you I used to drink. I used to be one of the biggest drinkers in this here town. And when I used to drink, I had plenty of friends. I ain't got no friends now since I stopped drinking.

In a similar vein, a younger man said:

A man has almost got to drink. If a man don't drink, he ain't got no friends.

Except for the few emancipated, the respectable woman doesn't drink or at least doesn't admit it except to intimates.

Drinking, as indicated, is in some respects a social or group phenomenon; it is an available accepted pattern of sociability and sharing. The rhythm of economic life, with its stretches of leisure and uncertainty, provides opportunity and reinforcement. Questioning of drinkers indicates that, for most of them, custom, curiosity, and social pressure were factors in the initiation into drinking. It becomes apparent then that the purely personal satisfactions that reinforce the drinking habit among many—relief from boredom or monotony, frustration, fear, and inferiority feelings—are at first secondary, although they eventually become primary motivations.

The fact that rarely is there an attempt made to rationalize or justify heavy and regular whisky drinking beyond "I just likes my whisky" or "I've just got to have me a little drink," indicates a feeling that drinking is something of a personal privilege or right, and underscores its nature as a type of self-indulgence and a means of self-expression. An old ritualistic drinker explained:

When I was a younger man I was just crazy after the women, but now that I done got old and can't do nothing, I done took up a worser habit—whisky.

A middle-aged week-end drunk and brawler who lacks status, even among chronic drinkers, because of his extreme "low class" behavior said:

Everybody knows I drinks. I tell anybody I can drink plenty of liquor and if there's any to be got I'm going to have me some. But I don't harm nobody. I tries to treat everybody right. The biggest harm is what I does to myself.

The desire to get money for whisky underlies the great bulk of small loan and pawning transactions among friends and acquaintances; there is rarely any attempt to conceal the purpose for which the money is wanted.

The pervasiveness of whisky drinking among the adult males and lower status women; the indulgent and tolerant attitudes toward it in all quarters except among the females who perhaps feel strongest about its effects upon family income and expenditures, status, and personal relations; the frequency with which whisky appears as a factor in nonmarital sex play, "touchy" behavior, and "having a good time," whether attending baseball games, hunting, or idling; and the lack of elaborate rationalizations or justifications for its use or abuse—all these indicate a near-successful integration with other aspects of the culture. Here, whisky tends to be an individual or family problem rather than a social problem. It is an essential aspect of normal social ritual and leisure-time activity; it eases personal tensions (while at the same time creating new ones) in a culture that has many "tough" features—status and respect hunger, limited access to rewards, a measure of economic uncertainty. It is also, for many, a temporary ego-booster and a gesture of defiance to family and community. The emphasis upon alcohol as a sort of personal and social "lubricant" suggests the importance of individual release and self-expression as values. It is significant that these same two values are important ingredients of the more active and emotional religious behavior.

DIONYSIAN TENDENCIES IN THE CULTURE

THE evidence shows that among the Negroes of Kent there is a significant disposition to escape the humdrum and monotonous. This, plus the seasonal character of economic activity, gives emphasis to leisure-time and idling behavior. Whisky drinking, tavern frequenting, and nonmarital sex experiences are patterns involving a certain amount of release and self-indulgence. Public release and indulgence in any area are frowned upon by the respectables, although it is probable that the design for release is no less strong among them even if channeled in other directions or levels. When we add a marked disposition to querulousness or "touchiness" and ingroup violence, we get intimations at least of a Dionysiac way of life, particularly among the lower status groups.

This lack of restraint applies primarily to ingroup behavior and is in marked contrast to the necessity for restraint in intergroup relations. The Kent Negro has two public personalities —one for the white community and one for the Negro community; they need not coincide. In fact, the incompatibility of the role demands of each may account for the high content of random and disorganized behavior in the Negro community. The concept, Dionysian, is not used here in an attempt to characterize a whole culture; rather it is used to "bring clearly to the fore the major qualities that differentiate" [2] this segment of culture from others. Ruth Benedict used the concept to contrast American Indian cultures:

The basic contrast between the Pueblos and the other cultures of North America is the contrast that is named and described by Nietsche in his studies of Greek tragedy. He discusses two diametrically opposed ways of arriving at the values of existence. The Dionysian pursues them through the annihilation of the ordinary bounds and limits of existence; he seeks to attain in his most valued moments escape from the boundaries imposed upon him by his five senses. The desire of the Dionysian, in personal experience or in ritual, is to press through it toward a certain psychological state, to achieve excess. The closest analogy to the emotions he seeks is drunkenness, and he values the illuminations of frenzy. With Blake, he believes the path of excess leads to the palace of wisdom. The Appolonian distrusts all this. . . .[3]

Gertrude D. Stevens, after an independent content analysis of field notes collected for this study, concluded that frustration-aggression and religion were two of the basic controlling patterns in the Kent Negro subculture. She pointed out:

2. Ruth Benedict, *Patterns of Culture* (New York: First Pelican Books Edition, 1946), p. 72.
3. *Ibid.*

It seemed clear . . . that the greater amount of events measurable as the immediate cause of aggression are those arising within the Negro section of Kent, verbal and circumstantial, rather than violent. The fact that they result in so much aggression indicates a "touchiness" of personality. . . . Drinking . . . seems to be antecedent to and coincidental with much of the aggression.[4]

The ranking of the types of initial acts in the aggression sequence based on the data Miss Stevens analyzed were: verbalization, sex patterns, attitudes, violence, law breaking, economic and competitive. The conditions of aggression ranked as follows: drunk (or liquor), suspicion, sex, caste, insanity, fighting, irresponsibility.[5]

"Touchiness" and the disposition to violence are more prevalent among lower status groups; in fact, this is conceded to be an ingredient of "low class" behavior and an inevitable accompaniment of public drinking and tavern behavior. However, such characteristics are not exclusive with nonrespectables.

A constant and highly significant element in the pattern of querulousness and aggression is the use of the profane and obscene phrase. Intent and tone are important factors defining response to cursing; the same expressions can be used jocularly, or impersonally for conversational emphasis and as extremely aggressive vocal gestures and deprecations. In any event, the very frequent use of profanity and obscenity—and the fact that such expressions are conventional for the nonrespectable, low-status male, in particular [6]—suggest the "out-

4. Gertrude D. Stevens, Application of Content Analysis to Anthropological Field Notes (unpublished M. A. thesis, Department of Sociology and Anthropology, University of North Carolina, 1949), p. 66.

5. *Ibid.*, pp. 65-66.

6. Knowledge of profane words and use of them is not confined to the lower-status groups, although there is undoubtedly a significant difference in incidence of both; and there is certainly more discrimination in their use among respectables. One certain way of identifying a nonrespectable woman is in terms of whether males curse freely around or at her, or whether she curses rather indiscriminately herself.

let" function; satisfaction is undoubtedly received from using freely words that are normally taboo. The words used are common elements in the substandard language of America; there is nothing unique about them, except probably the incidence of their use in certain settings and the psychological content for that group. In cultural terms, the pattern of profanity and obscenity among certain categories of the Kent Negro population, with its spontaneous use in certain situations marked by balking or frustration, has an adaptive function; it is "natural." The mechanisms involved are suggested in the following explanation of soldiers' responses to the frustrations, conflicts, and deprivations of army life:

Soldiers have the reputation of assuming less responsibility toward society's ideals and values. In the American Army the soldier often comes not only to realize this reputation but to accept it as a prerogative. . . . The expression of this self-image manifests itself in his thoughts, his behavior, his language.

In his image of himself, then, the soldier tends to feel a freedom from civilian society's taboos and controls. This image would, in most cases, never exist in an isolated individual; it is a feature of the crowd. In a group of similarly minded men these expressions are no longer taboo; on the contrary, they are often the conventional way of speaking. In his own mind, however, the soldier is aware that he is expressing what was formerly a taboo and is thus freer from social restraint. The expression of this soldier self-image is primarily in profanity.

The expression of obscenity obviously gives the soldier certain indulgences. Violating the taboos of language gives feelings of courage and freedom; it is in itself satisfying. It seems, however, that more can be derived from the given expressions than the mere fact that the soldier obtains indulgences, for each expression manifests something of a repressed sphere. In most respects, however, this is a field of study for the psychoanalyst.

As obscene words come into such universal usage and as seemingly indiscriminate usage, they tend to lose their original sexual significance. As casually spoken by soldiers, obscene expressions do not mean that the users actually are thinking on the sexual level; they are merely speaking the language of their social group.[7]

There are many analogous features. Profanity and obscenity in the Kent subculture are in part an expression of freedom from the restraints of the larger society; they give a sense of courage and freedom to the Negro who indulges. Obscenity does not always have its ordinary denotative meaning; it is the language of a special category of the population with complex psychological implications.

Hair-trigger sensitivity to word and gesture is accentuated by whisky drinking, but whisky is not a necessary condition. This sensitivity has compulsive features and involves the ego and "face." It is most commonly expressed as "I don't bother nobody and I don't allow nobody to do nothing to me." It is also marked by a significant element of fatalism: "If I gets killed, I just gets killed"—"I couldn't see nothing but for me to die." In looking at the disposition to violence and "touchiness" as a research problem, we must keep in mind that personal violence is something of a southern regional pattern and therefore there is a question as to how much is related primarily to—or aggravated by—the Negro's status. The nearby Stone Valley Bugle editorialized:

Shoot 'n' Cut

You know, in a year's time, quite a few people in this section get shot or cut up.

Oh, no, not YOUR family.

Oh, no, not YOUR kind of folks.

But you know what we're writing about: you know that in a year's time quite a few people in this section get shot or cut up.

Some white. Some Negro.

7. Frederick Elkin, "The Soldier's Language," *American Journal of Sociology*, LI (March 1946), 418-19.

It doesn't do anybody any good.

Sometimes "the law" doesn't even get to arrest anybody. Other times, somebody gets into court, maybe is sentenced. But that doesn't undo what has been done. . . .

What can we do about it?

There's just no sense in the cuttings and shootings.

Sometimes there's liquor mixed up in it. But usually it isn't the liquor that makes the trouble; it was just that somebody who is liquored lets loose. It would be hard to say whether the same person, cold sober, might not have done the same thing sooner or later.

No, it's something inside folks that causes them to do such things, that lets them do such things.

What can be done to change that "something inside folks" which ends up in shootings and cuttings?

Church going helps. Being self-respecting helps. Going to school enough when a child helps. Friends help. More attention by YOUR kind of people (who don't get mixed up in such things) to the lives led by the kind of people who do get mixed up in cuttings and shootings could help some.

In the same way that hardly a person or a family has escaped some contact with "the law," scarcely a person or a family has not been touched by violence and querulousness. Identifying references such as "he's a bad man to fool with," "he killed a man," "he'll cut you in a minute," "he slapped hell out of a woman," are frequent among lower status groups. A large number of persons, mainly men, are marked with knife scars on the neck and face, some of them having been cut or wounded several times. A young veteran who had just been cut in a Saturday tavern scrape remarked:

That's the fourth time I been cut. But there ain't nobody I know around here ain't got some kind of mark or something where they been in a ramble. I told my dad, I got a bad record behind me—four members of my family, aunts and uncles—is murderers. I tries to hold myself in because I done shot a "cat" once. I tries to avoid getting in a corner where you's got to do something.

There is significant conversational interest in disputes, scrapes, and violence. The majority of the adult males own and carry pocket knives; many nonrespectables feel uncomfortable and unprepared without them. Illustrative is the case of the young man on his way to church who retraced his steps home, and when he returned said: "I had to go back and get my knife; I just don't feel right without it." The gestures of drawing the knife or references to using it are frequent in jest and play behavior. The knives used are pocket knives with folding blades from three and a half to six inches long. In many cases when trouble is anticipated, the knife is carried "at the ready" that is, in an outer pocket open and ready for action. The most frequent technique used is the quick slash at the face or body; this is often a surprise attack. Stabbings or multiple slashings on the other hand usually involve some degree of premeditation or brooding and tend to exhibit significant sadism. In cases of knife play, the only elements of skill involved that suggest some training or aptitude are in the speed with which the knife is opened and made ready and the ability to ward off counter thrusts and strike quickly. For the most part, altercations involving knife play are not exhibitions of skill and finesse, rather they are one or more passionate and often wild thrusts that usually come at the end of an exchange of threats and/or blows. Persons are ranked in terms of their dispositions to use knives rather than in terms of skill.

A smaller number of persons carry pistols; a few carry them, especially when "going out" or anticipating attack or trouble. "Touchiness" of personality and hostility to intimates is indicated in the fact that a large number of altercations—both verbal and physical—involve relatives or close acquaintances.

That a great deal of this behavior is unpremeditated and rationally disapproved is indicated by the fact that persons who themselves have a record of violence or contentiousness will decry both. They will even advise others that such situations are not worth getting in trouble about. The point to be emphasized is that the typical person, given a situation and the proper cues, will act immediately: there is little disposition to "take things" from other Negroes. In many cases observed, the causes of violence have been objectively trivial or vague, and the incident is the inevitable culmination of an exchange of aggressive gestures.

Illustrative is the account by a well-known and active person in the community of his "reformation."

Dub pointed out that since he had stopped carrying a gun he had gotten along much better. If he were carrying a gun, he would, in fact, be looking for trouble—"and that is the easiest thing in the world to find." At one time he used to feel and tell himself that he wouldn't take anything off of anybody—"but I've got more sense now." The incident that "cured" him occurred on Christmas Gift Night at his home church just outside Kent. Fortunately, he had taken his gun from his pocket and put it in the house before leaving for the church with his family. While on the church ground, his children were shooting firecrackers. One of his fellow church members objected and told him that children who did such showed that they had no raising. Dub immediately attacked him; after a scuffle, he ran to a nearby house, broke the door in and grabbed a shotgun and returned. Luckily, other persons intervened. Dub says that he would have surely shot the man if he had had his pistol; that "learned" him. The police came but the participants would not prosecute each other. Dub told his opponent: "If I didn't do nothing to you while I was mad, I don't see the point in trying to harm you further when I'm in my good senses."

In this setting, it is well to note, a "bad guy" or a "tough guy" is not necessarily a braggart who parades his toughness—although there are a few; he may in fact be a mild-mannered person ordinarily. Usually he is a person who is known to have few qualms about fighting or hurting another person with little provocation. It is the code rather than mannerisms that makes one tough; each individual in self-protection is "tough" to some degree. This is hair-trigger sensitivity rather than chip-on-the-shoulder behavior.

The following is an account of an altercation between two "tough" guys who were friends and drinking companions:

"Snuffy" and "Cap" had been drinking together on the Wednesday afternoon half-day holiday. They were sitting in the poolroom exchanging small talk. What began as a joking exchange about the merits of the high school education of one of the bystanders developed into an exchange of curses and threats. The manager told them to take the cursing outside. "Cap" told the manager that he wasn't afraid of him and would willingly fight him even though he knew he probably couldn't beat the manager who was a larger man. "Snuffy" added, "Everybody knows I'll fight a m___ f___; I ain't scared." They got in the car of a friend, "Snuffy" in front and "Cap" in the rear; they continued to curse and argue. "Snuffy" took a swing at "Cap" with his knife; "Cap" jumped out of the back door of the car and started to run. When he saw the crowd watching, he changed his mind and started back with fists cocked. "Snuffy" took another swing at him with his knife and "Cap" ran again. "Snuffy" wanted to go home to get his pistol; he kept muttering: "I ought to kill that son-of-a-bitch."

"Snuffy" has a long stormy record; a friend describes him: "He's a nice fellow when he ain't drinking. But once you get to drinking with him, he'll turn on you in a minute if he thinks you're trying to take advantage of him."

Symptomatic of the sensitivity over status and respect is the often aggressive reaction to the use of the term "nigger" by a Negro to another Negro. Illustrative are these two instances:

"BB" is a mild-mannered fellow who is given to considerable beer-animation on Saturdays. He was dancing in one of the taverns with Mae Lee. As they finished one very passionate dance, Mae casually said something to him and used the word "nigger." "BB" asked her firmly not to use that word, saying that was not what he is. Mae stood her ground, repeated the term and told him that was all he was and that was what the white man called him. The audience laughed. The exchange continued and got more heated. "BB" invited Mae outside to settle the matter physically. Mae was on the verge of going outside to accept the challenge when the proprietor stepped in. Mae said that she would have gone out there and beaten the hell out of him; furthermore, no man had ever messed up her face or body like some girls had let them do.

Oscar and Albert were at a dance following a basketball game. Oscar saw a boy from a nearby community open his knife and mumble, "He called me a nigger," as he prepared to plunge it in Albert's back. Oscar pulled his knife and told the boy that if he tried that the two of them would have to cut it out. The boy desisted but later told his friends about it and "spotted" Oscar for them. Oscar was afraid that if he went to the taverns on a Friday or Saturday night that he might "get it." He later talked it out with the boy and explained that the both of them were drunk and meant no harm; they "got straight" but he continued to be concerned about the boy's buddies.

In the same vein of touchiness was the altercation between two middle-aged men, one a staunch churchgoer and member of the prayer band, over the facetious allusion to stealing:

Rex owed Cookie fifty cents on a pint of whisky that they had shared earlier. Cookie approached Rex before a group of idling men and boys and asked, in drunken facetiousness, for the money that Rex "had stole" from him. Rex reacted immediately and violently, saying that he had never "stole" in his life; he pulled his knife and said that, goddammit, he would cut Cookie's throat. In a teasing way, Cookie explained that he was just using that expression and meant no harm. Rex broke forth in a crying rage and began to curse and threaten; Cookie left and Rex said that, goddammit, he was going with him and "have it out." They were separated and no actual physical contact occurred.

Billy is a ritualistic week-end drinker. His record shows a marked disposition to violence: he has cut several persons seriously, broken a man's leg with a car jack, served time on the chain gang for fighting the police. He will state his creed quickly: "Nobody does anything to me and gets away with it." Yet he is not a bully. Not long after this study was begun, he was shot at point-blank by Archie, in whom he had earlier stuck a knife and held it until Archie collapsed. The trouble between these two was the climax of a tavern sequence in which Archie had challenged Billy: Archie had playfully emptied beer that Billy had bought, and then had taunted him to buy more so that he could empty it. Billy bought more beer, Archie moved to empty it; they fought, and Archie was seriously cut. The sequel illustrates a kind of fatalistic fearlessness and sensitivity, and a personal code:

One Saturday night Billy was at a house on Ox Row where several men, including one white man, were gambling. Archie was in the room; when Billy sat behind him, he remonstrated, saying that he didn't want Billy sitting behind him because he didn't know what Billy would do. After a brief exchange, Archie went next door, got a .22 rifle, returned and shot at Billy point-blank. The bullet went through the front of Billy's hat. Archie slugged Billy with the gun and would have continued to pummel him if a bystander had not separated them. Billy went home, got his shotgun, loaded all his pockets and the blouse of his shirt with shells and returned. By this time, Billy's relatives had been informed, and they went to the scene and tried to reason with Billy. He told them that he just wanted Archie to come out and talk with him, man to man. He called for Archie to come out and he asked Archie's wife to bring the children out; they refused to come out. Later, Billy said he was prepared to kill Archie if he had come out or to shoot enough shells into the house to set it on fire; the only thing that stopped him was the presence of the children in the home. He didn't "believe in hurting nobody who ain't done nothing to you. Them kids was innocent and I couldn't do nothing to hurt them; I got some biddies myself.

But if a man do me wrong, I'm going to get him—it's going to be either me or him. . . . Now if a man beat me fair-like, that's all there's to it. I ain't going to be mad the next day; me and him can go on being friends like ain't nothing ever happened." The police picked Billy up later; his mother ("Our children, they will do wrong.") put up $100.00 bond. At the Monday trial, Billy was fined $75.00. He felt this was the cruelest blow of all: here he was all bloodied up and had almost gotten killed—and on top of that had to pay $75.00!

The general attitude of most of the men "on the block" was summed up by one: "Billy was a lucky son-of-a-bitch. He's been asking for it a long time. The next time he won't be so lucky."

The one incident in Kent proper that resulted in death during the study,[8] although not necessarily typical, does illustrate something of the personal psychology that characterizes many. It represents the exaggeration of some of the normal tendencies implicit and explicit in this subculture: self-indulgence, touchiness, whisky-sponsored contentiousness and violence, and a certain fatalism.

"Corky" was a very dark, puckish character in his early twenties who stood in well with the whites of the town. Critics say his favorable position with the whites tended to make him a little cocky. When drinking, he would show exaggerated aggressiveness or sensitivity to slight.

"Rocky" was short, slightly deformed and reddish-brown in complexion. He was an illegitimate child with a record of delinquency, some of it allegedly involving attacks upon, and thefts from, members of his close family. After he had become a man, his mother married a man who had murdered a man and served time in the penitentiary for it. "Rocky" had spent several months in a hospital recently with a serious fracture received on the job. He was having trouble getting satisfactory compensation. "Rocky" shot "Corky" on Christmas Eve night outside the door of a tavern.

8. There have been three murders involving all Negro principals in Kent during the past two years.

On the afternoon of the day he was shot, "Corky" jokingly told a friend who was a regular drinker: "Death might be your Santa Claus." Later, with relatives and friends, "Corky" began the round of taverns. At the place he was killed, he was said to have been drunk and vomiting and "hard to get along with." He was advised to go home; his answer was "I ain't going nowhere. Go on and call the law; I'll get out. I got money." He had an altercation with "Rocky" that stemmed from a fancied insult: his wife was pregnant and "Rocky," who had not seen her in quite a while, remarked that she appeared to be getting fat. He struck "Rocky" and was given some support by his relatives. "Rocky" left to get his gun. When he returned, "Corky" stripped off his coat to go out the door after "Rocky," with the words: "If I've got to die, I'm going to die. I got to die sometime—might as well be now." "Rocky" shot "Corky" to death in the scuffle that followed.

When "Corky's" sister heard of his death, she exclaimed, "All I want to know is, did he have time to say 'Lord have mercy!'" A sequel is the fact that three weeks after "Corky's" death, his pregnant widow was arrested and jailed for being drunk and disorderly in a public tavern.

After several trial postponements, "Rocky" pleaded guilty to a lesser charge of manslaughter and was sentenced to eight years in the penitentiary.

The holiday murder described above served to illustrate certain things about the community and its responses. Persons tended to identify themselves as sympathizers, good friends, or relatives of the principals; those who identified themselves with "Rocky" were in the minority. The preponderant feeling was that this was a useless and unjustified murder; the first reaction of many people was that "Rocky" should hang or be electrocuted. A friend of "Corky's" said that the white folks up town had said that they were going to see that "Rocky" died; and if he got out they were going to take him out and kill him. Men, who themselves had had tangles with the law because of violence, shook their heads and pointed to the ex-

pected sentence of "twenty-five or thirty years for nothing."
The interesting point is that they agreed that "a man should
think"; and yet a part of their behavior pattern is swift retaliation in the case of slight or danger. Some pointed to the fact
that the next term of court would probably see four murderers
(including "Rocky") tried; in no case was there expressed—im-
plicity or explicitly—any justification for murder. In brief, this
murder during the holiday season shocked the community
into a certain soberness and served as a rallying point for a
mixture of sentiments and expressions: sympathy, denuncia-
tion, identification, pity, mild bitterness, confirmation of theories of retribution. "Corky" and his wife were the sympathetic figures; "Rocky" was almost universally rejected.

In the late Spring, "Rocky," while on bail, began to circulate cautiously among his friends and in the old haunts, much
to the surprise and indignation of many persons. "Rocky" was
optimistic about his chances of "beating the rap" and talked
easily to intimates about the incident. Insight is gained into
his conceptions of himself in the conversation in which he
moved from a discussion of his own case to a vehement condemnation of a man who had killed a taxi-driver in Stone
Valley in a dispute over a fare. He said this man was a dirty
son-of-a-bitch to kill a man over a taxi fare and that anything
was too good for him. He said that, if a man ever overcharged
him, that would be all there was to it. He added that he
wouldn't harm anybody unless they "hemmed him up," and
then he would try to "burn them up." He spoke with a sort
of casual respect and gratitude for his mother who had stood
by him. He pointed out that the only thing he disliked about
her was the way that she talked after he had done anything:
"A man don't like to insult his mother, but I swear it's hard to
stand all that talk."

Ingroup querulousness and the possibility of violence and
physical hurt are constant and expected risks characteristic

of the way of life of the tavern habitues, the chronic public drinkers, and the males and females who indulge significantly in nonmarital sex exploits. Indeed, to a significant degree it is anticipated in all areas of contact and group behavior. The small size and relative homogeneity of the community mean that in some way all people tend to have access to each other; this in turn means that everyone is influenced or is aware of this feature of Negro ways, whether he takes it for granted or has strong negative feelings. Those who have strong negative feelings are in some degree isolated and characteristically avoid active participation in many areas of group activity. In any event, the disposition outlined above indicates the importance of respect for the person as a pervasive value. Practically every Negro in this bi-racial situation tends to be respect-starved. When the opportunity affords, he will demand it, or satisfy his need for it indirectly or subtly, when whites are involved; the use of direct aggression varies with the person and the situation. Consistent with this "having to take it" is the Negro's behavior within his own group: it is the one place where he doesn't have to "take it." Aggressiveness and querulousness are symptomatic of a respect-starved group; they have a cumulative and persistent quality insofar as "touchiness begets touchiness."

THE PREMIUM ON "TREATING PEOPLE RIGHT"

THE Kent Negro's implicit and explicit emphasis upon appreciation for the person is clear when he exhibits his basic warmth, generosity, and hospitality to those who appreciate and recognize him as a person regardless of status. Friendliness, courtesy and kindness are important values that are graciously reciprocated; they are the chief weapons that can be used to break through sensitivity and suspiciousness. To some extent they become "values by contrast" in a society that is marked by a great deal of touchiness and latent resentment.

The burden of proof tends to be on the newcomer to the community and also upon those who, for any reason, are differentiated from the mass—the educated, the leaders, the conspicuously successful. The words "appreciate everybody," "treat people" are recurrent. Illustrative were the remarks to the writer of a woman who herself was of low status:

> You sure is like around here. . . . You appreciates everybody. Of course, you's got sense; you ain't like these ignorant niggers around here. Just because a person's done something bad, you ain't got to treat him bad.

There is great respect for the person who "can get out among the people." Where class lines are virtually non-existent and the range of statuses is small, personal characteristics loom large. There is a tendency for every person to think "I'm as good as anyone else"; at least, that is a frequent bristling response to the slight, or intimation of a slight. Yet, paradoxically, each person tends to have a personal definition of the limits of association; there is no person who would not define some others as unfit for association. Hence the paradox for the newcomer who seeks mobility: he can't afford to associate with just certain people, yet he is not supposed to associate with every "Tom, Dick, and Harry." But "Tom, Dick, and Harry" are as appreciative of recognition as anyone else.

In a society where so many persons have meager means, low status, and limited contact, the essential dignity of the "common people" is an important implicit value. The worth of ordinary people is implicit in a statement by the previously mentioned Billy: "It ain't your fault how much education you got. It ain't your fault it you didn't go to school. The only thing your fault is how you treats people."

Social Organization

CHAPTER **10** THE DESCRIPTION and analyses up to this point have shown that there are certain social habits and orientations that characterize the Kent Negro society as a whole; but it has also been indicated that different persons, groups, or categories tend to show or exhibit in some degree differential behavior. For example, it has been shown or suggested that there is some variability of behavior related to such factors as age, sex, and church affiliation and that it makes a difference as to whether one plays a respectable or a nonrespectable role. It is desirable at this point to examine in greater detail some of the divisions or segments of the society that have not been analyzed before and to note the bases of differentiation and the behavior correlates. The interest in this chapter shall be primarily on those aspects of social organization that have to do with social stratification, types of ranked social statuses and roles, and the functions and the participation in voluntary associations in this small-town Negro society.

CLASS

IF A class-organized society is one in which there is a well-defined system of ranking that distinguishes cohesive, self-conscious segments marked by differences in social honor and power, then Kent Negro society of today is not organized on a class basis. A clear-cut system of social ranking and basis of association or intimate access was not discovered. This does not mean that there is not level consciousness; it does not mean there is not a status pattern marked by different measures of prestige and privilege, despite the leveling tendency mentioned earlier. Rather, it suggests that numerically significant groups differentiated on a basis of intimate association or access are not present, and that the people themselves do not in behavior or verbalizations make references to or relate themselves to such prestige collectivities.[1] Since class consciousness represents a kind of organized or crystallized status consciousness, it is pertinent to note that Miss Stevens, on a basis of her analyses of the field notes for this study, concluded that status consciousness as a factor in behavior in the Negro community was relatively less important than aggression and religion,[2] and that "class consciousness was not so marked among the Negroes."[3] Insofar as there are status differences and insofar as the society is changing and becoming more differentiated, one might say that class is incipient, rather than full blown.

Socio-Economic Categories

Although it is possible to use a variety of external and discrete characteristics such as wealth, occupation, education, type of house, etc. to stratify the Negro population, it must be recognized that: (1) the strata that result from such measures tend to be the investigator's categories and need not coincide with group evaluations and imputations of honor; (2) the number

1. Infrequent references are made to people (primarily, some of the members of one family, the Thorpes) as being "up there" or as having money; and similarly references may be made to "low-down" people, but these are designations of social positions rather than of any existent class group to which they are assigned. "Low-down" and "better" or "best" when applied to people usually have reference to public behavior and leisure-time habits.

2. Gertrude D. Stevens, Application of Content Analysis to Anthropological Field Notes (unpublished M. A. Thesis, Department of Sociology and Anthropology, University of North Carolina, 1949), pp. 46-48.

3. *Ibid.*

and range of positions available for socio-economic stratification are limited by the size of the Negro community, by the extent and quality of Negro participation in the economy and the strength of his claims for rewards, and by his access to specialized services from other societies—as in the case of some specialized services which he gets from the local white community; and (3) no single criterion or combination of criteria is a fully reliable index of standards of life or of local norms of social estimation.

TABLE 4. ESTIMATED [a] PERCENTAGE OF EMPLOYED KENT NEGROES BY OCCUPATIONAL LEVELS, 1948-49

	Percent
1. Professional and semi-professional workers	3.0
2. Proprietors, managers, and officials [b]	1.5
3. Clerical, sales, and kindred workers	0.5
4. Foremen, skilled, and kindred workers	2.0
5. Operatives, apprentices, and semi-skilled workers	3.0
6. Unskilled workers and laborers [c]	90.0

a. The calculations are based upon an estimate of six hundred Negroes in the labor force and computations based upon the actual occupations represented in the investigator's file of persons and families.
b. Farm owners are included in this category.
c. Domestic servants and farm laborers are included in this category.

The occupational levels developed by Alba Edwards for purposes of classifying U. S. Census data [4] presumably represent differences in skill, economic position, and status. When Kent Negro callings and their estimated percentage distribution are classified according to an adaptation of this scheme, the approximate result would be as shown in Table 4. Such a classification of Kent Negro occupations would be inade-

4. *Alphabetical Index of Occupations and Industries* (Washington, D. C.: U. S. Government Printing Office, 1950); see also W. L. Warner and others, *Social Class in America* (New York: American Book-Stratford Press, 1949), pp. 132-138; and Frazier, *The Negro Family in the United States*, pp. 285-300.

quate and misleading as a measure of social esteem or style of life associated with these callings or the persons actually following them in Kent, and it has limited usefulness for comparing differentiation in larger urban societies because one will not always be comparing the same things. With respect to the latter point: the estimated proportion in professional and semi-professional callings in Kent compares favorably with the proportions found in large urban centers, and the proportion found in the unskilled category in Kent is far greater than the proportions found in such cities.[5] However, the callings represented are not necessarily comparable in terms of variety or range within a group, nor with respect to local rewards and esteem related to them. For example, the professional category in Kent consists almost entirely of teachers and preachers; one-half of the group consists of teachers in the local school who are looked upon and look upon themselves as outsiders temporarily in the community. And this teacher group—both those who teach in Kent and the local residents who teach in the rural areas—until the 1940's had annual incomes which were not significantly different from local workers in industry and service. Despite a generally high evaluation of the teacher category, there are individual teachers whose social esteem and economic condition are matched or surpassed by some domestic servants in this society. Similarly, the category of unskilled worker and laborer gives no dependable basis for predicting economic position, style of life, or social estimation. For example, among the most prized jobs are those of mill firemen and janitors, drugstore porter, and service positions with a "good" employer. Important factors in the evaluation of a job are its stability and—apparently as important—what a particular individual has been able to accomplish while holding that job.

5. See Frazier, *op. cit.*, pp. 293-298 for charts and figures depicting Negro males in various employment statuses in Southern, Border, and Northern cities.

In particular instances, it appears that what a person imputes to a job is more important than what a job imputes to a person. One might contrast, as cases in point, the definition of jobs and statuses of Bill Watson and John Long: Watson is a painter who would be classified as a skilled worker according to the Edwards classification; he works infrequently and has a reputation as a drunkard who spends his money on whisky. Long has been a mill fireman for more than twenty years, and he is also an influential member of his church and one of the fraternal societies. With reference to these two persons, people express themselves in this fashion: "Deacon Long has a good job; he's been working at the mill for years"; "Bill Watson makes good money when he works, but he don't do nothing with it." The steady job of the mill worker and his style of life are generally more highly valued than the irregular job of the painter and, in this case, the behavior of the person who holds it.

The extent to which occupation is a discriminating characteristic and has predictive value is indicated when it is related to other external characteristics such as quality of housing, education, church affiliation, indoor plumbing, and possession of an automobile. Tables 5, 6, 7, 8, 9, and 10 attempt to show the interrelationship of these factors for the 40 families designated as living in "nice houses." For convenience and ease of interpretation, occupational levels are coded numerically from one to six, that is, from professional to unskilled as in Table 7; and educational level is coded from one to four to cover the categories college, high school, grammar school, and no schooling. The data show that the higher level occupation as defined in this classification scheme is relatively more closely associated with what the community defines as the better housing; however, the large number of lower level occupations associated with better housing indicate that the relationship is by no means an exclusive one. The most striking association is between those classified as professionals (teach-

TABLE 5. SOME CHARACTERISTICS OF KENT NEGROES WHO LIVE IN "NICE HOUSES" [a]

Occupational Level [b]		Educational Level [c]		Church Affiliation [d]	Flush Toilet	Auto
Husband	Wife	Husband	Wife			
1	1	1	1	M.E.	x	x
1	—	1	—	M.E.		x
1	(housewife)	1	2	Baptist		x
1	1	1	1	Presbyterian		x
1	1	1	1	Presbyterian	x	
1 [f]	6 [f]	1	2	M.E.		
2	6	2	2	A.M.E.Z.		
2	6	4	3	Baptist		x
2	—	3	—	Baptist	x	x
2	2	3	3	Baptist		x
3	2	2	2	A.M.E.Z.	x	x
4	1	3	1	M.E.	x	x
4 [f]	1	2	1	M.E.	x	x
4	(housewife)	2	2	M.E.		x
4 [f]	1	2	1	M.E.	x	x
4	6	2	2	M.E.	x	
5	6	2	2	A.M.E.Z.		
5 [f]	3	3	2	Baptist	x	x
5	6	2	2	Baptist		x
6	1	2	1	M.E.	x	x
6 [f]	(housewife)	3	1	Baptist		
6	(housewife)	2	1	M.E.		
6	(housewife)	3	2	M.E.		
6	6 [f]	2	2	A.M.E.Z.		
6	6	2	2	A.M.E.Z.		
6 [f]	6	3	2	A.M.E.Z.		
6	6	2	2	A.M.E.Z.		
6	6	2	2	Baptist		
6	(housewife) [f]	2	2	M.E.		
6	6	3	2	A.M.E.Z.		
6	6	4	3	A.M.E.Z.		
6	6	4	3	Baptist		
6	6	4	3	Baptist		x
—	1	—	1	M.E.		x
—	1	—	3	M.E.	x	x
—	6	—	3	M.E.		
—	6	—	3	M.E.		
—	6	—	3	A.M.E.Z.		
—	6	—	2	A.M.E.Z.		
—	6	—	3	Baptist		

a. "Nice House," as described by a panel of Kent Negro residents.

ers, preachers, and undertakers) and good housing; constituting roughly 3 percent of the labor force, they have nearly 25 percent of the better housing. The unskilled and service group constitute about 90 percent of the labor force, and they contribute just over one-half of the major wage earners occupying the relatively good houses. Similarly, in terms of proportions, education makes a difference; roughly one in twenty-five persons over 25 has had some college

TABLE 6. NUMBER AND PERCENTAGE OF KENT NEGRO MAJOR WAGE EARNERS OCCUPYING "NICE HOUSES," [a] BY OCCUPATIONAL LEVELS

Occupational Levels	Male		Female		Total	
	No.	Percent	No.	Percent	No.	Percent
Professional, etc.	6	18.2	9	28.1	15	23.1
Proprietors, etc.	4	12.1	2	6.3	6	9.2
Clerical, sales, etc.	1	3.0	1	3.1	2	3.0
Skilled	5	15.2	0	—	5	7.7
Semiskilled	3	9.1	0	—	3	4.6
Unskilled, laborers	14	42.4	20	62.5	34	52.4
Total	33	100.0	32	100.0	65	100.0

a. "Nice Houses" as described by a panel of Kent Negro residents.

training while slightly more than one in five of the persons in the "nice house" sample have had some college training. That education is not necessarily associated with this characteristic is shown by the fact that persons with no formal education occupy about one in twenty of the desirable houses and constitute about one-twelfth of the adult population over twenty-five.

b. Occupational equivalent: 1-professional; 2-proprietors, etc.; 3-clerical, sales, etc.; 4-skilled; 5-semiskilled; 6-unskilled.
c. Educational equivalent: 1-college; 2-high school; 3-grammar school; 4-no formal schooling.
d. M.E. equals Methodist Episcopal; A.M.E.Z. equals African Methodist Episcopal Zion.
e. x indicates possession of item.
f. Individuals whose personal status is nonrespectable as defined locally.

TABLE 7. PERCENTAGE OF KENT NEGRO MAJOR WAGE EARNERS
OCCUPYING "NICE HOUSES" [a] COMPARED WITH ESTIMATED
PERCENTAGE OF EMPLOYED NEGROES, BY OCCUPATIONAL LEVELS

Occupational Levels	Percent Major Wage Earners in "Nice Houses"	Estimated Percent of Employed Negroes
Professional, etc.	23.1	3.0
Proprietors, etc.	9.2	1.5
Clerical, sales, etc.	3.0	0.5
Skilled	7.7	2.0
Semiskilled	4.6	3.0
Unskilled, laborers	52.4	90.0
Total	100.0	100.0

a. "Nice Houses" as described by a panel of Kent Negro residents.

TABLE 8. NUMBER AND PERCENTAGE OF KENT NEGRO MAJOR WAGE
EARNERS AND HOUSEWIVES OCCUPYING "NICE HOUSES," [a]
BY EDUCATIONAL LEVELS

Educational Levels	Male		Female		Total	
	No.	Percent	No.	Percent	No.	Percent
College	6	18.2	10	26.3	16	22.5
High School	15	45.5	17	44.8	32	45.1
Grammar School	8	24.2	11	28.9	19	26.8
None	4	12.1	—	—	4	5.6
Total	33	100.0	38	100.0	71	5.6

a. "Nice Houses" as described by a panel of Kent Negro residents.

TABLE 9. PERCENTAGE OF KENT NEGRO MAJOR WAGE EARNERS AND
HOUSEWIVES OCCUPYING "NICE HOUSES" [a] COMPARED WITH
ESTIMATED PERCENTAGE OF NEGROES OVER TWENTY-FIVE
YEARS OF AGE, BY EDUCATIONAL LEVELS [b]

Educational Levels	Percent of Major Wage Earners and Housewives in "Nice Houses" [a]	Estimated Percent of Negroes over Twenty-five
College	22.5	4.0
High School	45.1	20.0
Grammar School	26.8	68.0
None	5.6	8.0
Total	100.0	100.0

a. "Nice Houses" as described by a panel of Kent Negro residents.
b. Estimate based upon known educational status of a sample of the population plus a comparison with Census figures of 1940 for South Carolina Negro urban, rural non-farm, and rural farm populations.

TABLE 10. DENOMINATIONAL AFFILIATIONS OF KENT NEGRO MAJOR
WAGE EARNERS AND HOUSEWIVES OCCUPYING "NICE HOUSES" [a]
COMPARED WITH DISTRIBUTION OF ACTIVE CHURCH MEMBERS

Denomination	Major Wage Earners and Housewives Occupying "Nice Houses," by Denomination		Church Membership in Kent Churches	
	No.	Percent	No.	Percent
Methodist Episcopal	16	40.0	106	27.9
A.M.E.Z.	11	27.5	153	40.3
Baptist	11	27.5	116	30.5
Presbyterian	2	5.0	5	1.3
Total	40	100.0	380	100.0

a. "Nice Houses" as described by a panel of Kent Negro residents.

Although this list contains a heavy proportion of the people who are considered substantial and relatively influential citizens, it does not contain all of the persons who are looked up to as "better off" or as community leaders. For example, Mr. Sam ("Buck") Roberts, a large property owner and president of the NAACP and the fair association, is not represented, nor is Reverend Sampson, the militant minister, included. On the other hand, the list contains nine (or about one in eight) of the 71 persons included who are looked upon as nonrespectable because of their behavior and reputations.

The data further document differences among the three churches referred to earlier: [6] a relatively larger number of Methodists have higher level jobs, some college education, good houses, and flush toilets. The representation of the Methodist church is due mainly to the large number of Thorpes on its rolls.

THE FAMILY AND STATUS

THE Thorpes have eight of the 40 nice houses listed, seven of 16 household heads or housewives with some college education, and five of the 13 houses with indoor flush toilets. The Thorpe family—in particular that branch that is headed by "Miss Phoebe" Thorpe, the owner of the funeral parlor business left by her husband—tends to be "in a class by itself" in terms of family unity and pride, relative isolation or lack of intimate exchange with other families, and the obvious economic gap between it and other groups. They are the only family group about which there is consensus in applying status superlatives—"They're up there!" "They's mighty well fixed." "They're educated people." The Thorpe kinship group has stressed achievement, property, education, and family unity, and illustrates the function of the family in fostering or protecting individual status. The inevitable family skeletons,

6. See pp. 137-139.

frustrations, and minor crises in the history of this group also underscore the constant struggle waged by status-seeking groups against demoralizing and status-threatening influences in the local society and culture: whisky and drunkenness, extra-family sex, the impact of violence, and involvement with the courts.

It seems significant that the relations among these families marked off by wealth, occupation, and level of living are not characteristically intimate and close; each family tends to stand alone, sensitive to its good name and the possibility of attack upon it. Of the differentiated 40 families listed in Table 5, intermarriage of sons and daughters has occurred in only three instances: the older son of "Buck" Roberts married one of the Thorpe girls, and the younger son married the only daughter of Mrs. Robinson, the insurance agent.

In general, a much more important basis of social access and intimate association of persons is church membership rather than occupation, wealth, education, or family pride. In Kent, the great bulk of formal "social" activity and entertaining which involves visiting in homes or gatherings of large numbers of persons for recreation and interchange of experiences or hospitality is church-oriented or sponsored.

RESPECTABLES AND NONRESPECTABLES

THE most significant status cleavage from the point of view of the people themselves seems to be along the respectable-nonrespectable line referred to earlier. These broad status categories have behavior or role correlates that amount to two distinctive styles of adaptation to the cultural situation. In general, the respectable persons are defined by what they do not do. They are people who are careful of their public conduct and reputation: they don't drink whisky in public or get drunk in public; they don't frequent the taverns; they don't get in trouble; and they are proud of their lack of contact

with the law and the courts. The respectables are not clustered in any particular section of the town, nor does any of
the churches have a monopoly on them. Although the category
is not composed exclusively of the persons with the best jobs,
the most property, or the highest incomes, these features are
positively associated with the status. The reason is that respectability—or conventionally-moral conduct—is an expected
accompaniment of education and a good or responsible job.
People with education and economic advantage are looked
upon as persons who have achieved, and they are people who
have a standard of public demeanor to maintain; they are
people the nonrespectables tend to *want* to look up to. In
other words, being differentiated by education or economic
status not only involves the voluntary assumption of different
behavior standards but it also means having imposed upon
one a definite role: since they are people who are going somewhere—or aspiring to—they should act like it. For example,
a local businessman insisted on getting drunk publicly while
under an emotional strain related to a domestic crisis; a nonrespectable friend chastised him: "Man, don't drink. Let me
do it, not you. Let somebody do it who don't matter and who
they don't expect no better of."

In another instance, a person who was a college graduate
was drinking "white whisky" with another person with whom
he had attended high school and who had access to a large
supply. The first person sought to negotiate for a large quantity for personal use. He was told by his high school classmate:
"You don't want no white whisky. That just wouldn't become
you." A person may operate a tavern and be considered respectable. Good jobs and jobs that require some training or
skill tend to have respectability ascribed to them; however, the
personal behavior of the person in such positions may be such
that he is considered nonrespectable. A case in point is the minister (he pastors a church in another town) who persists in
carrying on an affair that is generally known and talked about.

Mere regular attendance at church is neither a sufficient cause nor a necessary condition to respectability although it does help to fix status and represents a partial claim.

Family status and name are not determinants of personal respectability. The family of Mrs. Robinson, the insurance agent, consists of herself, her husband, three sons, and one daughter; the only respectable members of the family, however, are the mother and daughter. "Miss Phoebe" Thorpe has one son, two sons-in-law, a brother, a nephew, and two brothers-in-law who are considered nonrespectable. On the other hand, there are families with a majority of their members in the nonrespectable category that have a member or members referred to as "the best of the lot" and who are looked upon as respectables. The following example of illegitimacy and intricate family relationships, although not typical, illustrates the point:

Rex Rucker, a railroad laborer, is considered one of the community's chronic drunkards; however, he is an enthusiastic member of the Elks. Rex has had two wives and three fragments of families. Joe Rucker, the young Negro who operates the motion picture projector in the town's only theater, is his son. Joe's mother herself is one of eight illegitimate children. Walter Brown is her half-brother; his father was Rex Rucker's first cousin. Rex has another son who was also born out of wedlock. This son, Luke, is one of the town's notorious "bad niggers"—a person who is quick to resort to violence and who boasts about it.

Prior to his marriage to a daughter of a respectable (but eccentric) farmer, Joe Rucker lived with his father. He neither smokes nor drinks. His father condemns Joe's mother for periodically returning to town and embarrassing her son. He says that Joe does not allow her around when she is drinking—which is most of the time.

Out of this background, Joe and Walter have risen to achieve respectability and stability through building a reputation for sobriety and work. Their backgrounds are well known, but the primary reaction of the community is to them as individuals with a respectable style of life.

The categories respectable and nonrespectable cut across all segments, levels, or groups in the Negro population—occupational, educational, kinship, religious. It is difficult to describe the persons in these categories in terms of precise numbers or proportions because the line between the two categories cannot be sharply drawn; there are some people who are considered more nonrespectable than others, and similarly there are some people who adhere more rigidly to respectable standards of conduct than others who nevertheless would be considered—and consider themselves—nonrespectable persons.

These facts about this cleavage should be restated here: there appear to be no institutional or organized group activities which are participated in exclusively by persons of either of the categories. It is difficult in this small society for a person to confine his contacts or associations solely to respectables without suffering extreme isolation, and the designations respectable and nonrespectable refer to aspects or emphases of total behavior, the great bulk of which for both categories is neutral or conventional and without value implications in this sense. Nonrespectable behavior tends to be more dramatic, unrestrained, and public, and therefore it looms larger in the public eye, and the persons who practice it contribute more heavily to the over-all tone of the society than their mere numbers would warrant. The nonrespectable category would include a small group of extremes—between five and ten percent of the adult population—known as chronically "bad" or "low-lifed" Negroes and a larger group—about thirty percent —of persons whose behavior with respect to leisure-time activity, whisky, and sex shows them as choosing this way of life with a minimum of apparent concern about reputation and associations. Respectables tend to be persons who, although they might engage in isolated or surreptitious acts which might be defined as nonrespectable—and may have frequent and close associations with nonrespectables—are concerned about their reputations.

Figures 9 and 10, respectively, show schematically the approximate relationships between occupational status and respectability and nonrespectability and between educational status and these categories in Kent Negro society. They indicate that the relative amount of respectability increases as education and economic status increase, but that nonrespectability tends to be an alternate style of life that is chosen by a significant number in each category. The next sections will designate persons and types within these categories.

Concretely, these are among the types of people who are considered respectable:

(1) A number of three- or four-generation families having relatively clear lineage, particularly in recent generations and having relative security and a tradition of success or achievement: The Thorpe family, already mentioned, is the best example. The Roberts family also has most of these characteristics; it is headed by Mr. Sam Roberts, a gruff, hard-bitten, active, elderly man who owns considerable real estate and has been farmer, carpenter, and store owner. He is probably the most influential and best known of the older men. It has been said that whenever Mr. Sam is connected with anything and the Negroes want to pick a leader or spokesman, they appoint Mr. Sam. He heads the local NAACP (National Association for the Advancement of Colored People), the Kent County Colored Fair Association, and is a prominent church and fraternal leader. Both the Thorpes and the Roberts are pillars of the Methodist church. One of the sons of Sam Roberts married a Thorpe; yet there is no intimate, clique-like social contact between the families. The two families combined have furnished the bulk of local college graduates,

FIGURE 9. Occupational levels of Kent Negroes in labor force in relation to estimated proportions of respectable and nonrespectable statuses

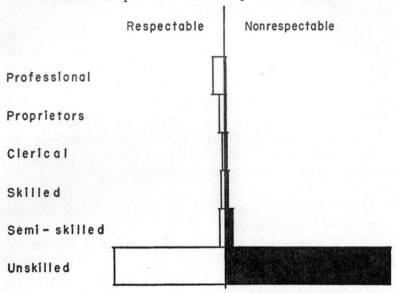

FIGURE 10. Educational levels of Kent Negroes over twenty-five years of age in relation to estimated proportions of respectable and nonrespectable statuses

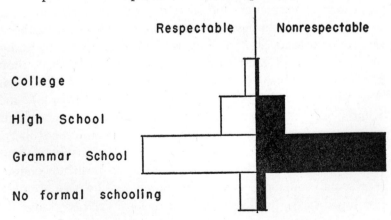

the majority of native school teachers, and much of the leadership in the Negro community. Although there are many other stable family groups with significant pride, no other family matches them for dominance, extent of influence, and over-all prestige.

(2) The secure widow: a person whose husband left her relatively "well-fixed" by way of property and insurance; or a person who by her own energies and thrift has achieved a measure of security. An example of the latter is Mrs. Louise Todd, the "flower woman" and faithful church worker:

Mrs. Louise Todd is a widow; her husband died 42 years ago and left her with "three children and one coming." She worked a "hoe farm" (worker furnishes labor and shares in proceeds to the extent of one-third) and did domestic work for five years. She never failed to show a profit. She decided to move to town so that her children might get better schooling. She is very profuse in attributing her success to the Lord and her prayers: the Lord blessed her and made her a strong woman who could and would work. Her twin passions are the Lord and her flowers.

When Mrs. Todd came to Kent, she raised vegetables for sale and did domestic work for awhile. She didn't like domestic work. One day while looking at a small bouquet of flowers she had made, she said to herself that someone would like that. She began to grow and experiment with flowers; she ordered and read a great variety of seed catalogues. She has been selling flowers on the streets and in the local stores and offices for over twenty-five years. Every available space in her yard is planted with flowers. She knows the names of all and can indicate genus and species. Her prize exhibit is a rock wall that she built herself. She tells proudly how she found and carried each rock and mixed the mortar.

(3) The successful farm owner or operator: a high status type by virtue of land ownership or control and independence. The successful farm operators maintain an above-average standard of living—good housing and equipment, diet, auto-

mobiles, clothing. There is a marked contrast between them and the poorer tenants; they are generally appreciated as symbols of success and enterprise among a people whose lives are colored to so large an extent by agricultural activities and who themselves are not far removed from a rural background. The high level farm incomes of recent years have added to their stature. The fact that most of the prominent ones of the area are using modern methods—mechanization, crop rotation and diversification, and soil conservation—increases their recognition as intelligent and serious economic operators. They are among the most solid citizens of the community. To say that a person is a farmer or has a big farm carries a significant connotation locally.

(4) The successful artisan: he is the energetic and reliable worker who possesses a skill such as bricklaying, carpentry, and painting. Reliability and personal reputation are important earmarks of success. The few successful artisans are in considerable demand among whites. They are concrete examples of "people who can do something." "When a man can do something, he's in demand." The most successful Negroes of the older generation have been artisans and/or farmers; to some extent this has colored the ambitions of the younger generation. The wish to be a carpenter, bricklayer, or electrician is a dominant ambition pattern among school boys as revealed in their autobiographies. One boy wrote: "I want to be a bricklayer. Because my uncle said there wasn't one in the family, and that you make a good piece for the work."

(5) The principal of the school and the school teacher; the status and roles of these functionaries have been described in Chapter 7.

(6) The undertaker: the size of the community, the lack of a Negro professional group, the limited roles played by teachers and preachers in the local community are factors that help define the role of the Negro undertaker and impose a variety of functions in relation to the Negro community. The

local undertaker has to be a friend and trouble shooter in life and death; he combines many of the conventional functions of the lawyer, doctor, preacher, banker, credit agency, confidential agent, taxi driver. Not untypical were the following events that took place at the undertaking establishment in the course of a single afternoon: a man came by to have an appointment made with a dentist in a nearby city; a woman came by to borrow fifteen dollars to get her husband out of jail; two youths got assistance with their draft cards; a man sought to get a house built for him; the pastor arrived to discuss church finances; a call came from a rural region fifteen miles away to pick up a patient and deliver her to a hospital that is fifteen miles away in the other direction; a lady acquaintance asked to be driven home; Western Union called to inquire about the address of a local resident. The undertaker must be a diplomat in handling preacher, friends, family, and insurance companies. The position as the most important Negro business-profession in the community and the necessity of frequent contact with white businessmen, professionals, and public officials mean that he must be skilled and restrained in public relations with whites. Leadership and liaison functions are imposed or taken-for-granted by both the white and Negro communities.

(7) The preacher: the religious and social functions of the church automatically make the preacher's role an important one. It is probable that local whites still think of the minister as the most influential and important person in the Negro community; the "preacher" or the "professor"—as any Negro who deviates from the over-all pattern is likely to be called by whites—gets a kind of patronizing respect from whites. The Negro community looks upon the preacher in quite a different way. The functions of the office—preaching and presiding over significant ceremonies such as the burial rites— are important; the individual minister is highly expendable locally and his prestige as a person may be low. He comes

to be a sort of part-time expert presiding with more or less satisfaction over traditional and necessary rites. In actual practice, he has a rather tenuous hold on his job, and his leadership functions are made difficult by the limited expectations of the congregation, chronic financial problems, limitations related to training or personal characteristics, and a factionalism in the church that is inherent in the gap between young and old, traditionalists and progressives. His lack of financial independence doesn't help his prestige or his self-confidence. The recurrent expression "These Kent Negroes are funny" is a vague common-sense recognition of an unstable situation and of the difficulties that beset the religious and other functionaries. In the case of the preacher one can distinguish three manifestations of status and role—the ideal, the preferred, the actual.

The ideal status and role of the minister would include the characteristics of a spiritual leader-teacher, a skilled orator, a good mixer with the people, a "good" man above reproach. This ideal is recognized as impossible and is used in the main as a stand from which incumbents can be criticized when criticism is desirable. The preferred role for the minister is that of an orator-diplomat who is highly effective in the pulpit and who does not rub anyone the wrong way. He is not supposed to be too zealous in checking up on members personally, nor is he to be too anxious to change things. He is to be available when wanted and expected but otherwise not to be too obtrusive or persistent in following out his functions as he sees them. He is not necessarily above reproach; he should be human but discreet. Departure from any of these is likely to bring criticism in terms of the ideal when actually the only fault is that the minister has been over-zealous; he has not known when to leave people alone. The bulk of the people want religion and the church on their own terms; the minister is supposed to conform.

The actual social rankings and behavior of the ministers

are highly variable. There are those who are poorly trained, undifferentiated in economic status, and without regular churches who are not thought of highly; they are preachers in name only, without influence and prestige, and they are rarely called upon to perform the functions of the office. The title "Reverend" when applied to them may have a hint of derision and condescension. Every local minister tends to be a "captive" of his church who is torn between "giving the people what they want" and being the required diplomat, and trying to be a leader who might strengthen the church physically and spiritually. Those who belong to organized bodies with a hierarchy of church officials are caught up in church politics to some degree and must please both the local congregation and the bishop. In at least one of the organized churches, a significant criterion of success on the local scene is the amount of money raised and regularly supplied to the conference; in two of them, a minister loses his effectiveness when he fails to please or placate the influential church leaders having access to his superior officer who has the power of placement. The ministers are ranked informally as to ability as pulpit orators, training, courage, and interest in community affairs, money-raising abilities, and the propensity to extramarital sex play. In practice, both office and person tend to be stripped of much of the sacred and spiritual quality, leadership and control are diminished, and the prestige of the individual minister cannot be taken for granted.

(8) The person with a "good" or relatively rare job: a "good" job is a stable job under good working conditions or an attachment to a white person of power or prestige. Among the "good" jobs of Kent would be some of the cooking positions, chauffeur for rich whites, clerk-porter in the drugstore. On the one hand, it is probable that selection operates to pick the more stable and responsible persons for such jobs. On the other hand, the very stability of the jobs makes that person "lucky" in this setting of limited economic opportunity, and

the reflected prestige of attachment to someone important reinforces individual prestige and influence in the Negro community. Like the Negro house servant of slavery days, these persons are in a favored position in three ways: (a) the stability of job and relative ease of employment; (b) the opportunity to achieve a favorable relationship with employers; and (c) intimate contact with "the ways of white folks." One of the best examples of an occupational and social type of imputed power and prestige is the cook. This doesn't mean that all cooking jobs are desirable and prestige-laden, nor does it mean that all cooks are *ipso facto* persons of status.[8]

In general, with the exception of teaching, the best job for the woman is that of cook for a person of prestige or wealth; those who are "good" employers represent premium jobs. It is indicative of change, however, that lately the premium job for women has been that of cook or helper in connection with the white school's free lunch program: the pay range is from seven to eleven dollars per week in contrast to the normal scale for domestics of five to ten dollars per week; working conditions and relations with supervisors are good; there is some opportunity to bring home surplus food. The eight women who worked in this program during this study had high morale; in general they were stable and respectable. All of them had worked "in private" previously; they preferred this type of work. Indicative of a developing preference for institutions as employment sources rather than private employers is the fact that also among the best jobs for women are those of nurse assistants at the local hospital. It is not meant to suggest that there is an absolute preference for domestic work nor that the abilities or skills of the local women are limited, it is rather to be emphasized that in a setting where

8. The cook's status depends upon skill, demand for services, stability and working conditions of employment, prestige of employers, the rewards that flow from having a patron-protector, and standards of personal conduct and living.

the majority of women work—and must work—job outlets are limited. This is their adaptation to the realities of the local scene. The woman who doesn't have to work or who has "never worked for white folks" is a fortunate and envied person.

The cooks are important persons in both communities. Stable and skilled, they tend to occupy positions of trust and intimacy in the white household. Reflecting prestige, secure in having a patron-protector, sophisticated in living tastes and techniques, better informed than their more isolated neighbors, the favored servants tend to be more poised and better livers and dressers. They are among the important pace setters in the Negro community. Incidentally, the cook is one of the most important "pipelines" between the Negro and white communities, carrying and interpreting selected news to each group of what is going on in the other's world.

(9) The businessman: the status of the businessman tends to be marginal and not too well defined, although there is some respect for the enterpriser, particularly if he appears to be doing well, and there is appreciation for the businessman's design for independence and "making some money." Attitudes and roles are not crystallized as in the case of some other functions. A factor that makes for a lack of clear definition is the incidental and limited character of business enterprise in the local community: the largest number, and in general, the most successful cater to the leisure-time wants and activities of the nonrespectable category. True, there are enterprisers among the "best and respected people," but that status had been achieved or ascribed before entering business. Attempts are made to tap or recruit persons with businesses for leadership or support functions, particularly in the church; a number of them are active church officers.

(10) The "good" or "nice" woman: this is a type about which there is consensus; it is about the greatest compliment that can be given a woman. It does not represent an emphasis

upon morality as such, although good personal reputation is an important ingredient. The emphasis is upon general manner and disposition. The women who are called "good" women or "wonderful persons" are above reproach and gossip; they are cheerfully cooperative; they are active and dependable in community and church affairs; and their range of congenial association is interdenominational. Marital status is not important. The few such persons about whom there seems general agreement are mature women who get added admiration because of the manner in which they have handled or reacted to personal or family crises. The male counterpart, the "good man," has, in general, the same traits, but he is much rarer in this community. These persons are near-crystallizations of the approved or ideal personality.

Difficult to classify is the person who is recognized as an eccentric but is not a derelict or dependent. In fact, the chief eccentrics of the town are highly active, fierce individualists. Their eccentricity lies in the main in their outspoken and dogmatic non-conformity. In two cases, the core of their obsessive behavior is religion. Both have a highly mystical streak: "God tells them things." One of these persons is Tom ("Cap") Slater or Briscoe; he is one of the many persons in the community who have or are known by two surnames.

"Cap" is a large, imposing figure who still clings to the symbols of his 35 years on the railroad—the watch, fireman's cap, and overalls. His retirement was hastened by illness. His great obsession with religion and the Bible is something new. He got religion and was baptized after his retirement. The railroad was his consuming passion; superficially, it appears that religion fills the void and holds together a life that would have been empty without the railroad. Despite his deep religious feeling, "Cap" doesn't go to church; he can't get along with the church members: "They call me crazy, but the trouble is—they don't want to hear the truth. I live by the Bible, that's what I do. . . . If I can't get along with you, I don't bother with you; I leave you alone. I've got my salvation! ... If I went to church I'd have to take sides. And their ain't no sides with Jesus; you're either with Him or you ain't."

"Cap" is obsessed with the Bible as literal truth and authority for conduct. He reads and cites it constantly. He argues vigorously and brooks very little opposition. He claims that he can foretell future events, and, characteristically, after death or a personal disaster, he claims that he knew the misfortune was going to happen. His characteristic gesture is to cock his head on the side and point upward "to God." His aphorisms are usually preceded by the rhetorical question: "What does the Bible say?" On drinking: "Touch not, taste not, handle not." On wealth: "Who is the richest man?—The man with salvation!" On charity and fair play: "It is better to give than to receive. If you don't give nothing, then what you have will be taken away from you. If you give, it will be returned many fold."

Most of "Cap's" neighbors are amused and critical: they call him crazy; they point to the fact that he is a hard, if not sharp, dealer in business matters; and they make sly references to his earlier personal life. He farms and does contract plowing in season and hauls and sells wood in winter. On himself: "There ain't another colored man in this here town who has made as much money as I is. But they don't know it; I don't tell my business. If they made as much money as I is made, you wouldn't be able to hold them. ... I charges two dollars an hour—take it or leave it. I don't work for nothing; they got to pay me. And I don't do no half-handed work; when I do a job, it's done. My time is worth something." On the side of his wagon, he has painted in crude letters: "MY WORK IS GOD ANT GOT TIME TO COME BACK STEP ON THE GAS."

"Cap" emphasizes that he is a happy and contented man, and he appears to be. In his dealings with whites, he shows a peculiar combination of marked deference and a certain permissive bluntness. He stresses that there are certain things that he will tell anybody—white or black. To some extent, his recognized eccentricity shields him.

Aside from the personal satisfactions involved in adherence to a certain way of life, the most significant reward of respectability is the "good name" which one enjoys in both the Negro and white communities; however, this gives no absolute assurance of complete immunity from the sanctions of either group. "Nice people," "decent people," "people who don't bother nobody and who don't get in trouble" are at once objects of respect and of sensitive surveillance. The respectables, if they act properly, can get some things done that involve the approval or support of whites; but on the other hand, many nonrespectables with personal relations with influential whites can get some things done also. The Negro community grants the respectables a modicum of respect also, but the ability of this group to translate this into leadership or power—other than the limited power related to church leadership and small business—is small in this particular setting. Respectability and higher planes of living are their own rewards in the Negro community of Kent to a greater degree than they are in the white.

Those who have a design for respectability tend to be most critical of other Negroes, i.e., those who "don't know how to act," "those who drag the race down," "those who have no getup about them."

Turning now to the nonrespectables, the following is a description of "low-acting" behavior that might serve as a prototype—or polar extreme—of the nonrespectable category:

Flo and Jack are expected to put on a "show" every week-end; these brawls are a matter of good-humored comment by neighbors; they always sound more serious than they are, for Flo and Jack have battled and threatened each other for many years without major tragedy. The house in which they live was left her by her father who was a rural minister. Flo is fairly active in church and is a faithful member of the Missionary Circle. When aroused by a drunken Jack, she talks in a loud voice and exhibits a remarkably colorful and profane vocabulary. Jack is a rather stolid man who walks with a stoop-shouldered gait; he is a heavy week-end drinker, a shrewd and pungent conversation-alist; when drinking, he talks freely about himself and his wife, punctuating the talk with threats and reminiscences about how bad he was (e.g., "I done killed one man and made time for it."); he makes a play for sympathy and indicates that he is mistreated and misunderstood—he has been known to break down and cry.

Most frequently the "show" begins early Sunday morning with an exchange of curses, charges and threats. Invariably, Flo orders Jack out of "my house" and shouts: "You ain't my husband no how; I ain't married to you." A typical morning: neighbors were awakened by a series of screams and a tirade of profanity—"Flo and Jack are at it again." Flo does most of the talking, repeating her demand that he get out and telling him over and over that he is not her husband. Flo tells Jack to go back to his old mother and further that she wishes his mother would die. (She explained later that she really didn't mean that; she was seeking the most effective way of hurting him.) She told him that she was going to poison him one of these days; he replied that if any poisoning were to be done he was going to give her some "lead poison" with his .38. She told him that she was going to call the cops and tell them to come and get him. When she went out in the street talking, the chief of police who had been listening from a hidden spot arrested her and fined her on the spot $25.00. Jack says that she paid it out of a hidden cache of $750.00 that belonged to him. Throughout it all Jack had been unusually restrained. He explained later that he was trying to show some respect to the wife of a neighbor. He said that he had had to put his wife in her place; that she had said something about his mother: "I'm all right, you can say anything you want to about me, but don't say anything about my old mama; I'll kill you!" He repeated that he was going to have to "kill that bitch yet." Later that evening they walked together as if nothing had happened.

Among the types of people included in the nonrespectable category are the following:

(1) The drunk or excessive drinker: the person who is a regular drinker or who gets "booted" often and is seen in

public drinking or drunk. A distinction would be made here between those who for a variety of reasons are rarely arrested for being drunk or disorderly and those who admit to a number of arrests and fines and expect more. The latter group shows no reticence or shame about experiences or expectations. A further distinction might be made between the "sociable drunk" and the "nuisance drunk." The "nuisance drunk" is looked down upon even by other inveterate drinkers. Lowest in status of those in this group are those who habitually get drunk off cheap wine. In general, nuisance drunks are termed "crazy." One young man whose parents and immediate kin would fall in the respectable category describes himself: "I know I'm crazy. People say I'm all right until I get one drink, and then I get crazy."

A chronic drinker describes a wine-drunk: "I don't see how that fellow can keep that stuff up and work every day. He's crazy."

Another chronic drinker who has never been arrested locally said about other drinkers: "All those peoples is damn fools. I might drink as much as they do. But when I commences to get that way, I goes on home and if necessary gets under the bed."

(2) The person who has served time for a criminal offense: there are several distinctions made: (a) those who have been on the chain gang or served time at the county prison camp; (b) those who have been to the state penitentiary; (c) those who have been arrested and even jailed for minor offenses but have never been to the "big jail" (county jail) or to court (county court); the inference is that those in the last group are the victims of common minor vices such as drinking or fighting, but that they are not criminals. In none of these groups is there reticence to talk about experiences or prison records. Much talk is of the sober matter-of-fact kind and does not involve the boast or the threat. In some instances, experiences might be related with great gusto and satisfaction

as personal adventures not without humor. The following is illustrative:

"Big Head," a shabbily-dressed, red-eyed person, was among the idlers in Burton's shed one Wednesday afternoon. He approached a friend and asked him if he would let him have enough to get a drink until Saturday, as he was sick and feeling bad. The friend bought a beer for him. He perked up and rejoined the group and began to tell of his troubles and experiences. He had to have $35.00 to pay on his car—which is really his wife's car; but he didn't worry about that because he had ways of getting money: "I'll have it in two hours, and I won't have to steal it neither. I got things I can turn into money. I'll take my coat in my hand and say, 'White folks, I wants such and such a thing.' And I'll get it, because they knows what I got and what I can do. My wife got plenty money but she wouldn't give me a thing, and I wouldn't ask her. The only time I gits anything from her is when I gits in jail. When I gits in jail, I just rears back; pretty soon, I hears a voice say 'Kid!'; I looks out through the bars and there she is. . . . One hundred dollars, two hundred dollars—even five hundred dollars ain't no money; I can make it fast. When they caught me that time for making whisky (they'd been looking for me for two years; they knowed all about me), I thought the judge was going to fine me. But he fooled me; he said, 'Boy, that'll be four months, no fine!' I didn't say a word; I had the money right in my pocket —but I went out on the chain gang and saved that money.

(3) The person who has brutally assaulted or killed another person: [9] these are not necessarily persons who are feared or ostracized; they are rather persons with distinctive negative reputations—curiosities in part and persons to be careful of in part. The usual reference is "X killed a man one time" or "He's a dangerous guy; he'll hurt you!" Although they are deviates, the community shows a certain tolerance for them;

9. There are at least four persons in the town who admit to having killed persons. The person who has sought to kill or "nearly killed" another is fairly common.

they do not lack for association or access to their chosen groups.

(4) The stool pigeon or procurer for whites: the term "pimp" is used locally to describe both types of group betrayal—carrying tales and getting Negro girls for whites. These are probably the worst things that a Negro can do so far as the Negro community is concerned.[10] Although there is a feeling among some that a number of Negroes when drunk or in trouble are likely to "put in" other Negroes, there are but two persons about whom there is general consensus. One of these is the illegitimate son of a white man who spends most of his time among whites; he is looked upon with great suspicion as a renegade and has been "read out of the race" by some persons. It is alleged that he is an informer and a procurer; Negroes specify the prominent whites for whom he has gotten girls—"and some nice girls." [11]

(5) The woman who goes with white men: this type of woman shares low status honors with the procurer and stool pigeon. If known, she is thoroughly ostracized and her move-

10. It is an interesting fact that the investigator never heard the actual expression "Uncle Tom" used in the context of everyday contact with the "man (or woman) in the street." "Uncle Tom-ism" is recognized as a type of behavior and frequent references are made to "Tom-ing" and "Charley-ing" around white people, but there is no one in the town who is called explicitly an "Uncle Tom." There are these possible explanations: (1) the chronic "white folks' niggers" are looked upon either as feebleminded derelicts who use their pose to get favors from whites or as renegades and stool pigeons who have "left the race" or who betray the race for personal advantage; and (2) since every Negro in order to survive has to do some "Tom-ing" at some time or another, obsequious or deferential behavior to whites is looked upon as a segmental characteristic rather than dominant trait.

11. The Negro male tends to be bitter and indignant because of an inability to protect his women. When approached by whites for information about Negro women, three general types of answers are reported: (a) an indication that one doesn't know, with anger or bitterness reserved for a later display; (b) the apocryphal reply suggesting that the white get a white woman for him also; (c) the laying down of impossible conditions; e.g., "Sure, I know where I can get a woman but it will cost you $25.00"; this combines tact and a certain amount of masked aggression.

ments carefully checked. A person who was pointing out different degrees of promiscuity among women conditioned her evaluation of some of the most promiscuous with a statement that she didn't believe that they went out with white men: "They stays with their own." There is one local woman of the very lowest status, by name of Sal, who spends a good bit of time while she is in town in jail; she has been asked to leave town several times but has always returned. She is known jocularly by an obscene name; she is known to have many men—Negro and white. There are many stories about her. One story told by a white doctor, who has since left the community, to a Negro: a prominent white is supposed to have been going with Sal; he contracted a venereal disease. He asked the physican if there were any way for him to have contacted the disease from Sal, since she was cooking for his family. The doctor is supposed to have said, "Not if that's all she did for you."

(6) The "bad woman" or "no good woman": this type of woman is not defined solely in terms of sex morality; she rather tends to be a person who is extremely indiscreet, loose, and unethical. In one instance, she is a person who has had higher status and is expected to act differently by virtue of certain advantages of education or income. The "bad woman" is the woman whom nobody respects; she is usually a heavy-drinking woman also. She tends to be the female counterpart of the male "nuisance drunk" in terms of persistence and a certain imperviousness to insult. The worst thing that can be said about a woman is that she is a "bat"—a synonym for the above terms. "A 'bat' will do anything."

(7) The bootleggers and numbers agents: these are something of an elite among the nonrespectables; they provide a desired service; they are conceded to be shrewd, clever and lucky, as is anybody who "lives by his wits." As a type they seem to be money-conscious, hard-dealing, and a little suspicious and aloof.

(8) The "slick cat": this type is rare in this small community and is the result of two things: (a) contact with the urban prototype of the "hep cat" and (b) dissatisfaction with local status coupled with a certain disdain for local people and ways. In dress and manner, he is blatantly deviate; in conversation, he tries to impress with his cosmopolitan background and experience; he is prone to brag of his cleverness and superiority.

Lonnie is a very dark fellow in his mid-twenties. He wears his hair long and "conked," and walks with a self-confident swagger. He is unusually neat and colorfully dressed with a heavy "zoot" accent—pastel shades and pegged trousers. He is an excellent and exhibitionistic dancer. His speech is sharper and quicker than that of the average native, at times bordering on an affected eastern brogue. He claims to have gone to college for about one year and uses that fact to establish status. He also stresses the fact that he has traveled—he was in the Army. He can talk glibly about many places and things; things he learned while in the Army and particularly while stationed in California. He is constantly talking about his getting ready to "cut out" for Harlem and "upstate." He is something of a "lone wolf"; he shows great disdain and distrust of local Negroes but is supremely confident of taking care of himself.

Lonnie's philosophy and creed suggest the person who has not made "peace" with the local situation and he has a significant quota of hatred and bitterness:

I've always got money; you don't see me fooling around with this piddling stuff like those guys. I play for high stakes; high stakes that's me. I know something. My motto is "fool the fools"; if they ain't got sense enough to hold it, they ain't got no business with it.
Look at me. I've got education; I've been to college—nearly a year—but where did it get me? Nowhere! ...I don't fool myself about the place of the colored man in the South; I'm black and I can't get rid of that. I'm educated, I'm the best dancer in town,

but I know they'll treat me like everybody else. . . . What's the point? I drinks my liquor and I have me a good time. . . . I'm always going somewhere. Come on go with me. . . .

You got to watch these Negroes. You got to feed the Negro with a long-handled spoon. Don't let him get too close to you, especially when they tries to get too close to you and you ain't known them long. Watch these Negroes who praise you so much and then go around and say things behind your back. If I got something to say, I say it to a man's face; that's why they don't like me around here. . . .

Don't fool with everybody. There's three grades of Negroes: first grade, second grade and the don't-give-a-damn grade. Watch them last ones!

(9) The town derelicts: these are slow-thinking, good-natured persons who are defenseless against the jibes and derision that come their way. They are obsequious among whites for whom they do odd jobs or from whom they cadge small favors, and they are timid among Negroes who assault their egos without fear of retaliation or reply in kind. One of these is Caesar Armstead.

Caesar Armstead is known as the "soda man"; he constantly carries a box of "bread soda" in his pocket and is said to be able to eat a full box in one sitting. One story is that he fed a box to a mule once and the mule died. Caesar has no fixed home; he sleeps in abandoned houses, on porches, in outhouses, and in the winter, in boiler rooms. He is pointed to as a has-been of good background. His father was a rural preacher and farmer. It is said that Caesar at one time held a federal job in a nearby town. It is generally believed that he has money sufficient for all his needs; it is alleged that he was detained at one time for possible commitment to the county home but could not be committed when the size of his bank account was discovered.

His decline is said to have started with a fight he had at a nearby church with a man about his (Caesar's) wife; he lost the fight and his wife. Caesar seems exceedingly grateful to anyone who talks kindly to him. His conversation has a broken, incoherent quality and he is likely to interject such questions as, "When you ain't done nothing they can't do nothing to you, can they?" He has been seen to approach the police squad car with hat in hand asking the same question with much fawning and "Uncle-Tom-ing," to the disgust of bystanders.

Voluntary Associations

The extent to which the Negroes of Kent group themselves into voluntary organizations is a measure of the range and quality of social interests of the population, and the characteristics of the members of the various groups give further clues as to stratification and the degree of importance status has as a basis for selective grouping. The degree to which organizations are active and serve as foci of activity for members and other persons is a measure of the impact of these groups and their purposes on the community. In considering organizational activity there is also a question as to the differences between mere formal affiliation and the kind of participation that produces a sense of belonging and active efforts to further organizational goals.

The materials that have been presented earlier describing the composition and mobility of the population, the extent of economic and social differentiation, and the significant orientations of the Negro community have relevance to this interest in the number, size, and functions of voluntary associations. Before examining specific organizations, the significance of some of these features may be pointed out.

Exclusive of the churches, there were at the time of this study 23 active formal groups that reported approximately five hundred and fifty active memberships (see Table 11). In a population that is about 56 percent female and predominantly adult, with approximately 62 percent over 21 years of age, 54 percent of organization membership (exclusive of churches) is female and less than 10 percent under 21.

TABLE II. TYPES OF ACTIVE KENT ORGANIZATIONS AND NUMBERS
OF ACTIVE KENT MEMBERS, JULY 1949

	Members		
Organizations	Male	Female	Total
Church related and sponsored			
Helpful Ladies (A.M.E.Z.)	—	22	22
Excelsior Guild (M.E.)	—	18	18
Missionary Ladies (Baptist)	—	46	46
Betterment League (A.M.E.Z.)	10	—	10
Fraternal League (M.E.)	9	—	9
Fraternal League (Baptist)	11	—	11
Young Helpers (M.E.)	10	13	23
Fraternal and Welfare			
Elks	23	—	23
Masons (No. 1 Lodge)	17	—	17
Masons (No. 2 Lodge)	27	—	27
Eastern Star (No. 1 Lodge)	4	27	31
Eastern Star (No. 2 Lodge)	1	10	11
Carver Protective and Burial Society (No. 1)	13	45	58
Carver Protective and Burial Society (No. 2)	7	10	17
Fraternal Aid Society	6	4	10
Education and uplift			
Kent Colored Fair Association	5	6	11
Jackson Parent-Teachers Association	13	41	54
Political, protest and reform			
Kent NAACP	39	31	70
Fair Deal Democratic Club	5	4	9
Athletic and recreational			
Kent Black Sox Baseball Club	18	—	18
Progressive Four Quartet	6	—	6
Gospel Harmonies Quartet	5	—	5
Jackson School Athletic Association	23	20	43
Total	252	297	549

Further evidence that organizational continuity, recruitment, and leadership have been affected by the changes in the composition of the population that have occurred in relation to migration and aging comes from the comments of residents. Older residents point out that there were many more lodges and societies when they were younger—twenty-five or thirty years ago—but that most of them "broke up" or "went under." It is said that at one time "there was a society for practically everything you could think of." Many of these societies were mutual aid groups. Before the spread of formal insurance and in a setting where capital and credit were lacking, these groups had significant religious, economic, insurance, savings, real estate, investment, fraternal, and display functions. Those that survive still perform many of these functions, but they are not as dominant and universal a part of the picture as were the older groups.

Symbolical of these societies that "went under" and of their declining force in the community are the innumerable ramshackle and weather-beaten lodge halls that are to be found in Kent and surrounding area. At one time, the church, the schoolhouse, and the lodge hall were usually located together and were to some extent interdependent; they were the focal point of community activity and enterprise. In Kent proper there are two lodge halls that are in a state of near collapse; one was built by the now defunct local chapter of the Odd Fellows. There are now in the community less than six men who were active in this organization. As trustees of an organization that failed, they have deeded the dilapidated building to the Field's Street Church to which a number of the leaders of the lodge belonged. The other building was built by the Fraternal Aid Society, which formerly had a very large membership. The ten members who now belong to the organization are the beneficiaries of the money that comes from rentals of the hall and adjoining grounds to such groups as the fair association and the local baseball team.

The most frequent causes given for the collapse or decline of organizations that flourished at one time are: "the older folks died out," "so many folks moved away," "somebody messed with the money." This suggests several things, among them the failure or inability of the older group to insure continuity by recruitment of younger persons; this may have been due to shortsightedness or the relative decline in the number of younger eligibles because of migration and/or the birth rate. Leadership and recruitment in all areas have been affected by the preponderance of older people and the excess of females in the population. Organizations have not had much continuity; each adult generation tends to establish its own formal groupings. This generation of young adults appears to be weaker in this respect than the previous generation.

Some of the members of older families who are now in their late thirties and forties had social clubs and a tennis club when they were younger. They say marriage and migration spelled the decline of these. Succeeding age groups have not established any such organizations; today there are no social clubs in the community; the functions are performed by groups with nominally other purposes. And there is but one formal youth group—a church-related organization. Indicative is the fact that the regional headquarters of the Boy Scouts of America sought to have a boy scout troop organized locally during the course of this study. Interest was weak and diffused; the leadership to crystallize interest and the personnel to lead a troop was not found.

The facts show that the voluntary associations are essentially democratic in that most represent good cross-sections of the adult population. There are no formal groups composed exclusively of respectables or of their opposites, the nonrespectables. There is some design for exclusiveness and prestige on the part of groups like the Masons and their female auxiliary, the Eastern Stars, and the Helpful Ladies, a woman's club of the Mount Prospect church; but even in these groups,

the membership nearly runs the gamut of the status scale—
only the extreme nonrespectables are not represented.[12] All
other organizations tend to be as democratic as the church—
to which many of them are closely tied in terms of ritual or
sponsorship. Some measure of the missionary or uplift design
is present in most of the organizations; that is, there is expressed interest in improvement of the person and the group.
A leader of the local Elks pointed out, for example, that the
reason his organization took so many men in was because they
thought they "could do something with some of these fellows
who drink and carry on so, and don't know how to act."

Important orientations and values of the Negro society—
e.g., race and religion, among others—are reflected in organizational activity and tone. The interest in improvement of political and educational status of the Negro group is formally
represented in the newly-formed local branch of the NAACP
(organized in 1947), the Fair Deal Democratic Club (also
organized in 1947), and the reorganization of the Parent-
Teachers' Association. Aside from the fact that these two
new organizations have racial improvement and protest as
explicit functions, the other adult organizations in their formal
and informal activities show themselves to be sensitive to ethnic
status and reputation. As in the case of the Elks mentioned
above, each organization tends to exhibit some implicit or
explicit design for improvement or uplift regardless of its
primary or ostensible function. One of the indications is the
constant emphasis upon the values of racial cooperation or
organization which is usually combined with a general con-

12. Members of the Masons have complained to the investigator that "they
take in most anybody." One Mason pointed out that "members are not supposed to have more than one wife but I know at least three who do have."
A man who has served time in the penitentiary for homicide pointed out
that he was a member of the Elks but regretted that he could not "make
the Masons"; when asked why, he said that his jail record was the only thing
against him. The Helpful Ladies is the only one of the seven church-related
clubs which votes to accept new members. Members say that up until this
time, the voting has been a mere formality.

demnation of Negroes for not being organized. The remarks of the speakers at the anniversary meeting of one of the fraternal leagues are illustrative:

After praising the officers and members for their community spirit (planning a playground, providing a heating system for the Field's Street church, and a flush toilet for the parsonage), the speaker exhorted them to carry on and asked the community to give them adequate support. Decrying the community pattern of talk and no action, he stated that one of the troubles of the Negro group was its lack of disposition to develop and follow its own leaders: "For four hundred years we have been following the white man, and where has it got us? Nowhere!" He then told the following topical joke to illustrate his point: "A Negro was trying to round up some mules that had scattered, but with little success. A man told the Negro to mount the gray horse standing near and ride him; all the mules immediately followed the gray horse (the mules symbolized the Negroes; the gray horse, whites). The speaker that followed tried to reinforce the point about race unity and cooperation with another story: A Negro had won considerable fame for his adeptness at flicking flies off the backs of horses with his whip while driving a wagon. One day, a bee alighted on a horse's back; the Negro did not move. The boss (a white man) asked why he didn't use his whip to flick the bee off; the Negro answered: "No sir, they's organized!"

The August, 1946 "Journal" [13] of the Helpful Ladies contained this editorial:

In this present day, commonly called the Atomic Age, a very trying situation has developed among us: race prejudice. Whether white supremacy over the Negro was started by German agents as a form of propaganda to slow up national defense work and give Germany a chance at greater victories remains unsolved. The Negroes, however, are steadily and rapidly climbing, and equaliz-

13. This journal is a handwritten regular report read to members "containing the latest religious news, current and social events."

ing themselves with the white race in education, home environ-
ments, and war production. One of the greatest present day
scientists is Dr. George Washington Carver, a Negro man. There
are also colored educators, radio and movie stars. The Negro has
risen from degradation and is scaling the mountain peaks of heights
unknown.

Seven of the 23 organizations are direct affiliates or elabora-
tions of the organized churches, and the three protective and
burial aid societies were originally organized around church
groups. Those groups which are not directly affiliated with
the church tend to make regular and prominent use of religious symbols—prayer and sacred songs—in meetings and
ceremonies, and with the exception of the groups that are
devoted to athletic and recreational purposes, the core membership and the leadership tend to be the same as those of the
churches. Like the churches, the emphasis on money in these
voluntary associations is acute and constant; money-raising
is a prime function—whether explicitly stated or not—and
amounts raised are important measures of organizational success and pride.

If one were to use the classification of organizations presented in Table 12 as an indication of the strength of various
interests in causing the formation of other than church organizations, the ranking of interests would be: fraternal and
welfare; religion and Christian brotherhood; athletic and recreational; political, protest, and reform; and education and
uplift. However, the three single organizations with the largest
number of members are the NAACP, the Carver Protective
and Burial Society (No. 1), and the Jackson Parent-Teachers
Association. It must be stressed that these figures represent the
numbers of persons affiliated and not necessarily those who
participate regularly in the normal activities of the group—
as measured by attendance at regular meetings. For example,
whereas the NAACP has more members enrolled than any
other organization, relatively fewer members attend its regular

meetings than any other Kent organization.[14] The secretary
of the organization reports that since its founding locally,
he has never seen more than ten persons in attendance. The
investigator attended four of the regularly scheduled meetings
that were actually held during the study; the largest number
in attendance was six and the smallest, three. Although com-
pletely accurate data are not available, the investigator would
estimate, on a basis of attendance at meetings of the various
organizations and the estimates of officers and informants,
that a ranking of types of organizations by proportions of
members normally attending regular meetings would approximate the following: education and uplift,[15] church related,
fraternal and welfare, and political and protest.[16]

TABLE 12. MEMBERSHIP IN TYPES OF KENT ORGANIZATIONS

Type of Organization	Total Number	Total Membership	Percent Total Membership
Fraternal and welfare	8	194	35.3
Church related	7	139	25.3
Athletic and recreational	4	72	13.1
Political and protest	2	79	14.4
Education and uplift	2	65	11.9
Total	23	549	100.0

Three types of interests are not represented in the formal
listing of organizations by names and types: they are eco-

14. For a discussion of this organization and some of the reasons for the
small amount of regular, active participation, see pp. 276-280.
15. Due primarily to the interest in the newly reorganized Parent-Teachers
Association.
16. The athletic and recreational are left out of this ranking because the
school sponsored athletic association which is composed exclusively of students attending school contributes more than fifty percent of this category;
and the other groups do not have regular meetings in the same sense that
other listed organizations do.

nomic, social, and "cultural." This does not mean that these interests are not present or that they are necessarily weak in this society; actually, as pointed out earlier, the fair association, for example, tends to be in fact an economic association and each group embodies some economic (money-raising, saving, disbursement) function. And similarly, many of the groups have important social and "cultural" functions, notably the church-related men's and women's clubs. However, it is probable that the community's organizational activity and ideals of public behavior are still too church-oriented to permit the functioning of a card club, for example, at this time; and it is also probable that general reading habits and interests and book-purchasing are not sufficiently developed to support a specialized literary club, for example.[17]

We will examine now the specific organizations operating in the indicated major interest areas, and we will note the functions of these organizations and their effects on the community and the characteristics of leadership and membership.

The six adult associations that are associated with religious organizations other than formal church groups are actually sponsored by leaders of particular denominational groups. Although there is nothing in the rules of any of them excluding persons of other denominations—or even persons who are not members of any church—each tends to draw its membership from a particular church group; each is popularly identified with a church; and each usually assumes certain material obligations to that church, such as aid in furnishing the church building or financial contributions. The six adult groups are one-sex groups, an organization for males and an organization for females associated with each of the three churches: Field's

17. There is no local library or regular bookstore in the community to which Negroes have access. During the course of the study, the investigator found no Negro families who are subscribers to any of the national book clubs.

Street Methodist Episcopal: the Fraternal League and Excelsior Guild; Union Baptist: the Fraternal League and the Missionary Ladies; Mount Prospect African Methodist Episcopal Zion: the Betterment League and the Helpful Ladies.

The duplication of these groups and the basic similarity of their functions indicate inter-church rivalry and imitation. The women's clubs have been active in their present form since the 1930's, but the present men's clubs were organized within the four years prior to this study. The first of these men's clubs, the Fraternal League of the Field's Street Methodist Church, was organized in 1946 by a pastor of the church who left the community in 1947. In January 1949, the Mount Prospect men organized the Betterment League, and the Baptists organized their Fraternal League in May 1949. The first club organized enrolled 32 men from all denominations; it was projected by the leader as an all-community, nondenominational club which was to "do something for all the men—including the men who hang around the whisky stores and 'on the block' and to try to improve the community." Apparently the group disintegrated after the organizer left the community; today it consists of a small core of nine Methodist men. The point is that the expressed interest in improving the community is a feature of all of these groups—both the male and the female—but, in actual practice, the primary efforts seem to be directed toward raising money in order that a contribution might be made to the church. And the interest in improvement is the interest of rivals because no apparent efforts are made to cooperate or pool forces for a community-wide objective. The men's clubs appear to have developed no formats or programs of their own; rather they have imitated the club rituals and public activity of the women's organizations.

The groups vary as to the extent of their activity, but the general pattern is the same. Some of the differences in the extent of activity among the clubs may be related to the leadership and membership characteristics of the respective groups.

The clubs are church-sponsored and to some extent reflect church rivalries; they draw their memberships from respective church populations, and thus differences among them are related to differences in membership and spirit among the church congregations which have already been described. The Mount Prospect Helpful Ladies appear to be the most active of the women's groups and the Mount Prospect Betterment League is similarly the most active of the recently-organized men's clubs. The male and female groups associated with the Baptist church are least active in terms of public programs and contributions to the church and community.

The Helpful Ladies consist of 22 young and middle-aged women; there are no young single women in this club. One of the members operates a store; all of the others work in domestic service with the exception of two housewives—the pastor's wife and the wife of the white school janitor. Nine of the 22 live in what are considered "nice houses." The officers and members of this club furnish a number of the officers and leading members of other organizations in the community; for example, the president is the presiding officer of one of the Eastern Star lodges, and the secretary is president of the Parent-Teachers Association.

The men's counterpart of the Helpful Ladies, the Betterment League, consists of 10 married men; eight of the 10 men have wives who are members of the Helpful Ladies, and the other two men have daughters who are members. The occupations represented are as follows: tavern-store operator (the president), janitor of school, chauffeur-handyman, truck driver, mill fireman (4), bank porter, minister. These are all considered respectable and steady working people. The president of the men's group, a tavern operator, is also business manager of the local baseball team; the secretary, a truck driver, is secretary of one of the Masonic groups; and another member is the second highest officer in the Elks.

The Excelsior Guild (Field's Street Methodist) consists of

18 young and middle-aged women, all of whom are married. With one exception, they are looked upon as respectable. Included in this group are six teachers—four of them active now in the rural areas; the other two retired from teaching after marriage. The remainder are full or part-time domestics with the exception of four housewives (including the two retired teachers). Nine of the 18 maintain what are termed "nice houses." The president of this group is a part-time domestic servant who is the mother of six children; although active in the Parent-Teachers Association and the Methodist Church, she has no other organizational affiliations.

The Field's Street Betterment League consists of nine active members whose ages range from about thirty to seventy; two are unmarried. Three of the members have "old-family" status but are considered personally nonrespectable because of chronic drunkenness and irresponsibility. Among the occupations represented in the group: embalmer, unemployed mill worker and part-time barber and farmer, carpenter, railroad laborer and part-time barber, drugstore porter, painter, bricklayer, part-time construction helper, and mill laborer. Three of the group—the unemployed mill worker, the part-time construction helper, and the drugstore porter—have wives who are members of the sister-club, the Excelsior Guild. Only two members have "nice houses." The president of this group, the railroad laborer and part-time barber is an officer in one of the Masonic groups; the treasurer is head of the Elks.

The Missionary Ladies group is composed of 46 Baptist women, not all of whom are carried on the local church rolls as active members. This group has a larger number of older women and pensioners than either of the other women's groups; 11 are widows and four are recipients of pensions. Four of the group are considered nonrespectables in the general community. Three live in "nice houses." Six of these women are housewives; the remainder, with the exception of one hairdresser (the president) are in domestic serv-

ice. The president and the secretary are among the youngest
persons in the group, and they are among the five persons
who are high school graduates. The officers and members
of this group tend to be primarily active in church affairs
and a large percentage of them belong to the two protective
and burial societies.

The Baptists' Fraternal League was the last of the groups
to be organized. It consists of 11 members who are with one
exception either officers in the church or part-time ministers;
with two exceptions, they are men who are over forty years
of age. Seven deacons and three ministers—two of them part-
time—are represented. The occupations of the members:
farmers and farm tenants (3), mill laborers (4), ministers (3),
and the janitor of the Negro school. One of the younger mill
workers—and the youngest deacon in the church—is the president; he is also the second officer in the more recently organized of the two Masonic groups. Most of the members are
active primarily in church affairs.

In the case of each of the clubs described in this category,
such features as meeting time, order of business and activities,
and financing tend to be the same. Meetings are scheduled
every two weeks in members' homes in round-robin fashion.
"Having the club" is a significant event for the host or hostess,
involving as it does some preparation and expenditure for food.
The periodic entertainment of the clubs provides for many
the chief opportunity for social hospitality and display. It is
an important social event for host and hostess with mild competitive features and accompanying anxieties and satisfactions.
Elements common to all meetings: the formal religious tone
and the ritual of prayers, religious songs, and individual Bible
verses prior to the business session; the formal program which
usually features a discussion of a religious topic led by a member followed by some types of entertainment; the collection
of twenty-five cents in dues from each member or person present; and the decided emphasis upon money matters.

These are nominal religious groups involving the active participation of about one in every six adults—mainly, but by no means exclusively, of respectable status—which have important social functions for participating members insofar as they provide opportunities for fraternizing and enhancing prestige or status by display and association with a group engaged in good works and money-raising. The separateness and rivalry of the groups is enhanced by denominational loyalty which prevents any of them from becoming effective on a community-wide basis or more explicitly secular in outlook.

The eight active fraternal and welfare groups may be divided into two types: the local lodges of national fraternal orders—the Elks, the Masons, and the Eastern Stars; and local burial societies. The Elks, the Masons, and the Eastern Stars are secret orders to which members are elected, usually by secret ballot; they have mystical rituals, ceremonies, pins, handshakes, ceremonial regalia, and idealistic codes of conduct and mutual aid. The pride in being a member of one of these groups—especially the Masons and the Eastern Stars—appears to be related to affiliation with strong and prestige-laden national groups,[18] the participation in a secret and presumably exclusive brotherhood, the opportunity for recognition and display associated with public ceremonies—the annual sermon, funerals, etc.—which demand the wearing of regalia and the enacting of mystical rites. These are probably the only organizations, with the possible exception of the Helpful Ladies, to which persons actively aspire and with reference to which the investigator has heard a person express regret at his inability to "make it."

To be a member of the Masons or the Eastern Stars is in general a desirable goal that has actually been achieved by

18. For example, the Negro Elks have over a half-million members and combined assets of over sixty million dollars. Cf. Frazier, *op. cit.*, pp. 367-386 for a description of the general characteristics and functions of Negro mutual aid and fraternal organizations.

about eighty-five adults out of approximately seven hundred; approximately eighty of these are considered active and financial members. The status of Elk is apparently more easily attained; officers estimate that there are approximately one hundred males in the community who have been affiliated at some time with the Elks. They list 23 men who are now active and in good standing. The obligations and expectations of fraternal status are taken seriously by active members. One hears such designations or explanations as "He's a Mason," implying distinctive status and behavioral standards. Members are supposed to "look out for each other" in terms of mutual aid and protection and to maintain a high-level ethical relationship in dealings with each other. There is recognition of this expectation even when behavior is contrary. An example of the recognition of the code is seen in the following incident:

Two men, one a Mason, took two sisters who were daughters of a Mason out on a drinking party. When they brought the girls back home the father cursed the group and threatened the men with violence until he saw that one of the men was his Masonic brother. This man had purposely made himself conspicuous, thinking that the fact that he and the father were Masonic brothers would give him some protection and ease the situation. The father indicated later that he was confused: the fact that his Masonic brother was in the car puzzled him; he couldn't figure out whether he was protecting his daughters as Masonic brothers had vowed to do, or whether he was being unbrotherly.

To be "called before the brothers" has some social control functions. Unbrotherly (or unsisterly) conduct, criminal activity, or immorality may bring fines, censure, or expulsion. During the course of this investigation, the Elks appeared to be more prone to "have a meeting on a brother" than the other groups, or at least it was easier to obtain knowledge of such proceedings in the case of this group. A case that involved considerable talk and wrangling within the Elks group and among "the boys on the block" involved the aftermath of a hunting accident to one of its members. Although the Elks lodge did nothing official to aid the unfortunate member, one member sought to raise money for him by soliciting whites and Negroes in the community who knew the wounded person. The person who did the soliciting was later charged with withholding some of the money collected. The matter was brought up in an Elks' meeting and the member was placed "on trial." After several weeks of wrangling, the matter was dropped without a decision. The important feature was the concern which the accused person showed and his attempt to muster support and testimony from Negroes and whites (including the Chief of Police, who was one of the persons who had contributed) in order to prevent formal censure or ostracism.

Nominal identification and expectation extend across race lines, particularly in the case of the Negro Masons; some differential treatment or recognition by white Masons is expected on the basis of parallel status. One example is seen in the reason given by a Negro Mason as to why the Negro, Jack Poe, who was beaten by a white mob, was not killed: "He was a Mason; one of the men in that crowd was a Mason and he wouldn't let them hurt him any more. If it hadn't been for that, they would have killed him."

The two chapters of the Masonic order and the two chapters of the Eastern Star order are the results of personal rivalries among some of the male leaders. The "other lodges" as they are termed by the members of the older groups were established by Reverend Stewart in protest against what he calls the inactivity and exclusiveness of the older group. The members of the older group say that he did it for reasons of personal gain and power; they accuse him of duplicity and unscrupulousness and point to other things he has done that

are supposed to indicate his character.[19] Reverend Stewart is
said to have adopted the very unusual stratagem of having his
lodge established by a white lodge of Master Masons because
the Negro Master Lodge would not permit duplication. He
is chief officer of the new Masonic group, and his son, the
secretary. Some members of the older group of Masons make
invidious comparisons between the groups, pointing out in the
main that the younger group was not discriminating in its
membership.

The older Masonic group appears to have in its membership more men who are older and more established in the
community by virtue of age, longer residence, and the families they have raised. It includes the following occupations:
the principal of the school, three ministers, a tavern-store operator, a filling station operator, an auto mechanic, two farmers,
a carpenter, two truck drivers, three mill workers, a barbershop porter, and a numbers writer. Nine of these men are affiliated with the African Methodist Episcopal Zion denomination, five with the Methodist Episcopal, and three with the
Baptists. Six of the group are on the "nice house" list. The
newer Masonic group has as its nucleus eight persons whose

19. Many residents deride and view with suspicion his attempt to build
a church and establish a Presbyterian congregation among the Negroes of
Kent. During the early part of this century there was a small Presbyterian
church which existed in connection with a private school for Negro children supported by white and Negro Presbyterians. With the erection of a
public school, the school was abandoned and the congregation declined to
the vanishing point. Reverend Stewart's father was the pastor of the church
and a teacher in the school. The present Reverend Stewart preached and
taught in several southern states before returning to Kent; he teaches in
one of the rural schools of the country, and his wife and son teach in the
local school. He says his prime ambition is to revive the Presbyterian church;
to that end he has solicited funds for many years. It is said that at one time,
the local white Presbyterians supported him and contributed funds until he
was unable to give a proper accounting. The only members of the church
are his family and the family of a part-time electrician who is considered
an eccentric. Reverend Stewart has succeeded in erecting the shell of a cinder
block building in which he has installed a dozen old benches, a used hand
organ, and a pulpit. He is frequently seen on Saturdays soliciting dimes on
the main street and in front of taverns.

regular employment is in the mills; with the exception of the fact that this group has but one minister,[20] the distribution of occupations is about the same. This group contains no members who are affiliated or identified with the Methodist church; there are six Baptists, and two Presbyterians; the rest are A.M.E.Z. affiliates. Only two persons of this group are on the "nice house" list.

The Masons and their affiliates, the Eastern Stars, purport to be the most selective organizations in the community; a comparison of their memberships with those of other groups, the Elks, for example, indicates a greater emphasis upon persons of some stability as represented by steady jobs and upon persons with good community reputations. The temporary effect of the split in leadership and the organization of duplicate groups was to heighten general interest and activity in the fraternal area: informants point out that the old groups had become relatively inactive; they made no attempt to recruit new members; meetings were poorly attended; and the impact on the community was small.

The Elks are less selective in membership; the leaders are not certain as to the number of persons now in the community who have been initiated into the order;[21] they point out that the policy has been to take in all who want to come in with the feeling that the group can do something for them. In design, at least, the Elks represent a close approach to an adult male organization with a community-wide base; in actual practice, they appear to be a loosely-integrated group without a program and strong leadership. Some of the officers and members say that what they need is an Elks Home or

20. Each of the organizations is headed by a minister who does not have a local church.

21. The investigator was unable to get an accurate roster because the records of all except the current year could not be found. An officer indicated that he had reported 23 members in good standing to the national office, pointing out that this was but a small percentage of "all the men who are Elks in this town."

club room—"some place nice for the men to go"—and with
that enthusiasm and participation would increase. In general,
the feeling among males seems to be that it is a good thing
to be an Elk and that every man, whether he is on the active
roster or not, is privy to the secrets and symbolism of the
brotherhood. There is also a feeling that it is good to be an
Elk because when one goes to other towns or cities, one can
always depend on brother Elks for hospitality and aid. The
very fact that the Elks are so democratic in their membership
policy probably mitigates some against real unity and a strong
program. The cleavage between respectables and nonrespectables that characterizes the community at large has some
force in the organization: for example, Elks' affairs—meetings
and parties—are apt to be rather lively affairs marked by
considerable drinking and random talk; the respectable members are prone to be privately critical of this behavior, and
some members no longer attend Elks meetings or affairs because of this. One measure of the state of the organization is
the fact that during the current year the group did not carry
out two of its usual activities: the annual sermon and the pres-
entation of Christmas packages to the aged and poor.

The burial aid groups tend to be tied in closely with the
churches and religious activities. Local meetings are held in
the churches; the quarterly gatherings are colored by the "old
time" religious emphasis. These are quasi-insurance groups
and although regular meetings of the "societies" are held, they
are poorly attended and fraternal activities are at a minimum:
customarily, they are dues collecting occasions on which the
officers accept and record dues, and the members bring—or
send—their dues and depart.

The two major local groups belong to a loose two-county
association of such groups. There are nearly fifty of these societies in Kent and the adjoining county with local memberships ranging from fifty to one hundred and twenty-five
persons. Their greatest strength is among rural people. Local

dues are twenty-five cents per person per month and these remain in the local treasury. Each local group sends a representative to the quarterly meeting where the size of the death benefit is determined and paid in cash to designated heirs. This is an all-day meeting usually held at a rural church and is featured by prayers, songs, sermons, exchanges of greetings, and the eating on outdoor tables of the food brought in baskets by members. This is the only occasion on which the elected officers, aside from the general secretary, perform official duties—the receipt of assessments, the calculation of amounts to be paid, and the disbursement of benefits.

The system works like this: Each group "represents" with a representation of $4.50 plus a death tax; this death tax is based upon the total number of persons who died during the quarter and is set at ten cents for each death for each person in good standing. For example, if a society had ten members, and five persons in the entire association had died during the quarter, this group would "represent" with a total of $9.50; this would go into a common fund, the net of which would be shared equally among the heirs of the five deceased members. As the representative of each group reports, he is cheered; there is pride and prestige involved in making a large "representation." At the summer quarterly meeting of 1949 which was held in a small rural church 14 miles from Kent, seven persons—two from Kent—were reported to have died during the preceding three months; the tax for each member of each participating society was seventy cents. After the officers had calculated expenses, they announced to the anxiously awaiting group that each of the seven beneficiaries would receive $185.30.

Membership in the burial societies is interdenominational, but approximately eighty percent of the members are Baptists; the rest are affiliated with the African Methodist Episcopal Zion Church with the exception of one Methodist—the lady who owns the funeral establishment. The chief officer of one group is a mill fireman, an A.M.E.Z., and the chief officer of the other is the funeral director, a Methodist. It is difficult to describe the members of these groups in terms of status, except to say that they are predominantly people of the middle and elderly age brackets and that very few persons of relatively high income and relatively high education are enrolled. In the great majority of cases adult members of family groups are enrolled together. The burial society is characteristically stronger in rural areas, and it is probably true that many of the members of these groups are persons who retain significant kinship and religious ties with rural areas and a preference for certain features of rural ways.

There are two organizations among Kent Negroes that are expressly devoted to group or race advance. In an earlier section,[22] we have indicated that these organizations—the Fair Deal Democratic Club and the National Association for the Advancement of Colored People (NAACP)—are local links with national and state organizations concerned with political activity, protest, and improvement of the Negro's status. Despite the purposes and goals of these groups, it is the investigator's feeling (based upon participant-observation and direct questioning) that these groups and their programs loom smaller in the conversations and thoughts of Kent Negroes than do the church-related and fraternal groups. However, this is no true measure of the importance of the organizations or of their influence on behavior and expectations. Both groups have been organized since World War II and the Fair Deal Democratic Club, in particular, has been most important as a rallying point during an emergency or crisis period—such as the period just prior to the Negro's re-entrance into political activity.[23] And although the local NAACP has never actually

22. See Chapter 8.
23. Ibid.

acted with respect to a local issue or a crisis, it does have the potential; and it does represent symbolic, if not active, identification with a powerful national group.

The organization of the Fair Deal Democratic Club was the result of cooperation between local church leaders and leaders of politically conscious Negroes in the capital of the state. Its chief functions were the raising of funds for the state organization and the mobilizing and educating of local Negro voters prior to the elections of 1948. The nucleus of the organization consists of less than a dozen older men and women, mainly from the African Methodist Episcopal Zion and Baptist churches. Their chief instruments have been the mass meeting and fund soliciting, and it is only in these ways that the broad participation of approximately one hundred and fifty persons has been obtained for specific and limited projects. Its power stemmed from its ability to obtain the limited cooperation on these specific projects of persons in the community who were otherwise not associated with the group; for example, although the influential Thorpe and Roberts families took no active part in the forming of the organization or the setting of policy, they cooperated in encouraging and educating the Negro voters and by taking part in public meetings where strategy was discussed. The significance of the church is seen in this organization by the following facts: the leaders and most active members of the group are either ministers or church officers; churches were used for purposes of circulating information and instructions; and the proceedings of the one business meeting held during the year the investigator was in the community were colored by the religious emphasis and ideology. These features, as well as the provisional character of the organization, are demonstrated in the following description of a meeting held in the spring of 1949; this was the first meeting called since the primary elections of the summer of 1948.

Reverend Sampson presided and keynoted the discussion. Five men and four women were in attendance; all of these persons are middle-aged or older. The group consisted of three ministers, two of them part-time; a farmer; a mill fireman; the wives of the farmer and one of the ministers; the daughter of one of the ministers; and a widowed domestic servant. Each of the men who is not a minister is a deacon or trustee of his church. Five members of this group are Baptists and four are African Methodist Episcopal Zion affiliates.

Reverend Sampson pointed out that since favorable federal court decisions had made Negroes in the state eligible for the regular Democratic Party of the state, there was some question as to whether there was any good reason for the group continuing under its present name as an affiliate of the Progressive Democratic Party (the Negro organization). He said, however, that the Negro's political fight was not over and that an organization such as theirs had watch-dog functions to serve; and then, too, it was probable that more calls would be coming for financial aid. He expressed disappointment at the poor attendance and decried the general apathy of Negroes.

The daughter of one of the ministers present reported on the proceedings of the state convention of the Progressive Democratic Party; she informed the group that state leaders suggested that the local groups retain their organizations. A collection of five dollars was taken to reimburse the delegate for the expenses of her trip to the state capitol. The report was followed by statements of support and determination from the men present; and the group decided to continue and to become more active. Reverend Sampson took the floor again and continued his references to the backwardness, the lack of courage, and the absence of cooperation among Negroes. With reference to the Ku Klux Klan, he asked: "Why be afraid of a white mask? There are other kinds of masks. What's going to stop *you* from putting on a black mask? ... If a few Negroes were to put on some black masks, there wouldn't be so many white masks." On lynching, he said, "What we need is some white folks to get lynched. I'm not advocating lynching, but if some white folks were to get lynched,

I'd bet you they would pass the law and put a stop to it." He suggested that in addition to developing courage, the organization would have to lead the fight on some of the evils "right on our own doorsteps": "Juke box" joints, whisky drinking, cursing, the immorality of youth, and the lack of attendance at Sunday School. These remarks were applauded and echoed with "Amens!" The members voted to assess themselves one dollar each in order to make a treasury; this amount was to be paid at the next meeting. After prayer, the meeting adjourned without setting a time or place for the next meeting.

The features that are significant about the Fair Deal Democratic Club are: it is the militant and action-oriented organization in the local community; its leader, aside from the fact that he is a minister, is not a long-time resident of the community; it has a provisional character, inasmuch as it is dependent upon an issue or a crisis to mobilize persons and support; and it probably is successful to the extent that it—as a provisional organization—seeks to do things which the local chapter of NAACP, with its leader a long-time resident of the community and with a larger dues paying membership, does not consider expedient.

One measure of the relatively small extent to which the program and activities of the local NAACP are a preoccupation or active interest of local Negroes is the fact that the investigator had been a participant observer in the community three months before he heard a reference to the local chapter or any indications of its existence. The secretary-treasurer, in explaining his departure to attend one of the scheduled meetings, said:

There's not much point in my going up there. Nobody hardly ever comes. There'll just be the three of us. Mr. Sam Roberts, Reverend Jennings, and I will just sit around the stove and talk and then leave. And that happens just about every month. These folks ain't interested in the NAACP; a lot of them's too scared.

The records of the organization indicate that between 1947 and 1949, a total of 137 different individuals paid the membership fee for the local organization; the actual dues-paying membership for any one year has been less: for the year 1948-49, there were 70 card-carrying members. Most of these memberships have been solicited and the dues are collected by one of the three officers, Sam Roberts, an influential farmer and property-holder; Reverend Jennings, a part-time minister; and Mr. Rose, the principal of the Negro school. Mr. Rose has been secretary-treasurer since the local unit was established; he says that no one else in the community wants the position because it would mean that that person's name would appear on all financial transactions, such as checks and money orders, thus revealing him to the white community. The principal says that a member of the school board protested his affiliation with the group when it was first founded and that he refused to discontinue it; he reports nothing happened or was said after this protest.

The membership, that is those who have paid dues, is a cross-section of the adult Negro population, heavily weighted with the people who are active in churches and other organizations in the community, and it is predominantly, although not exclusively, a group of respectables. Officers comment that most members do not hesitate to pay—or promise to pay—membership dues but that they are reluctant to have whites know that they are members or that they take an active part in the organization. Some members refuse to accept receipts for dues paid, some discard membership cards, and the vast majority refuse to wear membership buttons. There are but two Negroes who wear their membership buttons publicly; they are Sam Warren, an eccentric blacksmith who has served time in the penitentiary for homicide and who, during the course of this study, shot his wife; and Charlie Adams, a mill worker, of whom it is said, "He just doesn't give a good damn." Adams wears his pin on his hat.

The NAACP has no effective program locally; it is looked upon with gratefulness and pride as an external uplift organization that is doing things for the race; it is not looked upon now as an instrument for local pressure and improvement. The organization comes to be in fact a dues collecting organization which permits less than ten percent of the local Negro population to identify themselves in a practical and near-anonymous way with a militant national organization in a race-conscious fashion. The Kent Negro community has no tradition of organized and consistent pressure to improve status and to change local conditions, nor does it have a local leader [24] whose actions and program are considered consistently militant. The Negro in Kent has customarily depended upon his own ingenuity, favorable patronage relationships, and indirect methods to achieve some of the things that are important to him. Of course, there is general emphasis upon the values of organization. This is combined with a condemnation of the Negro group for not being organized, but this vague citing of a need for organization to promote collective ends is rarely defined in specific terms. The Parent-Teachers Association which was revived to effect improvement in the school and to secure accreditation for the school [25] and the Fair Deal Democratic Club when it had the specific end of getting Negroes to register to vote in the primary represent exceptions.

The two organizations in the community with explicit or presumed educational functions are the Parent-Teachers Association and the Kent Colored Fair Association. Of these two, the Parent-Teachers Association, which was described

24. Reverend Sampson is considered an outsider by the native Kentian. At any rate, he is a newcomer who in the normal course of events will stay in Kent only a few years anyway. After the completion of this study, Reverend Sampson was transferred by his bishop from the local church to a church in a community south of Kent.

25. This group and its membership have been described in the section on education. See pp. 162-164.

earlier, is the only one which has a broad community base and devotes itself seriously to community uplift or enlightenment. The Fair Association, which has some nominal educational functions, consists of 11 persons led by Sam Roberts; it is a stock company and all the shares are owned by six men and five women. The women are the heirs or relatives of deceased members. Informants say that control is maintained by this tightly knit group of old men, who are farmers or landowners, and the widows by refusal to sell shares to outsiders. When a member dies and leaves available shares, they are usually bought up by the inside group or sold to some carefully selected person. It is commonly understood that the group will sell no shares to any members of the Thorpe family; this is interpreted as due to both jealousy and fear of this prominent family group. The association makes its money from the annual fair which is usually held in the second week in October.

The two features of the fair are the exhibits and the carnival; the latter overshadows the former. The financial success of the enterprise depends upon the tie-in between the association, the traveling carnival, and the local police. The fair association furnishes the carnival grounds, has the right to charge admission (fifty cents in 1948), and gets an agreed upon percentage of the receipts of the carnival features and concessions. The police department furnishes added policemen and permits open gambling and risqué features. The fair officials are tight-lipped about financial arrangements and profits. However, the delicate balance among the gain-seeking agents involved is seen in the remark of the president that the white folks had seen them making a little money and were trying to "move in on them": the police had asked for $200.00 for policing the 1948 fair and threatened to furnish no future protection if it were not paid. In previous years the officials had tipped each of the officers ten dollars. The president felt that the police officers had seen the large sums of money coming in at the gate and sought a larger cut.

The exhibitional and educational aspect of the fair is secondary and according to informants it has diminished in importance and quality every year. The exhibits are placed in an old two-story unpainted lodge hall that is opened up annually for this event. The second floor is given over to exhibits of needlecraft, handicraft, and cookery, and the first floor has space for agricultural products. No livestock is exhibited. The chief exhibits were those of the rival church clubs. The agricultural exhibits consisted of two hams, some corn, and a few melons and pumpkins. Evidence that interest in exhibiting baked and canned products has waned is seen in the fact that several women when asked why they had not put items on exhibit said in effect that they just hadn't gotten around to exhibiting anything this year. This year judging of the exhibits was scheduled for 11 o'clock one morning but the judges did not appear until one o'clock in the afternoon. The only persons on hand were the officials and the booth tenders from the various churches, a group of less than twenty-five persons.

There are no recreational organizations among the Negroes of Kent that involve the active participation of all segments of the population, nor are there several separate organizations devoted to the interests or needs of different categories of the population. The two groups with explicit recreational functions are the Jackson School Athletic Association which is composed of students whose main function is to help raise money to outfit the athletic teams, and the Kent Black Sox, a semi-professional baseball team. The gospel quartets have been included in this group because singing is a hobby-like activity for the participants and they are responded to as forms of entertainment as well as worship.

The baseball club is a loosely-organized group of about twenty males; scheduling and business affairs are supervised by a non-playing manager (a tavern operator) and a treasurer (a bank porter). The only requisites for membership and a share in the income are the ability and the willingness to play baseball. Actually, there are not enough Kent men to field a competent team and the group hires four key men from Stone Valley each time it plays a game. Traditionally, Kent has had superior baseball teams; older men frequently reminisce about their playing days and the successes of former teams against teams from other parts of the state. This, plus the fact that practically every adult male has played baseball at some time or another, means that there is widespread interest in the team. The team has been a community enterprise in a real sense: its activities are followed by most of the Negro community and many whites; much of the equipment is donated by Negroes and "good white friends," mainly local merchants. One of the primary functions of the manager is to solicit local supporters and contributors. The intense interest in the game and the identification with the local team mean that the boosters of a winning team are quickly transformed into highly vocal critics and second-guessers of a losing team. The current team is a team which is said to have the poorest record of any team in recent years; its poor record is blamed in part on the fact that the star pitcher deserted his family to go to New York in the middle of the season.

The two gospel singing quartets are specialty groups that have religious, recreational, and economic functions. They sing in a heavily stylized fashion gospel hymns and topical sacred songs. The quartet-singing contest is a popular entertainment form and a minor source of income to the participants. Some of the groups go far to protect their records as singers of sacred songs. For example, a gospel singing group cannot have it known publicly that it can or will sing blues. However, quartets are looked upon by some of the more educated and sophisticated persons as caricatures of the "old-time" religious forms and, consequently, they are frowned upon by some church goers and ministers. The groups tend to emphasize showmanship and audience appeal and some critics accuse them of violating good taste. The local quartets get most of their songs from published sources, records, or radio broadcasts by similar groups. Basic arrangements tend to follow the same pattern: a member of one group pointed out that "the trick comes when we puts in the rhythm." Like baseball, the form and the activity tend to be familiar to most male youths, particularly those with a recent rural background. It is another means by which recognition is obtained for a few males.

On the whole, a significant amount of the behavior of Kent Negroes is not directly controlled or channelized by voluntary associations other than churches. The evidence for this conclusion is of two types: (1) the relatively small and limited range of organizational types and functions; the absence of clear-cut programs and effective leadership in many instances; and the small amount of active participation in some of the largest organizations; and (2) the figures indicating that only about one-third of the total population are active members of organizations: an analysis of duplicate memberships shows that 334 persons—275 of them adults—hold the 549 memberships tabulated; more than one-half of the adults have no active organizational ties; about one in three is active in one organization; about one in ten in two organizations; and about one in thirteen in three or more organizations.

PART THREE

INTEGRATION OF THE SUBCULTURE

INASMUCH as the elements of the Negro culture of Kent tend to "stick together" and fulfill larger needs related to survival and participation in this setting, they constitute a system. Ruth Benedict pointed out that

A culture, like an individual, is a more or less consistent pattern of thought and action. Within each culture there comes into being characteristic purposes not necessarily shared by other types of society. In obedience to these purposes, each people further and further consolidates its experience, and in proportion to the urgency of these drives the heterogeneous items of behavior take more and more congruous shape. Taken up by the well-integrated culture, the most ill-assorted acts become characteristic of its peculiar goals, often by the most unlikely metamorphoses. The form that these acts take we can understand only by understanding first the emotional and intellectual mainsprings of that society.[1]

Although there has probably never been a culture in which "all the social entities are nicely balanced with each other and the various unit patterns, complexes, institutions, and orientations 'gear into' each other smoothly and without friction or maladjustments," [2] there is in each cultural system "a strain toward consistency." In the organization of culture we find an indication of the degree of consensus in a society and possibly the most significant clues to the personality of its members. In addition to achieving internal integration, the customs of a society must achieve some balance with external, impinging ways.

1. Benedict, *Patterns of Culture*, p. 42.
2. Gillin, *The Ways of Man*, p. 498.

Consistency and Coordination of Ways

CHAPTER 11 — IT HAS BEEN indicated that the most crucial components of the cultural situation for the Negro of Kent are the "foreign" values of white Kent: the race-ridden character of life in the Negro community suggests that action and mental patterns are largely colored by the racial status of its members. The Negro society is contained, as it were, by law, custom, and the more or less imminent threat of force and violence; much of Negro culture consists of the adaptation to a pattern of containment or restriction. Following Benedict, the questions here are: To what extent are experiences consolidated (organized)? And to what extent do heterogeneous items of behavior take on congruous shape?

INTERNAL ORGANIZATION AND CONSISTENCY

IT IS argued here that the variation in this subculture is, in the main, one of emphasis and internal organization. Item by item, the significant values and goals explicit and implicit in the Kent Negro society are essentially accepted values of American culture: survival and getting along; opportunity and equality before the law; patience; religious salvation; self-expression and inviolability of the ego; friendliness and courtesy; property and "quick money." The greater emphasis and meaning given some of these, such as getting along (survival), religious salvation, and inviolability of the ego, stem from the realities of the local situation; they are adaptive in a real sense. Querulousness and the marked disposition to violence in some quarters suggest the fact that the culture does not provide easy or conventional means of attaining major ends. The impact of the dominant culture is such that it tends to make the achievement of conventional goals more difficult for the Negro. From one point of view, Negro culture is essentially warped or distorted; it makes for the rise and persistence of habits and orientations that are superficially inconsistent with value objectives; it makes for the substitution of less direct or conventional channels to achieve goals and possibly, in some instances, the substitution of new goals. The propositions advanced by John and Jean Arsenian are suggestive here:

... where a culture's paths make for difficult tension reduction the culture is tough.[1]

There is no simple way to demonstrate it, but for tough cultures with their tension-productive and tension-sustaining features, abortive and disorganized outlets for tension seem indicated.[2]

The major point at which local Negro ways show a lack of integration internally is where the habits and life-views of the respectable and nonrespectable categories clash. The respectable category holds the behavior of the nonrespectable in disdain and looks upon it with some shame and bitterness. Ostensibly, the behavior of the nonrespectable, with its emphasis upon querulousness and public self-indulgence and its gaucheries of language and manners, is not consistent with a basic desire for participation, opportunity, equality, and progress that has wide circulation. Among persons in both cate-

1. John Arsenian and Jean M. Arsenian, "Tough and Easy Cultures: A Conceptual Analysis," *Psychiatry*, XI (November 1948), 379.
2. *Ibid.*, p. 383.

gories, the things that are ultimately meaningful—respect for the ego and self-expression—are the same, but the paths chosen are different.

There is inconsistency between the idealized worth of cooperation and organization and the emphasis placed upon "going to the white man" individually and informally. High group morale is a desired goal, but it is inconsistent with the patterned sensitivity, "touchiness," and self-criticism. "Getting together" is a secular myth that obtains its force by contrast with the real situation. A joke that has had some circulation is a sardonic commentary:

God had instituted a test for those who were seeking admission to heaven: each person had to ask God a question He could not answer before getting in. Several whites tried to stump God with difficult questions but failed. A Negro man approached, and with some boredom God asked what his question was. The Negro asked: "When will Negroes get together?" Without hesitation, God said, "Come right on in, son!"

It is clear that the apparent inconsistency between religious expression and certain aspects of public behavior is not an inconsistency at all: religion has a kind of magical and analgesic function, and, as such, it is complementary to the harsher features of the culture. However, in the church association itself there are indications of inconsistency and disintegration. Prominent is the clash between the values involved in the Christian message and the avid interest in raising money.

Attitudes toward law are an important phase of the Negro culture. The general attitude combines respect, fear, bitterness, and resignation; this attitude may seem to run counter to a high incidence of law breaking. (In the respectable category there is an exaggerated avoidance of involvement or contact.) But, as has been pointed out, in the nonrespectable category, technical lawlessness involves something more than a mere lack of respect for the law: it involves the acceptance of—

and the adjustment to—a hazard or risk that is accepted as a part of the chosen (or imposed) way of life.

Again, all evidence points to a genuine respect for human life and an expressed belief that murder is hardly ever justified. This is true in the face of a heavy incidence of aggressive and violent gestures. The paradox is that although the rate of violence tends to be high, life is really not cheap; rather, a high premium is placed on personal pride. In cases of violence, this latter tends to be ascendant: the strong disposition not to be taken advantage of (this may reflect the turning of aggression against whites, because of the pervasive feeling of being taken advantage of by them, into the ingroup) and the need to meet any challenge to the ego or pride. There is present, of course, a pattern or tradition of violent behavior that becomes activated when the proper cues appear. This pattern of behavior is strengthened by the fact that the law in practice shows a certain tolerance or indifference to Negro intra-group conflict. For example, the "standard price" for "cuttings" is $75.00;[3] for some this is not too great a price to pay for their conceptions of self-respect and release of aggression. These patterns then tend to "gear into" or mesh with each other and other phases of the culture.

It is apparent that many patterns and institutions in the Negro community have a pragmatic, even makeshift quality; often logically inconsistent and unconventional, they tend to work or are made to work. This was seen in the case of the family. It is true to a large extent of the school and of all public activities affecting the Negro community where effective control is lacking and formal institutions and institutional agents are not present. Illustrative of the latter was the manner in which the polio benefit drive was organized and led in the Negro community. In the white community, campaign machinery and leadership were ready-made within the Chamber

3. It was recently raised to this figure, as the Chief of Police put it, "to stop some of this cutting that's been going on around here."

of Commerce and Merchants' Association. Although there were undoubtedly interest and "need" in the Negro community, initiative to the point of mobilizing could not, in the nature of the controls and sponsorship, be taken by Negroes. To make the activity community-wide it was necessary that Negroes participate or be serviced; special *ad hoc* machinery was set up. The initiative came from the controlling whites; they chose the Negro agents and intermediaries who were to carry out the functions in the Negro community. Three members of the white committee representing the larger committee called in the chosen Negro leaders and, in the only joint meeting held, outlined the program and expectations. The Negroes chosen were the school principal, two teachers who reside in the community but teach in the rural areas, an undertaker, and a tavern-store operator. Three of the persons chosen were members of the Thorpe family. A similar situation prevailed when attempts were made to induce Negroes to contribute blood to the county blood bank. One person was chosen by the whites to explain the program and solicit donors; the program was a failure inasmuch as the Negroes were not responsive.

Many practices within the Negro community represent acquired cultural traits that do not exactly parallel the original models, or they deviate from the conventional. The hairdressing complex already described is a case in point. The fact that some ways are transplanted with varying efficiency to a different setting means that actions and values are in some degree variant. It has been suggested that many of the gaucheries of manner that characterize portions of the Negro community can be attributed to relative isolation, to lack of training in the new way, to the fact that an available pattern has been incorrectly learned, or to the superimposing of new patterns upon old ways without rapid enough adjustments. Some of these variant traits are more "sticky" than others, and their persistence lends distinctiveness to the Negro subculture;

others change in time and approach or reach the conventional as sophistication increases. The important point is that gaucheries, lags, and improper performance tend to give a somewhat disorganized and inconsistent, or unbalanced, cast to much of Negro culture. The following case is illustrative of cultural awkwardness. At a recent funeral of a young veteran of the last war, three orders of services and ritual were involved—the religious, the fraternal, and the military. The functionaries were poorly trained and unskilled in the etiquette and mechanics of the military rites, and as a consequence several rules were violated; however, there were no indications that participants or observers were aware of incongruities. The distortion of conventional patterns and the inexpertness were due to lack of training in a specialty pattern—military burial—relatively foreign to this particular Negro community.

The fact that Negro society is "contained" and relatively isolated, and thus protected from outside censure of certain practices, helps to make for a persistence of differences. The Negro in general is acutely aware that in some things and in some degree he tends to be different, or is expected to be different; among these differences: sophistication of ways and manners and quality of group morale. On the whole, these differences tend to be taken for granted, insofar as they are not frequently speculated about or systematic rationalizations are not offered. There is vague and implicit rationale and search for reasons in such expressions as "a colored man don't get much chance"; "you can't do that down here"; "white folks act like a colored man is lower than a dog." On the other hand, ideas like "Negroes don't act business-like" or "a colored man is his worst enemy" have the effect not only of rationalizing behavior and status but also of internalizing the blame.

It seems, then, that three organizing principles give a kind of tenuous unity and meaning to Negro culture internally:

(1) the axiom that "white folks is white folks"; this is not only the recognition of a gulf between the groups; it also implies a set of expectations and taken-for-granted prescriptions with respect to behavior; (2) the religious myth of salvation; this is the promise of eternal reward at a relatively small price and an assurance that "Jesus will make it up to you"; and (3) group self-blame; this is a rationalization that has the effect of diverting blame from the larger cultural system and placing it upon one's own people and ways; there is also the important implication that personal and group destinies can be self-determined, i.e., improvement will come when the ways are altered or changed. The reverse of this proposition, which is just as logical, is rarely expressed explicitly even among those locals who have the intellectual function of interpreting or explaining.

ASPECTS OF EXTERNAL ADJUSTMENT AND INTEGRATION

It has been pointed out that the basic instruments of technology, economic distribution, government, and education are shared by Negro and white; in other words, Negro society is a social segment that gears into the larger community in functional terms, if not in the more intimate "social" terms. The respective ways of life are mutually interdependent and structured in relation to each other. As laborer, servant, and consumer, the Negro performs important economic and social functions in the larger social system that is Kent; in practical terms these are services for whites who are the controllers and chief beneficiaries of the system. As employer, controller of capital and credit, director of governmental services, professional man, and intermediary-patron, the white performs functions that are exclusive to him. The white tends to monopolize public power, respect, and privilege, and the means to achieve them. Reciprocal actions and values—cultural elements—tend to pattern and rationalize this unequal distribution. It is here that both conflict and adjustment occur between Negro and white patterns in the realm of actions, attitudes, and values related to status and to the distribution of—or access to—power, respect, and privilege. Conflict is made less acute or suppressed, but not eliminated, by alternate or substitutive patterns available to the Negro.

There are circumstances under which the Negro's desire to gain suitable and remunerative employment is thwarted or challenged because such a design runs counter to white designs or patterns. Similarly, his desire as a consumer to purchase tools or goods, his desire as a citizen to participate in governmental affairs, and his desire as a person to vie for or demand recognition, respect, and status may be thwarted or restricted. These are all wishes that must be satisfied within the larger society; lacking direct or easy access to these goals, the Negro characteristically makes available—or has made available to him—alternatives or substitutes. To illustrate the point, an example may be taken from the field of consumer goods: in the sellers' market for automobiles and mechanical equipment that was current during the study it was almost impossible for a Negro to buy a new car or tractor [4] in Kent; in a few instances, it was frankly pointed out that new items were for whites, second-hand or used for Negroes. These alternatives are available to the thwarted Negro consumer: he may wait until the market or attitudinal situation changes; he may have a white on whom he has some claim act as intermediary or sponsor and get the item as a favored person; he may shrug off the blocking in a sardonic humor or bitterness, retreating into the rationalization that "white folks is white folks"; he may choose the next best alternative or substitute: a purchase in another market, or, most frequently, the used or second-hand item. It is to be noted in the case of a goal such as this, or in the case of goals in other areas—jobs, politics,

4. This was probably true also—but to a lesser degree—of lower status whites, such as the mill villagers.

respect—that rarely is there direct attack or demand; in some cases there is no recourse (except moral), and in all cases the force of the survival and getting along value is strong.

The Negro is actually aware of the changes and possibilities of changes in the local white way of life; a change in that way means a change in his, and *vice versa*. There is evidence that some modification of behavior, attitudes, and expectations is occurring. Symptomatic are the expressions from both societies indicating that "things are not like they used to be." A white official remarked:

Some of the niggers are getting mighty uppity, even around here. Every time a colored man has come to my house since I have been in Kent, he has come to the front door. Fortunately, I have never had to ask one of them into the house—I have always been able to finish my business with him on the front porch.

Older white women are reported deploring the fact that "the niggers are such a sorry lot now." "You can't get them to do anything any more." "You just can't find a good servant any more."

The Negro counterparts emphasize, too, that times have changed and there is no longer the willingness to "work for nothing," nor the willingness to be absolutely deferential in all relations with all whites. For example, there are some business and idling relationships where the use of first names (or a nickname as a substitute) is taken for granted. A white salesman spent quite a bit of time idling around the Negro poolroom; sensitive to the fact that he was being called by his first name indiscriminately, he appealed to the proprietor, saying that he didn't mind him using his first name but couldn't he get the other boys to call him "Mr. Tom." The Negro youth who calls a white youth of his own age group "Mr. Dick" or "Mr. Robert" is likely to be an object of scorn and ridicule among Negroes. The nickname is an adroit way out; for example, a salesman, or a person who has amiable and extensive contacts with Negroes will be called by the name of his product, or given some such name as "Shorty," "Red," "Wheel."

Probably the most significant adjustment in patterns has occurred in the political area and in the sharing of governmental expenditures and services. Kent Negroes—less than one-hundred—have participated in the balloting for public officials in the recent elections; some whites have accepted the inevitable. It is important to note that the impetus for this changed state of affairs did not come from either of the local communities. A participant in the white community reported:

The prevailing attitude seems to be that "we *have* to let the niggers vote. But we can still make them as uncomfortable as possible and discourage them from voting in every way possible—indirect way, that is. There's nothing we can do about it now—we have to let the niggers vote now."

Opposing points of view in the white community with respect to the participation of the Negro in politics are highlighted in this reported conversation of a local white "liberal" with two other whites. The "liberal" argued that Negroes are human beings with hearts and souls and that they should have the vote just like any white man. The ensuing dialogue:

First man: I know that they say niggers and whites are just alike, but I think the Lord would have made us the same color if he meant for us to be alike.
Second man: That's what the Bible says.
Liberal: Well, don't you think there will be niggers in heaven?
Second man: Yes, I guess there will, but one of them better not sit down beside me, if I ever get there.
Liberal: But it's still a shame for us to take their tax money and then not give them any say-so about how we use it.
First man: Maybe some of them pay taxes, but I'll bet if you count up all the taxes that niggers pay and put it beside the taxes we pay, it would be just a drop in the bucket.

Liberal: Now don't get me wrong, I don't like the niggers any better than anybody else, and I'm not taking up for them. But we might all be better off if they were educated and able to pay taxes.

Second man: Do you think they can be educated? I don't.

Liberal: I've seen some of them that were pretty well educated.

Second man: And look what happened to them! Whenever you educate a nigger, all you do is ruin a good plowhand.

The ballot has served in some degree to increase individual self-respect and group consciousness; it is a symbol of improved status and a possible instrument of group advance. It is probably an important step in putting some relationships between the racial groups on a more impersonal basis; perhaps rewards and distribution of favors will eventually come to be the result of political power and pressure rather than the patronage or protection offered an individual because of a favored position. Recent events indicate that the change will come gradually rather than dramatically, because both patterns exist side by side. In a recent election, despite a plea by leaders for a vote on a basis of group self-interest, some persons voted on a basis of advice from, or connections with, white patrons. The Negro political leader and/or boss will probably arise as an important liaison between the two racial groups. At this stage, the functions of political education and leadership are dispersed among several persons and organizations; activity and interest are spasmodic rather than constant and organized.

Of a piece with these changes are indications of more equitable shares of public services and expenditures as seen in teachers' salaries, expenditures for school improvement and services, and improved streets and trash removal service. Such changes, although small, are significant because they tend to foster and make active a feeling that things are not necessarily fixed and that the Negro's position will improve—possibly in Kent before it will in some other places, for the Negro who remains there tends to think of himself as being relatively better off than most Negroes in the South and many in the North. This type of ethnocentricity has its complement in the white community. An observer reports:

> The whites believe that there are lots of "good niggers" in Kent, but that this is not true of the nearby industrial cities. . . . In these cities, "niggers are uppity" and do not know their place.

The fact that the two societies exist side by side and, together, form the larger society of Kent means that there must be channels and agents of communication and power linking the two groups. A certain minimum of consensus based on the adjustment of expectations must be achieved and maintained, services must be available and control implemented. Interchange and interaction take place at all levels and at all times. The type and quality of the contact and interchange are highly variable, as are the agents. Generally speaking, the formal and official means of communication and control are in the hands of whites, as well as the power to initiate and terminate relationships. The means available to Negroes in relation to whites tend to be informal, unofficial, and *ad hoc;* power manipulations tend to be indirect rather than direct. The only official and public Negro agents linking the two societies or aiding in the carrying out of community functions are the Negro school teachers. The undertaker often acts as an agent of the public when he performs services for indigent clients. The significant areas of interaction and exchange, and the respective personnel or media involved, are outlined in Table 13. They are ranked roughly in order of frequency of current contact or significance of impact.

In few areas of Kent life is the interaction between members of the two racial groups free and without status implications; the closest approach to relationships that are not significantly colored by status are some of the idling and leisure-time relationships where some whites "shoot the bull," play

TABLE 13. CATALOGUE OF INTERGROUP CONTACTS

Area	Persons or Agents	
	White	Negro
1. Work	small-business employers, supervisors, co-workers	laborers, artisans
	housewives and families	servants, cooks
2. Goods and Services	owners, clerks, salesmen	consumers
	insurance agents	policyholders
	professionals	patients and clients
	bankers	clients
3. Government and Public Service	police	public lawbreakers
	courts	lawbreakers, spectators
	social workers	clients
	school superintendent	school principal
	politician	unofficial and unacknowledged contacts
4. Information	newspapers	subscribers
	radio	set owners
	motion pictures	patrons
	informal informants with established relationships	informal informants with established relationships
5. Leisure and Recreation	selected idlers, spectators and participants	idlers, spectators, and participants
6. Special or Selected Church Events	selected ministers	congregations
	selected congregations	choirs, singers
	mourners of Negro friend or servant	mourners
	mourners	friend or employer
7. Illicit Sex	selected males	selected females

pool, and on occasions drink and gamble with Negroes. In
some commercial relationships, where a buyer's market pre-
vails, the Negro is treated as an "equal" and business values
tend to over-ride other considerations. In short, greater
emancipation is achieved in the idling and market-place relationships. Even in idling behavior only a few whites are involved, but they tend to come from all levels—professionals,
truck drivers, loafers. The white idler, if he wishes, can intrude upon almost any Negro idling or leisure-time situation.
As one Negro put it: "There ain't nothing the Negro got that
is his. You could put up the best colored place in town and
you couldn't keep them out if they wanted to come in." Some
Negroes resent the presence of whites in the Negro poolroom
"when they got a place of their own uptown that they don't
allow a colored man in." Some accuse the Negro proprietor
of being afraid to discourage white patronage.

There is no formal segregation at Negro athletic contests;
a number of whites invariably attend and move freely about.
The Kent Black Sox baseball team has played white teams
from the area without incident or protest. White patrons constitute a significant part of the crowds at the annual Kent
County Colored Fair; the Kent County Fair that is held in
nearby Stone Valley does not permit Negro attendance. At
the last colored fair, white police jostled Negroes out of the
way in order to permit white patrons to get favorable positions
in the admission line. A Negro woman left the line and said
loudly:

I thought this was our fair. This is the onliest thing we has in
Kent during the year. That man (cop) up there pushing us back
and putting his own kind in front. And this is supposed to be
our fair. Goddammit, don't go in there. I wouldn't go in there
for nothing now.

It has been pointed out that in general the role of the Negro
in intergroup relationships is passive and subordinate; the

initiative for social intercourse is not his and he is unable or unwilling to erect formal counter-barriers. Some relationships between whites and Negroes tend to be more impersonal than others, but the general tendency is for relationships to take on a personal tone within the framework of status definition. The bi-racial social system of Kent to a large extent works through informal and personal channels. Increasing impersonality and greater initiative for the Negro would be marks of emancipation and indications of the decline of the system. Some Negroes and some whites have vested interests in the maintenance of relationships that are not formally defined or channeled. For the individual Negro they are means of getting favors, maintaining claims, and acquiring the incidental status that comes from having an "in" with someone. For the whites they are a means of maintaining control without formal recognition of Negro claims or status; they also help to preserve a fiction of *noblesse oblige*, an ingredient of the "good white folks" myth.

As an upper status group with greater access to the new, presumed knowledge of conventional manners and techniques of living, and control of public means of communication, local whites are one of the important sources of new knowledge and techniques in the areas of living and making a living. The white community serves as a "cultural filter" [5] for much that comes to the Negro community; much is transmitted in an informal, second-hand manner; much is copied from white models with varying accuracy; and some things are probably withheld or censored.

Characteristically, the Negro servant and the person who has had extensive contact with whites is aware of, and often comments on, "what the white folks like" and the fact that "the white folks are doing it this way." The ways of white folks are recognized as being the conventional, the stylish,

5. The more mobile and sophisticated Negro serves the same function within the Negro community.

the proper, or the more sophisticated; it is in this sense that they are models or goals for Negro behavior. Leaders and the educated lead the way in advocating changes in Negro ways, but in many cases—church procedure and burial rites, for example—resistance is met, because these practices have somewhat different meanings in the context of Negro life and derive their character from different group experiences and needs.

Although the ways of local whites are important models and sources for the Negro, he is sensitive to and learns from other areas also. His behavior tends to be a compound composed of influences from his own past, the local white community, the larger world as revealed by education, travel, and the influences of mass media. An illustration of the way in which new habits, techniques, and skills are acquired—and their varied sources—is seen in the introduction and integration of the poolroom into the local Negro culture.

A poolroom for Negroes was recently opened by a "responsible" Negro after the intercession of influential whites who assured him it would be all right. This was the first poolroom with standard-sized tables in the Negro community for more than a generation. Only men in their late fifties or sixties remember the earlier poolroom; they are not significant for the present pool-playing generation from the standpoint of imparting skills or providing a demand for pool. This is emphasized by the fact that middle-aged men insist that this is the first poolroom for Negroes in Kent.

Antecedent to the standard-sized tables, from the point of view of providing a pattern of activity and an opportunity for men who are now in their forties to have acquired tastes and skills, was a small coin-operated table that was available in the early 1930's. The tastes and skills of this group provided some leaven for the naiveté of most persons in the younger group when the current poolroom was set up a few years ago. The questions are: How did the present generation of Kent Negro pool players learn to shoot pool and from whom? What kinds of patterns of play have developed? How does the poolroom, as "something new," fit into the total situation?

The following sources of knowledge and influence can be identified: older Negro men from the local community who retain interests and skills acquired in an earlier period; Negro male migrants to the community who brought an interest and skills; older and younger males who have returned to the community after acquiring the interest and skill elsewhere—visiting, working, serving in the armed forces; Negro and white transients from other centers, including salesmen and agents; two Negro youths who have access to a private table owned by their white boss; local whites who, for a variety of reasons, frequent the Negro poolroom and compete among Negroes and themselves (local whites have a poolroom of their own; Negroes have worked there but are apparently not significant in this instance for transmission purposes); the proprietor of the white poolroom who informally imparts trade news and developments to the Negro proprietor; published rule books and game and equipment descriptions.

Youths of high school age and just beyond constitute the backbone of support; they are recruits of the pattern as are rural youths who frequently come to town. The first manager of the poolroom was "Bosco," an old carnival man who had "been around." "Bosco taught many of the youths the fundamentals of the games—how to hold the stick, the variety of games, how to play "position" and "make the cue ball do what you want it to do"; he points out that most of the youths he taught can beat him now. Assiduous practice and constant play have resulted in the maturation of a group of young experts. More skilled Negro and white transients provided models and competition and introduced a variety of gambling games. As one player put it; "There ain't no more 'fish' (weak players or 'suckers') now; everybody can shoot pool now."

Significant for the total picture is the fact that there is a local ordinance that youth of high school age are banned from poolrooms; it is enforced in the white community but not in the Negro. When the subject was broached by the manager to one of the under-age youths, the youth immediately obtained written permission from his mother to frequent the place; now, the question is never raised with any of the boys. Indicative of the nature of the Negro community and the as yet undefined status of the poolroom is the fact that school boys and teachers are often shooting at the same time. Also significant is the fact that local white policemen often shoot pool with Negro men there. One person explained that it was only among Negroes that the officer could play pool publicly; if he went into the white poolroom it would be bad for morale and enforcement, but he can play among Negroes and they will not presume upon an apparent intimacy—rather they dare not. Incidentally, many Negroes resent the fact that whites can play on their tables, but they cannot play on the whites' tables; they feel that there is absolutely nothing that they have that is safe from invasion of whites, if the whites desire to intrude. Management can not protest or fully heed the protests of Negro patrons because he must "keep on the good side of the whites; they can close me up in a minute, if they want to."

The poolroom is one of the newest elements in a culture that doesn't see a great deal of change or innovation and which has limited institutional devices for Negro leisure-time activity. These factors explain in part the uses, the meaning, and the atmosphere. The poolroom has not yet become a problem; i.e., it is not generally defined as a threat to established institutions or values; it may yet be—in which case clientele, atmosphere, and meaning would probably change.

Striking a Balance

There are few Negroes in Kent who come from outside of the state or from urban areas; the background of the vast majority is rural or small town Piedmont. The great bulk of the Negro population consists of persons who were born and raised in Kent or who migrated from nearby rural areas of Kent County. There is no great clash between rural ways—

and specifically the ways of rural Negroes—and the ways of Kent Negroes. True there are those who state emphatically that they prefer the town to the farm, but the fact is that a marked rural streak as manifested in much of the economic activity and the consequent style and level of living, and in certain aspects of the social organization is an essential component of Kent culture. Kent is in the midst of a rural area, and the style of life of Kent residents is dependent upon close integration with rural ways and resources. Kent Negroes, even if not predominantly rural, tend to retain significant ties with rural institutions and persons. Identifying distinctions are made between "country" and "town," but they are neither sharp enough nor frequent enough to set up status categories. Observation indicates that a large number of the nonrespectable category are relatively recent migrants from the rural areas, but their rural background figures only incidentally in the definition of their status; for example, "He's from out in the country and don't have much education," or "That happened when they was in the country; you know how folks in the country do." The latter statement might be made in an explanation of sex or family irregularities. These two possibilities seem reasonable: rural migrants to Kent tend to reinforce a local pattern of behavior that is congenial to them and not radically different from what they have been used to because the gap between town and country here is not large; rural migrants fill in the gaps left by migration to larger urban centers of natives or earlier migrants from rural areas.

The point to be stressed is that these town ways are neither markedly strange nor uncongenial to rural Negroes; and rural ways are neither strange nor uncongenial to the Negroes of this town.

At the same time, there is hardly a family in which one or more of the significant adult members have not spent some time in Northern and Southern urban centers. In the 1920's many men who have since returned to Kent went North on

"transportations"; some of the women have worked as domestics in the North and returned; many men who probably
would not have gotten the chance otherwise acquired an
acquaintance with urban centers of the world during the
recent war; and there are some persons who make regular
pilgrimages to Northern urban centers. This direct contact
of adults with the outside through work experience, travel,
and communication with relatives in other centers, plus the
close proximity of a major Southern urban center and several
other cities of different size and "temperament" from Kent,
tends to dissipate insularity and makes for a certain sophistication and flexibility. The Kent Negro is not a "hick," and his
ways are not solely those of the folk society; nor are they
entirely secular.

It appears that the Kent Negro, in adapting to what would
objectively be termed a "tough" situation, has created and
integrated customs and values—a culture—that not only permits survival but offers him, in this time and place setting, a
modicum of satisfactions, though these satisfactions may be
obtained by substitute paths and indirection and at high personal and social cost. It is strikingly true that among the adults
who have remained in Kent, or who have returned there,
there seems to be no great disposition to "escape" physically—
no overt individual or collective yearning for distant or larger
places. Life for the Kent Negro who stays—and therefore for
the significant part of his culture—starts with the oft-stated
premise: "You've got to live here." And, for the many who
choose to live in Kent, the subculture attempts to provide
features that will remove this theme from the realm of resignation and of abdication of the human demands for self-respect. The "success" of the culture must be judged in terms
of how well and how long it can do this in view of the increasing pressures of many "foreign" elements and the necessity
to integrate them.

A View of the Whole

CHAPTER **12** IN SUMMARIZING the way of life of the Negro in this particular community of the Piedmont South of today, it is appropriate to include the following: first, a resume of the subculture, indicating its essential nature; second, a brief comparison of the ways of the local Negroes with the ways of local whites; third, an indication of the quality and the range of individual responses to this subculture; and, fourth, a statement of some of the research problems which are suggested by this study. Our first interest is in pulling together and restating some of the main features and bases of the "blackways of Kent."

A RESUME OF THE SUBCULTURE

THE "blackways of Kent," like the small town in which they have their setting, are a composite of old Southern ways and emergent new Southern ways, of the rural and the urban, the folk and the secular. They share and reflect the functions and the vicissitudes of the small Southern town whose people are not concerned directly with farming: "a grouping of centralized services in a clustered settlement which is the essence of a town, and which, at a higher grade, is the hallmark of a city." [1] Understanding of the ways of the Negro in

---

1. Robert E. Dickinson, *City, Region and Regionalism* (London: Kegan Paul, Trench, Trubner and Co., Ltd., 1946), p. 22.

the town is helped when it is realized that he follows few of the primary occupations with which the town is concerned. To a large extent, the Negro's culture is a reflection of the fact that the bulk of his economic function is in terms of what M. Aurousseau calls "the secondary occupations . . . concerned with the maintenance of the well-being of the people engaged in those of a primary nature." [2] Unlike the culture of those people who control the primary functions of the town, the Negro culture does not reflect directly the effects of any clashes having to do with the conflict between old ways and classes, on the one hand, and competing new ways and classes, on the other. And the design for retention of a particular way of life, or the aggressive pushing of individual or class interests in social, economic, and political terms, are relatively weak.

The pragmatic Negro subculture of Kent has achieved a sort of unity that is based mainly upon the facts of color proscription and race anxiety; its persistence in time is related to a certain passivity and the marked adaptability it has shown historically. The "success" of this subculture must be judged in terms of (1) how well and at what costs it performs its specific adaptive functions; (2) how long it can persist in view of internal inconsistencies and the increasing pressure of many "foreign" elements; and (3) the extent to which it engenders group pride and high morale instead of ambivalence. Given the culture as it is, high morale is difficult to attain. Such could only be achieved under two conditions: the approach to an all-Negro society with a full complement of institutions and with a measure of authority (power) and initiative localized within the group, and the opportunity for greater individual achievement and participation in the larger society. The maximizing of the latter would of course mean

2. M. Aurousseau, "The Distribution of Population," *Geographical Review*, XI (1921), 567; cited by Dickinson, *ibid.*, p. 23.

integration and would eliminate the prime basis for the sub-culture. At any rate, the ways of Kent Negroes have variant features, and a social organization sufficient to distinguish them as a subculture in their own right, with congruent social struc-ture, orientations, and personalities.

The features that make this subculture different from con-tiguous and surrounding cultures with which it is in interac-tion are not differences in kind; they are rather differences of emphasis that result from the particular problems the local Negro has in getting the satisfactions—or seeking basic goals—common to American culture. An anthropologist, after read-ing the field notes and the manuscript for this study, con-cluded that "it is quite obvious that certain anxieties play a more important part among these people than they do in societies generally and that culture has evolved as more or less an adjustment to these anxieties." [3] For summary purposes, it is pertinent to repeat here a conclusion that was stated earlier. Item by item, the significant values and goals explicit and implicit in the Negro society of Kent are essentially the ac-cepted and prized values of American culture: survival and getting along; opportunity and equality; patience; religious salvation; self-expression and individuation; inviolability of the ego; friendliness and courtesy; property and money. The added emphasis and distorted meaning given some of these, such as getting along and survival, religious salvation, and in-violability of the ego, stem from the realities of the local situa-tion; they are adaptive in a real sense. The big society does not provide direct and easy or fully conventional means of attain-ing major ends; nor does it encourage initiative. In one sense, the subculture is essentially warped or distorted. It makes for the rise and persistence of habits and orientations that are superficially inconsistent with value objectives; and it makes

3. Letter from John Gillin, September 28, 1949.

for the substitution and persistence of less direct and less
conventional channels to achieve satisfactions.

The Kent white tends to monopolize public power, privilege, and respect and the means to them. Reciprocal patterns
of action and thought—cultural elements—tend to fix and rationalize these inequalities of distribution and access. It is here
that both conflict and adjustment occur between Negro and
white ways and expectations. Conflict is made less acute or
suppressed but not eliminated by the alternate or substitutive
paths to satisfaction that are created by, or made available to,
the local Negro. The distinctive feature about life for the
Negro in Kent is that a significant amount of his behavior is
guided by cultural patterns that are alternate, substitutive, or
ad hoc in character. The subculture is essentially a set of adjustment devices for the restricted; it is geared to adjust to the
demands of life now and not to carving out or initiating that
which is new or different. In retrospect, this society, lacking
as it does a large body of active myth or tradition related to
past glory or achievement and without the initiative or power
to structure change in the future, is geared to the present and
not to the past or future. It accepts change, recognizes it,
wants it, and with some optimism expects it—but up to very
recent times it has not mobilized or pointed efforts to effect
change. Changes have come to it from the outside.

Life for the Kent Negro who stays—and therefore the significant part of his culture—starts with the oft-stated premise:
"You've got to live here." That this does not mean complete
resignation and abdication of the human demands for self-
respect is due to the fact that the culture provides alternate
and substitute paths by which satisfactions can be achieved,
but at significant personal and social cost.

As previously noted, three organizing principles give a kind
of tenuous unity and meaning to the subculture: the axiom
that "white folks is white folks"—this is not only a recognition

of a gulf between the groups and differences in power, but it also implies a set of expectations and proscriptions with respect to behavior; the religious myth of salvation—this is the promise of eternal reward at relatively small price and an assurance that "Jesus will make it up to you"; and group self-blame—this latter is a rationalization that has the effect of diverting blame from others, fate, society, etc., and placing it upon one's own people and ways; there is an added implication that personal and group destinies can be self-determined, i.e., improvement will come when the ways are altered or changed. Like other features of the subculture, there is no necessary logical consistency among these elements.

SOME COMPARISONS WITH THE WAYS OF KENT WHITES

IT SHOULD be stressed again that Negro and white ways of Kent do not represent discrete differences in kind; they are each aspects of the total Kent pattern and have many more features in common than in contrast. In a sense, each group is a sub-society with the differences between them stemming from the consequences of the distribution of power, honor, and the ability to initiate change. Power is used here in the sense that Max Weber uses it, as the factor affecting "life chances" and determining "classes," "status groups," and "parties."

In general we understand by "power" the chances of a man or a number of men to realize their own will in a communal action even against the resistance of others who are participating in the action. . . . Power, as well as honor, may be guaranteed by the legal order, but, at least, normally, it is not their primary source. The legal order is rather an additional factor that enhances the chance to hold power or honor; but it cannot always secure them.

The way in which social honor is distributed in a community between typical groups participating in this distribution we may call the "social order."

Now: "classes," "status groups," and "parties" are phenomena of the distribution of power within a community.[4]

Implicit and explicit in the discussion of the local community has been the fact that the locus of effective power is in the white community and that the culture of the Negro community is colored in a significant way by the lack of power and initiative; conversely, we expect the white society—or significant parts of it—to show the effects of power in its ways and social structure. Although Weber's formulation is to a degree "economic" and in terms of the market, his concept "class situation" has some merit as a means of relating the Negro group's ways and status to those of the white group,[5] insofar as they may be defined in terms of "the typical chance for a supply of goods, external living conditions, and personal life conditions. . . ." [6]

In its largest sense, the "world of white folks" in Kent and beyond is, for the Kent Negro, a world that is marked by the different incidence of certain material objects and more sophistication on the average. It is characterized by values and emphases related in the main to primary economic functions, status and power, easier access to cultural instruments and goals, and greater freedom of expression and movement. Implicit in the folk expression, "The white folks got everything," is the fact that these things—power, status, honor, material goods, and greater freedom—are important to the Negro too, although he is denied direct access to them. They are actually shared values. The following section indicates some of the likenesses and differences in emphasis and social structure between the two societies.

There are actually two white cultures in Kent with which

4. H. H. Gerth and C. Wright Mills (eds.), *From Max Weber: Essays In Sociology* (New York: Oxford University Press, 1946), pp. 180-81.

5. This is suggestive despite the fact that in Weber's scheme, the Negro would be a "status group" with caste features. *Ibid.*, pp. 186-89.

6. *Ibid.*, p. 181.

the Negro culture interacts in some degree; there is the "town" culture of the upper class whites and the mill culture of the mill villagers. In status and behavior, the Negro is probably closer to the mill villagers; in contact and identification he is closer to the "town whites." The materials that form the basis for this limited comparison are taken mainly from the field notes and preliminary statements of fellow students[7] who studied the respective communities using methods similar to those used in this study.

Miss Stevens'[8] content analysis of the field notes for this study and for the study of the town whites provides one basis of comparison. Miss Stevens found that frustration-aggression, religion, and status were dominant patterns in both communities but that the incidence and the content varied markedly between the two cultures. She concluded:

It is clear that in explicit references, the frustration-aggression pattern is more prevalent by far than either of the other categories in the Negro and the white group alike. It appears more than six times as often in the former notes than do word references to status, and nearly three times as often as religion. In notes from the white community, it is more than five times as common as status and nearly five times as frequent as religion. In either case, religion outnumbers status in allusions by single words or simple expressions. In the white community, however, mentions of status are very little less frequent than religion, whereas in the notes from the Negro community, religion is mentioned 2.3 times as often as status.[9]

Miss Stevens adds:

It is evident that the aggression, religion, and status patterns differ markedly in character when comparing the representation

7. Ralph C. Patrick, Jr. studied the "town" culture in 1947-48 and J. Kenneth Morland the mill villages in 1948-49.
8. Gertrude D. Stevens, Application of Content Analysis to Anthropological Field Notes (unpublished thesis, University of North Carolina, 1949).
9. Ibid., pp. 44-45.

of the two communities. Aggression in the white community appears as almost entirely verbal, whereas more than half of the expressions of aggression among the Negroes are of a violent nature. The church takes on a very different aspect in the white community from that of the Negro. References to religion as a spiritual phenomenon are comparatively frequent among the colored people, but the church pattern of the white community has very little of spirituality in direct references. Finally, it would seem from the chart of status consciousness that the white community referred to high status more often than low, and also more often than did the Negroes; on the other hand, the Negroes mentioned low class more often than did the white people, but less often than they did high class. Class consciousness was not so marked among the Negroes...[10]

The class structure of "town whites" is more clearly defined than that of either the Negro society or the mill village. Status consciousness and the status struggle are also more acute; in fact, the significant aggression and hostility which marks the town of Kent is directly related to the status struggle. Miss Stevens points out that "the real character of the religion in the white section was shown to be not spiritual but a facet of the prevailing conflict pattern, with status at stake, instead of saving souls." [11]

The power and status orientation of the dominant white culture has no real counterpart among Kent Negroes, primarily because these are stakes for which the Negro cannot play because they involve economics, politics and government, and public honor. Patrick points out:

In the realm of politics and government and economics, competitively defined in our culture, there was much evidence that the common values necessary for competitive activity had broken down and that competition had been replaced by group conflict. In politics, one group resisted the usurpation of power by "low

10. *Ibid.*, pp. 57-58.
11. *Ibid.*, p. 78.

caliber," "uneducated," "people who came from nothing." The other group attacked the former as "a bunch of old fogies who think they are the cream of the crop because their grandfathers chiseled the hell out of all the poor folks in the county." In the economic sphere, aggression and resentment were directed against the "outsiders" or the "people who had made themselves rich" on the breaks and on sharp practices.[12]

Patrick concludes with respect to the "town whites" that:

The conflict situation ... is essentially a struggle of groups oriented toward different norms and different modes of relationships. As a result of certain historical factors, the dominant group in Kent took on a cultural orientation toward traditionalistic norms, toward evaluations of persons on the basis of their position in a kinship system organized in terms of particularistic relations, and toward functional diffuseness of status and authority. But within the last decade the dominance of the traditional culture of Kent and the positions of the "Old Kent" people have been threatened by the influx of "newcomers" and "outsiders" culturally oriented toward rationalistic norms, toward evaluation of persons on the basis of their achievement in an occupational system organized in terms of performance, and toward status and authority within functionally specialized fields.[13]

The Negro society is significantly less differentiated than the "town whites'"; its frustrations and aggressions are in terms of the color line and the denial of individual respect rather than in terms of status ranking within their society. Aggression in the Negro community tends to be more internalized and oblique. Miss Stevens concludes that the materials suggest "the surface character of aggression without a great deal of pent-up feeling [in the white society], which is corroborated by a further comparison with the Negro section. . . . About one-fourth of the frustration expressions were followed

12. Ralph C. Patrick, Jr., Group Conflict and the Social Structure in a Piedmont Southern Community, p. 3. An unpublished manuscript.
13. *Ibid.*, pp. 22-23.

by mentions of aggression [in the Negro community]. In the white section, about one-half of the frustration mentioned is followed immediately by aggression." [14]

Although the mill whites, to a significant degree, share the low status and the isolation of the Negro, their roles in the occupational and political structure provide the basis for a differentiation and mobility that is denied the Negro in Kent. Morland reports.

. . . the mill people form a class group . . . a class that is near the bottom rung of the social scale. But there are wide variations among the mill people themselves. The town people constantly refer to the great difference between the people in the Cromwell village and those in the other mill villages. Also they say that the Townsend group is on the lowest level possible. But within each of the villages there are various differentiations among the mill people. . . .

The most obvious differentiation is between bossmen ("second" hands live in the villages; overseers and superintendents do not) and regular workmen. The bossmen have better houses which are equipped with flush toilets and running water. Their houses are usually larger and receive repair more promptly than do other houses. With better pay, they are usually able to have better furniture and better automobiles than the other workers. They dress better, wearing a coat with matching pants and often a tie, even when they go into the mill. . . . The bossmen and the more "respectable" mill workers attend downtown churches or the Cromwell Baptist church. Those further down the scale . . . attend the Church of God and the Wesleyan Methodist. [15]

The mill worker has problems of adjustment and consequent anxieties quite similar to those of the Negro in Kent. There are parallels between his adaptive behavior and that

14. Stevens, *op. cit.*, p. 74.
15. J. Kenneth Morland, Milton: A Cultural Study of the Cotton Mill Villages of a Piedmont Town, pp. 32-33. An unpublished manuscript.

of the Negro. The points at which the behavior and the orientations are most similar are in religion, whisky, sex and the family, and leisure-time activity. Again these are all basic and common patterns in the local community, but here, as in the case of the local Negro, the emphases appear to differ. The following excerpts from a preliminary statement by Morland have their almost exact counterparts in the descriptions of the Negro subculture:

Salvation from sin, which comes in accepting Jesus as Lord and Savior, is central in the religion of the three mill churches. . . . There are three or four revival meetings each year. . . . "When we all get to heaven . . . When we all see Jesus" is a song often sung.

The holiness sects have intense emotional expression on occasions. . . . In the midst of a song or prayer someone might become "happy" so that "his cup overflows." The result is that he will dance up and down the aisles, shout, sing, jump over benches and even fall exhausted on the floor. Women seem more prone to do this sort of thing than men. . . . The Cromwell Church is much more dignified. The preacher shows emotional stress but the congregation sits quietly, almost stolidly.[16]

Men usually go alone on hunting trips, on which they drink and exchange dirty jokes, usually about sex. Women like to fish about as well as men, but they have no time for such activities because of greater home responsibility.

Drinking is an important release. . . . It appears that drinking, like the holiness services, provides an emotional release that is not gained in the daily round of living. After a few drinks, the mill worker sheds his usually reserved nature. . . . Both the drinking sessions, often accompanied by fighting, and the religious ecstasies

16. This variation compares with the pattern of the Field's Street M.E. Church described in the section on Religion. The impression is that there remains a larger quota of fundamentalism and puritanism in the expressed doctrine of the mill churches than in the Negro churches of contemporary Kent.

appear to perform the same function of emotional expression. Otherwise, the day-by-day expression of the mill workers is one of reserve, almost repression.

.   .   .   .   .   .

Those who drink "too much," i.e., those who get drunk every weekend and thereby neglect their families are looked down on, even by those who drink. . . . People in the villages distinguish between those who are neat and clean and those "who live like cattle." Usually these are non-church families and indulge in all the church-termed vices of drinking, gambling, and sexual laxity. They are improvident and do not carry insurance. But as long as a parent provides for his children he is not in the lowest stratum. In the villages, other than Cromwell, there is a great deal of sexual laxity, and some of the wife's offsprings are recognized by everyone as having been fathered by someone other than the husband. . . . People who do not pay their debts are put in a low category.[17]

It seems clear that both the mill village and the Negro society have cultures that retain significant rural features; both are derived in part from the anxieties of a low-status, relatively isolated group; both exhibit significant malaise, when judged by town standards. Of course, it must be remembered there are many signs that there is a significant amount of culturally-induced malaise in the "town society" as well. We have no accurate measure of the respective amounts in the three societies, but we can say that the bases and content should differ significantly, especially as between the mill villagers and the Negroes, on the one hand, and the "town folks" on the other. Color as a factor defining power, social honor, and economic participation would make a significant difference between the orientation of the Negro and mill villagers, although their "cultural situation" and "class situation" are quite similar.

17. Morland, *op. cit.,* pp. 27-34.

TYPICALITY AND INDIVIDUALITY OF RESPONSES

THE preceding analysis of the content and organization of this subculture provides a basis for predicting and "understanding" in a gross fashion the life pattern of the Negro in this setting at this time. The fact that what was called in Chapter 1 the cultural "script" is acted out by actual persons raises questions as to uniformities and variations in responses and interpretations, as well as the quality of the interaction between persons and culture. The analysis has provided us with the significant traits which would go to make up the composite approved personality in this subculture at this stage of its evolution; this would be an ideal-type with the following key components: friendliness, ingroup honesty, "knows how to treat people," "doesn't get in trouble," "doesn't associate with every 'Tom, Dick, and Harry,'" "knows how to carry his liquor," discretion in sex play, "doesn't let everybody know his business," ability to do something that is economically significant or in demand, "treats his family nice," goes to church, and shows a certain discreet courage and frankness in dealing with whites. These traits, in combination, would represent the best and most balanced adjustment to the local situation. The idealized type of personality is at once a product of and a component of the subculture. And it must be distinguished from the generalized behavior which results through patterns of overt culture and the significantly varying behavior of individuals which reflects the manner in which actual persons interact with the culture and interpret and carry out their roles.

Since one of the basic themes of Kent Negro culture is "white folks is white folks" and the whole weight of the culture is directed toward inculcating this value and defining roles in accordance with it, the typical person's role has a large content of conformity, overt passivity vis-a-vis whites and the external world, and a design for adaptability or survival. External conformity cannot be gainsaid, but mental patterns vary widely from resignation and indifference through good-humored tolerance and patience to cynicism, gnawing bitterness and resentment bordering on overt and dramatic aggression. And then there is a significant amount of aggression of various kinds that is subtly or indirectly expressed. There is some tendency for the occasions on which aggression is expressed to increase both because of greater tolerance on the part of whites and the Negro's changing conception of his role. Despite this, caution, reserve, and even a certain duplicity in dealing with whites are personality counterparts of the universal recognition of "how far to go with white folks." These are attributes of the Negro's role in relation to whites and are parts of the standard equipment which he gets jointly from the Negro and white cultures. They are to be distinguished from the facets of his personality shown primarily in the Negro community. To a large extent certain generalized traits are reactions to the role played in relation to whites: the tendency to define and evaluate social relations with Negroes in terms of race, touchiness, self-expression and indulgence, and neurotic-like individuation. The content and quality of this behavior or disposition varies in terms of individuals and in terms of membership in the respectable or non-respectable categories.

Despite the over-all conformity, a striking fact about Kent Negro society is the manner in which individuals stand out and are distinguished by their neighbors and themselves. In Negro Kent everyone tends to be a "character." There is adaptation and conformity but with a distinctly individual twist marked by an organization of responses that often border on the queer, the colorful, the whimsical, or the stubbornly "just different." "He's a mess," "She's a bird," "Old man Jack is something" are typical expressions marking the casual and day-by-day evaluations of people by other people. There is a "story" about practically everybody in the community. Identifying incidents, colorful characteristics and human-interest bits are constantly associated with persons—not so much to place them on a status scale but rather to individualize them and mark them out as different. Much, but hardly all, of this is to be expected in a small town where everybody knows everyone else and contacts are relatively frequent and personal.

As highly personalized tags, the very common nickname or distortion of name takes on added significance in this context. These substitutes for given names are widely used and often proudly borne; they are intimate characterizations of persons or significant facets of their makeup or life history. They are cited here because they reflect the individualizing tendency and the range of personality types in the culture. They tend to fall into the following general categories: the shortened or twisted version of given names; descriptions of mental or physical characteristics, which may be inverted, as "Shorty" for a tall person; topical or anecdotal, which are descriptive of a specific incident or experience involving the person; exaggerated compliments used in an established joking relationships; traditional or stereotyped; and the miscellaneous. Among the names and their meanings or allusions: "Double Head"—large head; "Pencil"—very tall, slender legs; "Big Mary"—a male with big ideas; "Classy"—proud and meticulous; "Gee"—"around mules so much, practically born in a stable"; "Yes, he did!"—the person's favorite expression; "Blood"—"fought as a youngster so much he bled all the time"; "Pie"—"took white woman's pie from her window"; "Knowney"—"he always knows so damn much more than anybody else"; "Radio"—talkative woman; "Lovely"—"he was such a lovely baby"; "Colonel," "Governor," "Mrs. Roosevelt," "Mr. Truman," etc.—mock deference for manner and bearing used in joking relationship; "BH", "WH", "CT", etc.— initials of given names; and also such miscellaneous names as "Duke," "Flat Top," "Bob Steele," "Daddio,"

"Sweets," "Weeze," "Frog Eye," "Miss Liz," "Horsefly," etc. Of course, many of these names have a masked aggressive content; they represent what is known as "hard joking" and in many ways are similar to and perform functions akin to the profanity and obscenity mentioned earlier.

There is an important emphasis upon setting off personalities; apparent satisfactions come with being recognized in a distinctive way and through arousing specific expectations. Such individuals as the bawdy tale teller, the person with access to whisky, the know-it-all, the eccentric or slovenly dresser, the ladies' man, the rough guy, the person with a past, the churchgoer, the person who has always got money, the athlete, the singer, the owner of the late model car, the hunter, the professor, the boy who drives for the undertaker, the prayer-expert, the person with important connections testify to the wide range of types and roles. And the quality of the responses and expectations connected with them underscores the significant in-group emphasis upon recognition and respect in a status-starved society.

In a society in which "being somebody" [18] and maintaining the ego are important, being reacted to as personally distinctive for any reason whatsoever is the most elementary and significant level at which recognition can be achieved and maintained. This is adaptive behavior and is suggestive of chronic anxieties in the subculture related to ego-satisfactions. And the fact that so many people tend to be "characters"— they are recognized as being "different" and they themselves get satisfactions out of the fact—supports the hypothesis that there is a tendency for the organized systems of response of many—if not most—of Kent Negroes to be neurotic-like.[19]

18. "Being somebody" in this society tends to be defined in individualistic terms inasmuch as class, family, and occupational differentiation are not wholly crucial determinants of rank and association.

19. The forthcoming analyses of the Rorschach protocols for a sample of this population will throw added light on this apparent tendency in the culture.

This hypothesis is consistent with what has been called the "toughness" of the local culture; it is consistent with the other features that occupy and preoccupy persons in the subculture. As indicated, these emphases—the orientations and values—tend to be functionally linked, and they are colored significantly by the same situational factors—the most important of which is the color line and the manner in which it defines power, honor, and access. The typical Negro of Kent, who has to adopt a design for conformity and who is to a large extent the victim of categorical treatment, tends to develop as a counter-balance a personality structure with significant emphasis upon individuation and patterned non-conformity within his own group.

SOME QUESTIONS AND PROBLEMS

IN THE course of this study some specific problems were uncovered for which only tentative or partial answers could be given—in view of the aims and limits of the project. Also, as we consider these findings in relation to the descriptions of similar subcultures, there are problems of a general research character that are suggested. These problems and questions are worthy of further study because answers to them will augment and check these findings; and in the case of the broader questions, they will provide some basis for organizing and collating our knowledge about a number of subcultures which have some features in common. Among the specific problems, which, if pursued further, would augment this study are the following:

The manner in which differential morbidity and mortality affect the body of Negro customs, actional and mental, directly and indirectly.

The behavior and anxieties related to dress and personal adornment; in particular, a question such as the comparative importance of hair type and grooming and skin color as prestige and differentiating factors.

The factors other than size that affect the number and range of institutions and functionaries in a subculture. The *ad hoc* and ancillary character of institutions.

The low-degree class differentiation, and the point at which incipient class behavior and structuring become full-blown. The criteria which will be important in the evolution of classes in the subculture.

The mechanics, the agents, and the course of cultural interchange between this society, the local white society, other Negro societies, and the larger society. The extent and nature of what the anthropologists call transculturation.

It is not within the province of this study to compare exhaustively the ways of the Negro in the small town of Kent, which is in the Southern Piedmont, with the ways of the Negro in different time and place settings. However, it is clear that the full meaning and significance of the Kent subculture will not be achieved until it is compared with other Negro subcultures. Among the studies available are: (1) the studies of the Negro in the Black Belt and deep south: Charles S. Johnson's *The Shadow of the Plantation*, life in a rural Alabama county in the early 1930's; John Dollard's *Caste and Class in a Southern Town*; Hortense Powdermaker's *After Freedom*; Allison Davis and Burleigh and Mary Gardner's *Deep South*, all studies of rural and urban patterns in Mississippi counties in the mid-thirties; (2) studies of all-Negro communities: Mozell Hill's "All-Negro Societies in Oklahoma," [20] small-town life in racial homogeneous southwestern communities; and (3) the studies of the Negro in the urban North: E. Franklin Frazier's *Negro Family in Chicago*, the Chicago Negro community in the late 1920's and the early

20. Unpublished Ph.D. dissertation, Department of Sociology, University of Chicago, 1946.

1930's; Drake and Cayton's *Black Metropolis,* the Chicago Negro community up to the early 1940's.

If one is thinking in terms of a continuum of community types from small rural to large urban and from homogeneous and compact to heterogeneous and dispersed, or if one is thinking in terms of different regional settings, there are obvious gaps in this series. In any event, these studies should provide the basis for some comparisons and general conclusions. They suggest the possibility of a typology of American Negro subcultures in terms of specific content and the bases of organization or cultural integration and the relation to the dominant or over-all culture. Just a superficial examination of these studies of the Negro reveals a gross similarity in custom and social structure and comparability in mental responses,[21] with, of course, allowances being made for size and the specific time and place setting. This suggests desirability of making explicit and testing this hypothesis: Negro society in the United States is shaped and guided to a significant extent by an evolving national subculture, which, although a variant of the national culture, exhibits growth, patterning, and a gross national "character" all its own. And further, this national subculture has appropriate regional variations.

Another impression which a review of this study of Kent in relation to other studies gives is that, in research terms, we are approaching the saturation point insofar as concrete studies of the general customs of the Negro and the structure of his society are concerned; what seems indicated is added emphasis upon the manner in which individuals respond to and interpret these generalized patterns. Increased concern for intensive comparative personality studies and the range of types within the Negro society is needed to fill out the pic-

21. It is also significant that with few exceptions the core data and the findings tend to be alike regardless of the methods or theoretical orientations used by the various students.

ture and complete our knowledge of the subculture and what it means to live in it.

In conclusion, this study of the "blackways of Kent" is a study in cultural imperatives; like his fellow human beings in other settings, the Negro here has carved out a way of life that is more or less appropriate to the demands of a tough cultural situation; his ways are adaptive in a real sense. To a greater or lesser degree, the Negro in Kent shares this problem with all people who are concerned about how they are treated and about their status. An important key to the understanding of the subculture is the sensitivity to the treatment of people. Billy Strong's statement goes far to state that sensitivity and to indicate the roots of much that goes on in Kent Negro society: "It aint your fault how much education you get. It aint your fault if you didn't go to school. The only thing your fault is how you treats people." How the Negro people treat themselves against the background of the manner in which they are treated in the larger society is the story of the *Blackways of Kent* and a basic problem in the study of any subculture.

INDEX

Index

Abortions, 15, 90-91
Advertisements, for hair straightener, 58-59
African Methodist Episcopal Church, 136, 231, 272, 273, 275, 276, 277, 278
Aggression, against whites, 209-210, 252 n., 316, 317
Agriculture, 118
"All-Negro Societies in Oklahoma," Mozell Hill, 326
All These People, Rupert B. Vance, 12 n.
Alphabetical Index of Occupations in the United States, 225 n.
American Journal of Sociology, 211 n.
An American Dilemma, Gunnar Myrdal, 12 n., 15 n.
Apoplexy, 12
Arsenian, Jean, quoted, 290
Arsenian, John, quoted, 290
Athletics, Negro, 161-162, 257, 283
Atlanta University, vii
Attitudes, of the Negro, 28-29; toward other Negro communities, 36-37; toward hair, 56-63; toward medical treatment, 75-78; toward sex, 83-93; toward illegitimacy, 88-90; toward higher education, 106-107; toward whites, 109-113, 195-202; economic, 123-128; intra-racial,

126-127; interracial, 144-145; toward the police, 177-180; toward law, 291-292
Auroussea, M., quoted, 310
Automobiles, ownership of, 33; purchase of, 296
Auxiliaries, church, activities of, 145-148

Baltimore Afro-American, 30
Baptist Church, 66, 89, 134-135, 136, 139, 148, 190, 231, 265, 267, 272, 273, 277
Baseball, 284
Behavior, 3-6; effect of natural factors on, 16; zodiac as guide to, 79-80; sexual, 83-91; among children, 100-102; religious, 137-148; emotional, 153-154; of teachers, 157; mental restraints on, 196-197; cultural patterns of, 312
Benedict, Ruth, quoted, 288; mentioned, 289; *Patterns of Culture*, 208 n.
Bible, The Holy, 132, 246, 298
Black Metropolis, St. Clair Drake and Horace Cayton, 8 n., 327
Bootleggers, 253
Boy Scouts of America, 259
Brutality, of police, 180, 188
Burgess, E. W., quoted, 94; mentioned, xi
Burial societies, 262, 274-276

331